SUDDEN MONEY™

SUDDEN MONEY™

Managing a Financial Windfall

Susan Bradley, CFP
with Mary Martin, PhD

John Wiley & Sons, Inc.
New York • Chichester • Weinheim • Brisbane • Singapore • Toronto

This publication is designed to provide accurate and authoritative information in regard to the subject matter covered. It is sold with the understanding that the pub-lisher is not engaged in rendering legal, accounting, or other professional services. If legal advice or other expert assistance is required, the services of a competent profes-sional person should be sought.

Library of Congress Cataloging-in-Publication Data:
Bradley, Susan, 1949–
    Sudden money : managing a financial windfall / Susan Bradley ; with Mary Martin.
        p.   cm.
    Includes index.
    ISBN 0-471-38086-5 (cloth : alk. paper)
    1. Finance, Personal.   I. Martin, Mary, 1966–   II. Title.

    HG179.B713 2000
    332.024—dc21   99-055829

Printed in the United States of America

10 9 8 7 6 5 4 3 2 1

I dedicate this book to my family, Frank and Kathleen my parents, and to my nine siblings. And to my grandparents who passed on a legacy of love and giving, I am their grateful beneficiary.

CONTENTS

THE SUDDEN MONEY EVENTS

ACKNOWLEDGMENTS

t turns out writing a book is a very personal experience, and it took longer than I ever thought it would take; it was also more difficult and more rewarding than I had originally imagined. Without the support, encouragement, expertise, and vision of many people this book would not have been written. I would like to particularly thank the following.

Sasha Millstone for her sense of timing and her vision and critiques. Shelly Fernstrom whose friendship and opinions I relied upon.

My clients have continually shown me the subjective side of financial planning. I am grateful to my clients for their willingness to share their lives, their hopes and fears with me, thus allowing me to offer wholistic financial planning. These individuals and families continue to be a great source of knowledge. I thank them for their patience during this writing project.

To Linda Chodor my friend and assistant, without her it would not have been possible to serve my clients while writing this book.

I received valuable technical support and professional wisdom from divorce attorney Odett Bendeck and personal injury attorney Christian Searcy. I also am grateful for the knowledge and input of Chip Bauder JD.

To the members of the Nasrudin Project, a think tank of CFPs exploring the psychological and spiritual side of being a financial planner. I thank you for helping me know it was time to give voice to my subjective side. Members such as Cicely Maton, Tahara Haria, Dick Wagner, and Terry Welsh offered knowledge, inspiration, and sense of community that has been nourishing.

To all the financial advisors who contributed stories and insights to the Sudden Money experience, particularly Philip Baily of Charlotte, N.C., and Barbara Bouchey of Saratoga, N.Y. They were both involved in gathering material and the early formation of the book. I thank them for their guidance, contribution, and patience.

Mort Fishman, the best businessperson I know and a friend for life.

Estate planning attorneys Michael Tillman and Byron Woodman for understanding my message the first time they heard it. I learn from them each time I have the privilege of working with them and the families they serve.

Deb Englander, the first editor to really understand that the Sudden Money experience is a separate kind of financial event requiring its own planning discipline.

Carol Mann, my literary agent, who took the project and kept going until we found the right home for the book.

My Dad, who could not stop himself from asking when the book would be done each time I saw him. I am glad we all lived long enough to experience the completion of this project.

Most of all I am grateful to Marytaresa Martin, my developmental editor, for her project stamina, literary skills, humor, and friendship. Without her this book would not have been written. Thank you.

INTRODUCTION

have been a Certified Financial Planner for 18 years, and my practice has evolved from dealing with general family planning to the unique needs of Sudden Money™ recipients. The evolution was slow at first. Somewhere along the line, I just started seeing new clients who had recently acquired an amount of money that was more than they were accustomed to dealing with. I noticed that the problems and concerns they had were a bit different from those of my other clients.

I began informally studying and comparing them, keeping track of their similarities and differences. At about the same time, I started to notice more and more stories about windfall recipients in newspapers and magazines and on television. The stories covered what these people do with their money and the problems that the money seems to cause. And while lottery winners who go from rags to riches and then back to rags are a favorite of the media, I discovered that millions of people of all ages and from all socioeconomic levels get windfalls every year. Yes, millions.

The number is in the millions because the windfall is a relative concept. If you have been working from nine to five and are making $45,000 and you inherit $75,000, you become a Sudden Money recipient. The same is true, however, if you win a $15 million lottery. It is the not the amount of the Sudden Money as much as your past experience of having access to and being responsible for that amount of money. If you earned $500,000 a year and have significant savings, the $75,000 inheritance might be welcomed, but not overwhelming.

And precisely because this is a relative concept, the phrase "sudden wealth," which I hear a lot, does not seem appropriately descriptive. After all, if you are the sudden recipient of $50,000, are you necessarily suddenly wealthy? That would depend largely on your definition of *wealth*, which many would argue is more a matter of state of mind than of high net worth. To me, wealth is a sense of security and well-being, and knowing that you have the ability to maintain that state of being. The amount received might not mean immediate wealth, but it can mean the potential for future wealth, if handled well from the beginning.

I decided to try to ascertain why it is that some people really did end up wealthy (according to just about anyone's definition) after getting some Sudden Money, and some people ended up worse off than before they got their windfalls. My initial hypotheses were that those individuals whose windfall experiences were less successful either didn't get any financial planning advice, or the advice that they did get was in some way substandard. While both might be true to an extent, I now know they miss the mark.

The real issue is that there is a lack of understanding, on the part of Sudden Money recipients as well as most financial planners, about the complexity of the windfall experience—particularly the importance of the emotional component. This book project was borne of the desire to map out the Sudden Money Process, so I could create an owner's manual for my own clients and demystify the process for other planners and their Sudden Money clients. I wanted to create a vehicle that would give everyone an equal opportunity to turn their windfall into lasting wealth.

I officially began this owner's manual project by amassing windfall stories of all kinds and identifying the events that appeared to be the most common origins. I found that there are eight events that show up over and over again. Those eight events are:

1. Winning the lottery
2. Taking a lump sum retirement payout
3. Insurance settlements
4. Divorce settlements

5. Intergenerational inheritance (both intergenerational and from a spouse)

6. Spousal inheritance

7. Becoming overnight sensations in entertainment or athletics

8. Stock options (the most recent phenomenon)

While I was defining the events that were most common, I couldn't help notice that there was one thread that ran through every story, and it had nothing to do with financial planning as I was taught. That thread was the impact of the money on the emotional state of the recipient and the subsequent impact of the new emotional state on how the money was handled. In fact, many people were so influenced by their emotions upon the receipt of the money that they ended up losing most of it within a couple of years.

In addition to the emotional component to the Sudden Money experience, there was another common element to most of the stories I found, and that was the lack of preparedness due to the element of surprise. Think about it. If you knew you were about to get a windfall, you would (I hope) try to educate yourself about what to expect as a result of the transformation of your finances. But if I just gave you a $500,000 check right now, you'd have so much to think about (such as what car you'd buy or where you want to move to), that you probably wouldn't have the time or the inclination to find out *what you should be thinking about.* Therein lies the problem.

Furthermore, many people purchase lottery tickets every week and already have a plan for what they will do with the money and how they want their lives to look. However, fantasizing is just that. There is no dress rehearsal for Sudden Money; you don't know how you will react until it actually happens to you. But you can prepare yourself for certain decisions and problems that seem to be universal for windfall recipients.

Sudden Money: Managing a Financial Windfall, will teach you what to expect so you don't make the same mistakes that other windfall recipients have been making for decades (and probably much longer, but I can't say for sure). In defense of those before you who have squandered or otherwise lost their new money, there has never been a system that educates people in this country about what to expect in such a situation. And before now, there hasn't even been a book. There was simply no way to prepare.

This book will explain the Sudden Money Process, which begins with the receipt of the money (or the awareness that it is coming) and continues through three phases: (1) preparation and planning; (2) investing; and (3) monitoring, giving, and sharing. I will describe what to expect from your experience both financially and emotionally, and help you maximize your windfall.

I also address the eight Sudden Money events separately, as each has its own unique set of tax consequences, insurance and estate planning considerations, and emotions, all of which affect the timeline and outcome of your experience both financially and emotionally.

Recently, a nonprofit organization called the Forum for Investor Advice conducted what I believe is the first study on windfall recipients (*Survey of Large Cash Payout Recipients*, 1998).* The study questioned over 700 individuals who received $20,000 or more at once and found that retirement payouts and inheritances were the most common events precipitating the windfall. It also found, as I did, that the emotional reaction of the recipient was a crucial factor in the behavior of the recipient as an investor.

Furthermore, the study supported my contention that finding an appropriate financial advisor is vital. In fact, I suggest a team of advisors, including an attorney and a therapist, each of whom is as knowledgeable and experienced about the Sudden Money experience as possible. The impact of a financial windfall should not be underestimated, and I hope to make the public, the financial services professionals, and the windfall recipients in particular, aware of the uniqueness of the Sudden Money Process. It is also my hope that writing this book will begin a new specialization within financial planning: one dedicated to the orientation of Sudden Money recipients.

Considering that the money to be transferred or otherwise manifested over the next two decades will be the largest in American history, there is no underestimating the impact of the availability of a process that will make that transfer easier and more meaningful.

---

* Forum for Investor Advice, "Survey of Large Cash Payout Recipients" (1998).

I view the anticipated flow of Sudden Money as a resource to be harnessed. If most of the recipients use their windfalls to increase their financial security, health care, education, and philanthropy, the benefits will be felt far beyond the recipients. If the money is eventually passed on to future generations who further develop its potential, the benefits of each well-handled Sudden Money experience will be profound.

SUDDEN MONEY™

What Is Sudden Money™?

define Sudden Money as the unexpected receipt of an amount of money that is much larger than you are accustomed to dealing with. Unfortunately, all too often, when you are the recipient of a much larger sum of money than you are used to, you probably won't know how best to handle it. We have all read stories of lottery winners and entertainers who became multimillionaires overnight and then spent the next couple of years in legal battles. Their fortunes dwindle quickly, and soon they are left with nothing—or even worse, bankruptcy.

While these stories may be true, the reality is that lottery winners and entertainers are not the only people who struggle with windfalls; their stories just sell the most newspapers and magazines. As it turns out, however, the $20 billion that will be paid out annually in U.S. lotteries alone over the next couple of years is only a fraction of the trillions of dollars of Sudden Money that will land in the hands of unsuspecting recipients.

Inheritance

The largest transfer of wealth in the history of America is now taking place. Its total is in the trillions of dollars, and it will change hands via intergenerational inheritance. Many of the heirs will have been raised in families with considerable wealth, and many will be introduced to personal wealth for the first time. There is no guarantee that either group will be successful with their new money. After all, some wealthy individuals do not teach their children about money management. The simple fact is, unless someone tells you how to prepare yourself to receive a large sum of money, you won't be prepared.

Young people with large inheritances have always found ways, through their money, to communicate how they feel to their elders. Preparation for a large inheritance should include learning how to communicate directly, rather than acting out. This is easier said than done, but I am hopeful that *Sudden Money* will provide some of the guidance necessary to make the inheritance process, regardless of its size or the age of the heir, more meaningful than just money changing hands. (However, just because you grow up with money does not mean that you are prepared to assume responsibility for the management of your inheritance.)

Stock Option Wealth

There is a new wave of wealth in America, and it is coming from the increasing use and value of stock options. No longer reserved for the highest-level management, stock options are becoming a standard part of compensation packages throughout the entire corporate ladder. They are found everywhere from blue-chip companies to brand new start-up companies that have yet to go public. It is estimated that the current value of stock options in America's major corporations is $11 billion. Over 6 million people hold many of those stock options right now.

Stock option wealth makes sensational headlines as technology companies go public or merge. It has become the norm in that industry for employees to accept low compensation and long hours in exchange for the opportunity to participate in the growth potential through stock options. The most dramatic example I've seen is *Fortune* magazine's coverage of the 40 wealthiest Americans under the age of 40. It notes that the average cash compensation of the Internet executives on the list is $151,200, while their average net worth is $1.5 billion dollars.

Most of the Silicon Valley megamillionaires claim that money is not what makes them happy (otherwise, they would have quit after their first 10 or 20 million). Instead, they desire to make their mark on the world, to change the world during this window of time and technology that might not last. They work at a frenetic pace, and some don't even know how much money they have. Someday, however, they will all have to deal with their money and their feelings about it. Whether they plan to use the money to purchase things, to finance new start-ups, or to fund medical or technological research, they need to have a plan that factors in their desires, their insurance considerations, and their tax consequences.

Most financial planners are not accustomed to creating plans for clients who are 40 years old and worth several billion dollars. There are so many nuances with options, and the status of new technology companies fluctuates wildly, so learning about and keeping current with stock options can be difficult and are definitely time-consuming. My hope is that a new generation of planners will grow out of necessity.

Divorce

You may be wondering why I consider divorce a Sudden Money event. After all, the average divorce takes over a year from start to finish, so the resulting settlement can hardly be called sudden, right? Not really. The reality is that the entire process is so full of distractions and details that the settlement recipient is often, ironically, caught off guard when the money finally arrives.

Divorce is an event especially fraught with emotions, and if they are not properly dealt with, they can wreak havoc on your finances. You might be surprised by some of my recommendations. However, I assure you that though they may seem counterintuitive, they are based on years of watching people (mostly women) make the same mistakes over and over again.

When Two Become One

Much of what is true for divorcees is true for widows as well. The loss of a spouse is a life-changing event with profound impact on the surviving spouse. Whether the grieving process begins with a diagnosis of a terminal illness or with word of a sudden death, it usually takes at least a year after the death of a spouse before the survivor feels the clarity and peace necessary to make major financial and lifestyle decisions.

Unfortunately, many widows either take the wrong action at the peak of their grief and soon live in regret, or they are so paralyzed by their grief that they don't act on the few things that do warrant their attention. When I heard that an estimated 80% of widows living in poverty were not poor before their husbands died, I knew I had to figure out why this was occurring and to try to rectify the situation. This book is my beginning.

Insurance Settlement

Another group that has difficulty holding on to their Sudden Money is the population of insurance settlement recipients. I recently had lunch with the managing partner of a law firm handling a class action lawsuit for women with silicone breast implants. The settlement these women were being offered ranged from a minimum of $125,000 to over $1 million. I asked him how many of the women would have any of this money a year after they received it. He flatly responded, "Not many." He added that many had already spent the money. He knew of women who had bought cars and/or houses with the *anticipation* of the money. Others were mentally spending it over and over again, waiting for the chance to actualize their financial fantasies as soon as they received their checks.

Some of the women felt they could afford to spend the money because they had not had the negative medical side effects that were the basis of the lawsuit. They were told that medical complications could arise at any time and, if they did, the women would no longer have any legal recourse.

The women on the lower end of the settlement spectrum had not had medical problems, and they had the opportunity to have their silicone implants removed or replaced with safer saline implants. This was a wise way to spend a portion of the money, but the balance of the money would probably be spent in short order. This was a real shame because, for many of these women, this would probably be their one shot at having a significant amount of money to invest for their future. Without guidance and advice, this opportunity could be lost—maybe forever.

Retirement

Again, without guidance and good advice, particularly good tax advice, the money from your lump sum payout could be lost in a flash. In my experience, there is so much confusion about retirement benefits and their implications that I found myself second-guessing what I was taught and reresearching the entire subject.

The confusion I speak of comes not just from employees, but from employers, financial services professionals, and even tax specialists. This was the most complex chapter to compose, and it might also be the one most likely to change due to changes in tax law. Finding a financial advisor who is well versed in tax consequences of retirement plans is vital for this group of Sudden Money recipients.

Winning the Lottery

There is no other Sudden Money event like winning the lottery. The money doesn't represent an end to years of legal battles or years of employment. Nor is it an attempt to compensate for a painful catastrophic event. In fact, what makes winning the lottery so exciting is also what makes it especially difficult: the element of surprise. Even people who buy lottery tickets every week are astounded when they win.

The problem is that there is no way to prepare to win millions of dollars. That lack of readiness makes you vulnerable to all of the classic blunders of people who receive windfalls, and a couple of new ones. *If you have won a lottery and you haven't spent most of your money by the time you get around to reading this, you are an exception.* If you haven't even decided how you will take the money, you are in the optimal position. However, regardless of where you're at, if you have any lottery money left, you can still learn about how to maximize it.

Athletes and Entertainers

Of all the Sudden Money events, this is the most volatile because it can be thought of as a series of windfalls. Why? Because the reality is that very few athletes or entertainers are certain about what their income will be in five years. Some people become overnight sensations, only to disappear from the public eye and to resurface, often reinvented, years later. Others aren't as lucky. Due to this possibility, I recommend treating earnings as capital to secure your future: as the only money you will have for your retirement.

Athletes and entertainers are in a complex position with regard to the types of income they get (and how many people get a piece of it), their tax consequences, estate planning, and several other aspects of financial planning. An advisor who understands your pressures, as well as your technical considerations, is as important as a good manager in whom you can trust and confide.

The Sudden Money Process

Regardless of the origin and the amount of your windfall, *Sudden Money* can help you maximize it. For the first time, you are in a position to benefit from the collective experiences of scores of people who were once in your position. If possible, do not do anything with your money until you have read about the three phases and the chapter devoted to your windfall event. There is nothing more important than preparing yourself for the life-altering journey that begins with Sudden Money.

The Three Phases of the Sudden Money Process

Many of the issues, decisions, and challenges that Sudden Money recipients encounter are the same ones that they would have faced on their more gradual journeys to money maturity. But then a situation is thrust upon them, and they feel like they have less time to figure out what is going on in their financial lives; more people want to advise them, go into business with them, or borrow money. And new friends come out of the woodwork. This is not uncommon, nor is the wave of confusion that comes over them when they realize that their Sudden Money has the potential to change their lives forever.

Fortunately, I can report that much of the confusion that comes with Sudden Money can be eliminated. The windfall begins a process that is predictable and is marked by three phases that are universal. Once you know that what you are experiencing is normal, and then you find out what to expect next, much of the stress and confusion that accompanies Sudden Money dissipates. Once your anxiety is at a manageable level, you will be able to allow your Sudden Money to help create the financial success you seek.

Asking for Directions Is a Good Thing

Think of how you feel when you are lost while traveling to a new and important destination. Your tension increases, particularly if you are in a hurry. As you try to find your way, you don't pay attention to other traffic—or the scenery—and consequently you increase the probability of having an accident as well as getting even more lost. Then you ask for directions. You are told that you are on the right road after all, and that your destination is simply farther down the road than you expected. You immediately experience a sense of relief and can proceed comfortably knowing what landmarks to watch for to confirm that you are still headed in the right direction.

- *If you have received your money and have yet to make any decisions.* This is your scenario. Following the guidelines of the three phases will give you the directions you need to arrive at your destination.

- *If you have received your money and have made some bad decisions.* You might need direction to get back on the right road. It might take a little longer to get where you want to go, but you can still get there.

- *If you have yet to receive your money.* Understanding the three phases will give you the opportunity to know the directions cold before you begin your trip. It will also give you the opportunity to get familiar with the new neighborhood before you actually embark on your journey. This is the most fortunate position to be in because it will allow you to comfortably begin—and progress efficiently through—the three phases. You will arrive at your financial destination with the least amount of worry and start enjoying the benefits of this success as soon as possible.

The Three Phases: The Condensed Version

The Sudden Money Process has three sequential phases, and each phase has to be completed before you move on to the next one. The sequence is very important, and to be successful with your new money you must not get ahead of yourself. *Phase One* is a time of preparation and planning for the investment and lifestyle decisions you will be making in the second phase. *Phase Two* is a time for action: putting your money to work by investing. *Phase Three* is defined by the monitoring of your annual progress toward the goals you have set, and sharing your wealth with your family and community.

Each phase has distinct activities: things to learn, decisions to make, and goals to accomplish. Following the guidelines of the three phases will help you remain on an orderly, progressive path toward building a solid financial foundation.

Without following a step-by-step program, it is easy to fall into the common trap of making decisions before you are really ready and, consequently, making inappropriate decisions. If you commit to following the recommended three-phase program, your chances of successfully building financial security and truly enjoying the potential of your new money will be greatly increased.

Everybody Is Unique, But . . .

Each person will go through the three phases in their own way, on their own timetable. The guidelines for each phase were developed based on years of work with Sudden Money clients and hours of listening to the stories told by scores of Sudden Money recipients. Over and over again the same elements are present when someone succeeds with their new money. Likewise, a different set of common elements is consistently present when problems and unhappiness are created. I have included many of the stories to give you some vicarious experience and to help you see how the steps I recommend have worked in real-life situations.

Understanding the process and the dynamics of each phase will help you to avoid making unfortunate investment and lifestyle decisions. For instance, if you take action before you are prepared, you are likely to make some regrettable mistakes. A classic example of this is gifting. If you immediately start giving money away without understanding the long-term impact the gifts will have on your future finances, you yourself may be asking for handouts someday. Throughout the book I have provided several examples of gifting gone awry; I urge you to finish the book before you give *anyone* money.

Decisions, Decisions . . .

While you might feel overwhelmed or pressured to make decisions, *there are very few things you really need to think about now,* no matter where you are with your Sudden Money. For now, I advise you to

- Stay calm and not make decisions based on your emotions.

- Seek professional advice. For example, everyone needs to see an accountant and to find an experienced financial planner, and everyone can benefit from time with a good therapist.

- Avoid the pressure from others to make decisions you feel you are not ready for.

- Stick with my advice, even if it seems counterintuitive or if you feel like your progress is very slow.

Take a few minutes to read the rest of this chapter. Before you dive into your Phase One work, think about the entire sequence in a very general way. Reflect upon the idea of Sudden Money being an event that begins a journey. Before you embark on that journey, it would behoove you to educate yourself about what to expect.

Your journey has a definite beginning and clear landmarks along the way. It requires you to make decisions, and those decisions will affect your journey and its outcome. At any point, you can stop and rest or regroup, but if you plan your trip effectively from the start, you won't need to. Planning effectively from the start involves clarifying who you are, how you feel, and where you want to go.

Phase One: Preparation and Planning

Phase One is the anticipation and the planning for the receipt of the money. This is your time to get ready to make the decisions that will have lifelong consequences (e.g., where you will be living and whether you will begin or end a career). During this phase, emotional bookkeeping and financial planning are your most important tasks. These tasks involve determining how you feel about your new money, listing the range of choices you have because of it, and deciding which goals you'd like to accomplish with it. Finding a financial planner and becoming familiar with the investment process is a necessity.

The desired outcome of this initial stage of your Sudden Money Process is a financial plan that you have created with the help of the advisor you carefully selected. This plan, which is a list of your current and future desires and goals that are feasible, will be transformed into an investment plan in Phase Two.

Phase One has four parts:

1. Decision Free Zone (DFZ)

2. Chute of Emotions

3. Search for the Right Advisors

4. Goal Setting and the Reality Check

Phase One should be a time when you make as few decisions as possible. Instead, it is a time to *prepare* to make decisions. Part of preparing yourself is having a thorough understanding of your emotions. For this reason, most of Phase One takes place in your heart, your soul, and your mind. It is a time to think, to wonder, and to question, and it is critical that you spend whatever time you need to find the answers to the questions you will be asking yourself. If the amount you are receiving is large enough for you to make major changes in your lifestyle, Phase One could take over a year. Regardless of how long it takes, the time you invest in Phase One might be the best investment you will make during your Sudden Money Process.

The Decision Free Zone

The Decision Free Zone (DFZ) is about providing yourself time and space where you are free from the burden of making unnecessary decisions. The DFZ will be discussed in detail in Chapter 3, as will the few decisions that you *do* need to make. For now, know that Phase One is a time to understand your new feelings and your new financial position. To get the most from Phase One, you will want to begin to work with a financial planner and possibly a therapist.

POSSIBLY A THERAPIST? Your financial planner will need to know your emotional state; therefore, *you* will need to know your emotional state. This information will help your planner correctly guide and advise you.

It is not your planner's job to counsel you through the grieving process or through any of the other intense emotions that arrive with your Sudden Money. Even if you are not aware of any strong emotions, it is a good idea to discuss your feelings about the new situation you are in. As Phase One is the time for you to plan your future, and your emotional state will affect your decisions, reaching clarity regarding your emotions is of paramount importance. Though your finances may seem more factual and like safer ground, they do not exist in isolation of your emotions. Most bad financial decisions are due to unchecked emotions.

The Chute of Emotions

Several of my Sudden Money clients have used the metaphor of a chute when describing the emotional part of the windfall experience. The range of emotions that rushes through you can be overwhelming and confusing, and if you act on any part of it, you have the potential to cause yourself immeasurable financial grief. Even when the windfall is not so sudden, such as in the case of divorce settlements, the experience is not easy because of the emotions involved. My experience and my research show that one of the most influential factors in the success or failure of a Sudden Money Process is how the recipient deals with the set of emotions that accompanies the windfall.

Throughout this process, the emotional component may shift or completely change. It will be essential for you to understand your emotional swings and to learn to not react immediately to them. You need to try to define where you are emotionally, because many emotions emerge in a subtle way and go undetected until damage has been done.

Search for the Right Advisors

Even experienced investors and financial advisors need advice when it comes to Sudden Money. Taking the time to find the person who is right for you is vital to minimizing your stress and anxiety and maximizing the potential of your windfall. I'll show you how to find that person and tell you what you should expect during your search.

Goal Setting and the Reality Check

Once you feel comfortable that your decisions are not being dictated by your emotions, it's time to think about what you want from your new money. I suggest you create a Bliss List: a list of all of the things you want, without considering if they are feasible. Your next step will be to refine that list based on the financial reality of each item. I have developed the Reality Check exercise to effectively determine exactly how much money you have and how long it will last, given the different variables that will affect it. Inflation, your age expectancy, and the return on your investments will all affect the longevity of your money; you and your advisor should approach this issue in a systematic way before you make any major purchases.

Overview

Phase One: Planning

Goals. Understand yourself emotionally, understand your needs as an investor, find out what your new range of choices includes, and find an advisor who will help you develop a plan to manifest your most important present and future goals.

Decisions to make. Make only essential decisions and take this time to *prepare* to make all the other decisions you will make once you are out of the DFZ. The essential decision everyone shares in Phase One is whom they will hire as their financial planner.

Things to do. Sort through your feelings, list your short- and long-term goals, determine what your risk tolerance is, select a financial planner, and then take your information to that planner, who will help you create a financial plan to reach your goals.

Phase Two: Action

The financial planning you do with your advisor in Phase One will identify how much income your new money can safely sustain and when the optimal time is to begin investing. Your Phase One discussions will also help you shape lifestyle choices, such as what kind of home you can afford, whether it is wise to open a new business, and whether you can stop working.

Phase Two is the time to put your money to work to support the choices you have so thoughtfully made. While this might sound pretty straightforward, you cannot effectively do it until you know who you are as an investor. You will discover that there are some investments that are more suitable to your investment personality than others. I have included a tool to help you figure out what kind of investor you are so that you will be able to better grasp the subsequent discussion about the basic investment vehicles.

The overview of the main investment types includes the risks associated with them and factors that influence their fluctuations. You should start thinking about these issues as soon as possible because you will be addressing them when you meet with your advisor. You do not have to wait until you understand how investments work before you start working with your financial planner. Part of their job is to educate you on the range of investment choices. However, knowing more about yourself and investments enhances the quality of the planner-client relationship.

    Goals. To feel confident that you have taken the necessary action to manifest the goals that are most important to you. You will begin by choosing investments that support your financial plan.

    Decisions to make. Investment purchases should be based on your risk tolerance and the time horizons of your goals. Selecting the appropriate investments to support lifestyle decisions is the hallmark of Phase Two.

    Things to do. Meet with your advisors and review your goals, your philosophy, your family needs, and your ability to deal with risk. Make an implementation list of specific actions you will take (e.g., the purchase of investments) and when you will take them; then, execute each item.

Phase Three: Monitoring and Sharing

Phase Three lasts longer than the previous phases: It lasts for the rest of your life, and beyond. This is the time for you to watch your plan unfold. Your job now is to become a good steward of your wealth and to monitor as your money grows and works for you and for others you care about. You will always have decisions to make, but now they are refinements and adjustments because the overall planning and investing for the big picture have been accomplished.

    As time goes by, you will acquire more knowledge and more money maturity. You will need to respond to changes in the economy, in your family, and within yourself, but this part of the process should not be as overwhelming as the initial stage was. You will learn that no investment is without risk, that tax laws do change, and that your feelings about your money, your family, and your community change, as well. You will learn that money alone does not solve all problems and that it alone is not responsible for creating hopeless situations.

The turning point of Phase Three is when you realize that you have enough money and income for your own needs, and when you begin to think about passing your wealth on to your loved ones and sharing some with charitable causes. As with many of the other topics discussed in this book, both estate planning and charitable giving deserve their own entire book. These topics typically come later in the Sudden Money Process, but they are often the most rewarding aspects of having wealth. I have begun to address them here, and I will continue in my next book.

Goals. To learn to become a good manager of your money. You will work with your team of advisors—your financial planner, attorney, tax advisor, and perhaps your philanthropy advisor—to monitor, adjust, and plan the sharing of your growing wealth. You will feel a sense of increasing fulfillment in your life and a confidence that you are living within your means. When you share your good fortune with others, you will experience money as a source of deep satisfaction.

Decisions to make. Every year you will have different decisions to make. You will review your investments in light of your current needs and objectives. You will also monitor the results of your investments in terms of how they performed and how much risk you took to get your returns. If an investment is underperforming or creating more risk than you want, you must decide when to sell and move the money elsewhere.

Things to do. It will be important to set up a way to effectively monitor your progress and to become aware of legal and economic changes you are going to have to respond to. Typically, this is done through your advisors; however, it will always be more powerful if you are involved. Involved means at the very least that you are reading the mail you receive from your advisors, including your monthly investment account statements. It also helps if you establish a habit of reading the financial pages or listening to the financial news. You should have an annual review meeting with each of your advisors, and more often with your financial advisor.

The quality of your future depends upon your thoughts and actions of today and every day. The impact of what you choose to do or not to do will always emerge somewhere in your life. Following the recommendations within each of the phases detailed in this book will help you to make more conscious choices and create a future you will find fulfilling and satisfying.

PHASE ONE

The Decision Free Zone
What It Is and How to Handle It

The number one rule when receiving Sudden Money is to create an environment that is free from emotion-based decisions and free from the influence of others. This is what I call the Decision Free Zone (DFZ), and it is a place everyone needs regardless of how much they have received or how experienced they are with money. This chapter explains what you should and shouldn't be doing when you first receive your new money.

Whatever the amount of your windfall, your first mission as a Sudden Money recipient is to deal with your feelings about its origin and your feelings about money in general. This decision free period should be used to find out what your choices are and to think about what you want to do with your money. The key point is that the DFZ is not a place to go to hide from the emotions generated by the windfall process. Instead, it is a time to experience your emotions in a place that is not cluttered with inessentials such as investment decisions. The only decision that is essential for everyone during the DFZ is the selection of a team of advisors (i.e., a financial planner, an attorney, an accountant, and possibly a therapist).

Possibilities . . .

If you now have enough money to totally reinvent yourself, or if the source of your money is a loss, such as a divorce, an accident, or the death of a loved one, you probably have serious decisions ahead of you. On the other hand, if the amount is modest you may have a more narrow range of choices immediately ahead of you. Just remember that a modest amount of Sudden Money may not alter your life today, but if managed properly you may have future retirement choices otherwise unavailable to you. The DFZ is your time to discover and define your personal range of possibilities.

Patience . . .

The first instinct of many people is to invest all of their money immediately. There is nothing wrong with waiting awhile before you plunge into the stock market. In fact, all good financial advisors will agree that it is much better to accept the low interest rate of a money market account or a CD than to make hasty, questionable investment decisions. The low interest you will receive from safe and available investments during your DFZ time will not harm your financial future. However, the negative consequences of not allowing yourself to experience the emotions that emerge after the receipt of your windfall *can* be very harmful to your financial future.

The primary reason I advocate patience and waiting before you invest is that you are likely to end up changing your mind—several times. Any financial planner will tell you that one of the worst things you can do with money is to keep changing your mind about where it is going. When you act hastily you invariably have to conduct some damage control, which begins with getting yourself out of your original decision. This can be both costly and stressful. *The worst investment plans I've seen are those that have been totally rearranged within the first year.*

Be patient. Don't make long-term or unchangeable decisions. Better yet, don't make *any* decisions about your money beyond putting it in a safe place. Parking your money in a safe place gives you time to careen down the "Chute of Emotions" (Chapter 4), which is associated with the windfall experience.

Your Advisor's Role

Your advisor can help you select the best place to park your money. Together, you can explore issues such as:

- Should you use taxable or tax-free money market accounts?
- Do you need all of your money to be immediately available by writing a check, or do you need to get a higher interest rate by tying some of it up for a short period of time (e.g., a 6-month CD)?

Chapter 5 will help you choose an advisor.

How Much Time Should You Spend in Your DFZ?

It depends. The DFZ is not defined by any particular amount of time. It is common for widows and divorced women to take a year to acclimate to their new circumstances. Some people think that is a long time. Some don't. The point is to not rush yourself or allow anyone else to rush you.

It's okay to go slowly. I encourage you to take time to gather information, understand your options, ask questions, read, and spend quiet time with your thoughts and feelings. Joining a support group and working with a therapist will also help you to sort through your new situation. Meanwhile, keep in mind that it is normal to feel out of control and overwhelmed in the beginning. Much of that intensity will dissipate as you acquire knowledge, get a handle on all the paperwork you now face, and spend time with your financial planner developing your personal financial plan.

Your time in the DFZ should last as long as you need in order to feel comfortable about beginning to invest your windfall. Part of feeling comfortable is clarifying how you feel *about your money* before you start to use it. It would be unfortunate at best to allow your emotions to have too much influence over your decisions. Your money could end up going to all of the wrong investments and all of the wrong people, never allowing your windfall to reach its potential.

If you are looking for a distinct end to your DFZ, it is the time when you are feeling in control and confident that you are working with the right team of advisors. You should thoroughly understand the plan you have developed and the kinds of investments you are going to buy. You should be able to explain what you intend to do with your money—and why—to your grandmother, who has never had investment experience.

Sandra was 54 when her husband, Carl, who was also 54, died suddenly. Sandra never worked outside of their home, and Carl's income was enough to provide a comfortable life for them. If Carl had survived until he was 65 years old, they would have received a generous pension. Instead, the pension was only 25% of his salary. As for their retirement savings, they would have grown sufficiently by Sandra and Carl's mid-60s and would have nicely supplemented their pension. However, at the time of Carl's death, the savings weren't enough to provide for Sandra's needs.

Sandra's family was justifiably concerned and wanted to help. Her family members were not sophisticated investors, but they knew that she had very little room to make mistakes. An uncle looked through the Yellow Pages and found several financial planners for her to speak with. Sandra chose the one she felt most comfortable with and whom she thought understood her emotional state the best. The planner's advice was to take time to process all of her professional recommendations as well as all of the suggestions she was getting from everyone else.

Over the subsequent months, Sandra vacillated between feeling strong and clear, and fragile and confused. Her planner told her that she would be ready to start making investment decisions when she was able to clearly explain her financial plan to her family. Eventually, she was able to articulate her goals, her concerns, and how she was planning on managing her money to get where she needed to go. She told her family: "I know I need to live on this money for the rest of my life. I know my income will be less than I am used to, so I have made a budget and I will move to a smaller house. I am investing in bonds for income and stocks for growth. The stocks will pay me some income, as well. I'm leaving Carl's IRA and 401(k) money alone until I am 60 years old, and I'll start collecting social security at age 62."

This information let her family know that Sandra had a plan, understood her situation, and was making logical decisions. It also made them feel that Sandra was in good hands with her advisor and that she would not need their intervention. Sandra made sure to tell them that she appreciated their concern and that they were welcome to ask questions in the future.

Taking this approach can go a long way toward establishing healthy relationships with people who are concerned with your well-being. They probably don't want or need to know all of your private details, but they do want to know that you have a sensible plan, that you have an advisor who seems to be appropriate for you, and that you are unlikely to go off the deep end and lose your money and your future security.

Guidelines for Your Stay in the DFZ

1. *Don't give up control.*   Your friends and family will most likely be anxious to give you advice, and they might even want to assume control of your finances. There are very few situations, however, where relinquishing control over your money is a good idea.

When an amount of money suddenly manifests in your life, it is common to feel overwhelmed and to want to turn the money over to someone who has experience. This is especially true if you are busy with your career, dealing with debilitating emotions such as guilt and grief, or if you have always had a fear of handling money. But as easy as it may seem to let someone else take care of your money, keep in mind that it is your life and your future at stake. In the long run, you will be better off maintaining control of your own financial affairs.

In the beginning, it might seem impossible to navigate your way through the maze of decisions you are faced with. But give it time. Once you have a solid understanding of the basics, you will begin to develop the confidence you need to make lifestyle and investment decisions at the appropriate times.

Working with a financial planner and a tax advisor is different from giving someone total control over your investments and your income. The idea is to maintain control while getting the advice of professionals who know the nuances of personal finance better than you do. Most planners will work with you through your DFZ, and then they will help you set up an investment portfolio when you are ready.

If at that point you think that you might want to change your investments or your income, or even move your money to a different advisor, you should have that right. That is not a right to be underestimated. Later, you might want to take over some of the investing, so maintaining your right to do this can become very important. No one will ever care about your money and your needs as much as you do.

2. *Work with an advisor to create your financial plan and to establish your tolerance for risk.*   Preventing yourself from making decisions based on emotions and protecting yourself from the influence of others are the primary reasons for seeking help in the beginning of your Sudden Money experience. Most people lack objectivity when it comes to their own affairs, and even financial advisors need the advice of other experts regarding Sudden Money. Remember that the goal during the DFZ is to keep your money intact while dealing with the emotional issues that arise as you carefully develop a financial plan. That's not as easy as it may sound, even for seasoned investors.

A divorce attorney I know found herself in a surprising position. After her divorce, she used her settlement money to set up a private law practice. Her intention was to create more time to spend with her children. What she had not thought about when she was contemplating leaving the large practice she had been working for was how much time it takes to start a business.

After a couple of years of very long workdays and lower-than-desired earnings, she is now trying to sell her practice, and she is looking for another means to support her children. However, selling a small, struggling law practice is not easy, and her chances of getting all of her money back are slim at best.

After years of seeing her clients make similar mistakes, this attorney is demonstrating that she is as human and as vulnerable as her clients are. She is also demonstrating that many professionals who are excellent at diagnosing the problems and needs of others are not as effective when it comes to their own lives.

---

3. *Understand the implications of the transition to wealth management.* Even if you are an experienced investor, Sudden Money puts you in new territory, and you will need objective professional guidance. The windfall represents a quick transition from the *accumulation* phase of your financial life to the *wealth management* phase. It means your goals will probably change along with your tax bracket. In addition, estate planning decisions, which may not have been pressing, may suddenly be very important.

It's worth repeating: *Before you invest your new money, you should understand your new financial position from a wealth management perspective.* This vantage point will help you clarify your investment needs, and it could also help you recognize the need to add new investment strategies that were not appropriate before your windfall. All of this is most effectively done with the help of the right financial advisor, who may take some time to find. Chapter 5, "Search for the Right Financial Planner," will help you through this search.

4. *Make a list of necessary decisions.* Many windfall recipients feel disoriented during the early part of their Sudden Money experience. Their priorities change from one month to the next as they learn about the choices that are available to them for the first time.

Remember that while you are in the DFZ, your mission is to make only those decisions that are essential. This is where you need the advice of an experienced financial advisor. As a first step, I suggest that the two of you make a list of all of the decisions you need to make. Then comes the expertise of your advisor, who should be able to sort the list chronologically and to explain when and why you need to make specific decisions.

In many cases, you'll have the option to decide not to decide. For instance, you'll probably need to decide *how you will receive* the money, but you won't have to decide *how to invest it* until later. This is common in divorce settlements, pension payouts, and some insurance settlements.

When you *do* have a choice, you will probably have a deadline by which to make your election. Considering a tight timeline can add tremendous pressure; I recommend preparing yourself to make this kind of decision as soon as you are made aware of it.

A child was severely injured in an accident and his parents sued for damages. This money would in no way be considered a windfall, as it was to be used for the recovery of past medical expenses and toward payment of future medical expenses. The legal process took several years, and the anticipated outcome changed frequently. Meanwhile, the immediate medical expenses caused considerable strain within the family.

When they finally heard that their settlement was imminent, all the family wanted was to collect the money and to end their stress. The manner in which they would receive the money, however, had serious consequences that they had to thoughtfully attend to. If the money received in this type of settlement was a lump sum, it would be considered a recovery of damages and, therefore, would not be subject to tax. However, the income that they would receive after the money was invested would be taxable. On the other hand, if the money was received in the form of lifetime income rather than a lump sum, the income would be tax free.

They had never invested money before, and the thought of making an investment mistake was overwhelming. They chose to take enough to pay the existing medical bills and to receive a guaranteed amount annually. Now, 10 years later, the income is not enough to cover medical plus living expenses. In addition, there is no money for any unexpected major medical costs.

If they had taken the time to learn about investing and to find an appropriate advisor, they would have made long-term projections and discovered that they needed more income. Furthermore, their advisor would have shown them how it was possible to create that income by using the right investment strategy.

Necessary Decision—Anything That Will Affect Your Tax Bill

When it comes to retirement payouts, divorce settlements, and life insurance settlements, the choices you make are tax sensitive. You will be well served by working with your financial advisor, your tax advisor, and your attorney to reach a clear understanding of the tax implications before you make decisions. Once you know your options and their consequences, you will be prepared to make decisions and take action. Furthermore, some aspects of your tax situation do not involve making choices, but you need to know about them to effectively plan for your future. As soon as possible, find out how much of your money is taxable, at what percent, and when all payments are due.

Marge had stayed home to raise her children and to support her corporate husband, Steve. He filed the taxes, paid the bills, and managed the investments. Their divorce was final in October, and Steve's accountant filed a joint tax return for their final year together. Marge had a lot going on in her life, and paying attention to the final tax return was not high on her list of priorities.

During the subsequent year she spent time completely isolated, not dealing with the full reality of her life circumstances. She had not filed quarterly taxes nor had she thought of the capital gains taxes she would owe because of the investments she sold. Her alimony was $120,000 a year, and she owed income tax on it. She also owed capital gains tax of $60,000 on the $300,000 profit she made from selling the investments.

Marge had to sell more investments to get the cash to pay the IRS. Her taxes were prepared in March, and her new accountant made sure she started filing quarterly taxes. Marge not only had to pay the previous year's taxes, but she had to pay the April quarterly payments as well. This new tax reality made Marge scale back on her spending in order to ensure her quarterly payments were available.

Are You in a New Tax Bracket?

Your Sudden Money may have put you into a new tax bracket. This is yet another reason that it is important to work with a tax advisor early on. You will need to know how much of your income you can spend and how much should be sent to the IRS as a quarterly tax payment. When you are receiving a paycheck from an employer, your income taxes are typically withheld and sent to the IRS in your name. When you receive income from investments, taxes are not usually withheld, unless you specifically request withholding. Therefore, you may be growing a tax bill and not be aware of it until you file your taxes, which may not happen for a year. This is not a good surprise to have.

Not knowing your tax consequences can lead to a very high tax bill. That tax bill may put you into a cash flow bind or even require you to borrow money to pay your taxes. Then, the interest you will owe on the borrowed money in effect further increases your tax bill.

Furthermore, when you aren't clear about your taxes, you can easily establish a lifestyle that you really cannot afford. For example, if your investments are producing $100,000 a year, you really have $60,000 to $70,000 a year to spend after federal and state taxes are paid. If you are spending 30% to 40% more money than you have, you wind up digging yourself into a deep hole of debt.

Unnecessary Decision—Relocation

A common issue for windfall recipients is the immediate urge to sell their home and move to a new area. This is a major life decision that is difficult to undo if it turns out that you are not happy in your new home. To avoid this complication, I suggest you go to your desired new area and rent an apartment or a condo. Spend some time there. Go to the grocery store, read the local paper, go to the church or the synagogue you'd be joining, and take yourself out to eat. Determine the cost of living beyond the price of the homes in your new area. Become familiar with the real estate taxes and homeowners' association fees. Above all, take your time. I recommend that you take a year to make a relocation decision.

Unnecessary Decision—Early Retirement

A natural impulse of people who receive windfalls is to quit their day job. While retirement may be a possibility for some people, I caution *everyone* to meet with a financial advisor to make sure that their money will last without the fear or the reality that it will run out. The last thing you want is to be 10 years into an enjoyable retirement and then to find out that you have to go back to work.

When calculating how long your money will last, you must factor in inflation, which will boost your cost of living each year. In addition, you should stick with conservative estimates of how much you will need to live on and include a reasonable amount for unexpected events, which we all have experienced and will continue to experience. The Reality Check in Chapter 7 will help you with your longevity of money calculations.

A personal injury attorney I know uses the following metaphor when advising his clients about how to handle their settlements. *Picture yourself about to start a long walk across the desert. Your water supply is finite; if you drink it all too soon, you won't have another source to drink from. If you were going to make a mistake, it would be to drink less rather than more.*

Obviously, the water symbolizes the settlement money. It must last a long time, so it is better to live on a little less. Translation? Assume a low investment return and higher inflation when you are making future income projections.

5. *Delay gifting until you really know what you have.*   People give their money away for a number of reasons. Some feel guilty that they have money and their friends don't; some are fearful of the changes they see coming as a result of their windfall; some think they have more than enough money, and they good-heartedly desire to share their fortunes.

Whatever your motivation for gifting is, I suggest you postpone gifting until you have a firm grasp of your new financial position.

If you have plenty to share, your planner will make that clear and will help you work out a giving plan. The key is to determine that you do indeed have enough to give some away. Too many windfall recipients give away their money only to discover that they will need it in the future.

If you feel you absolutely must give some money away immediately, at least try to mitigate future damage by making small gifts. Explain that you are unsure of your taxes and other new requirements that have come with the money, so you are not in a position to make large gifts. It's not just an excuse—it's the truth.

Rose had the good fortune of being able to sell her late husband's business within a year of his death. The amount she received seemed quite generous: $2.5 million. Rose wanted to share the proceeds from the sale of the business with her three children, so she gave each child $250,000 and kept $1.75 million for herself. She planned to invest her money and estimated her investment income at about $85,000 a year. That amount, along with social security, would be only half of what her husband had been earning, but if she was careful she could get by on it.

However, since the sale occurred in February and she didn't get around to meeting with her accountant until October, she hadn't thought about the taxes that would have to be paid on the $2.5 million. Her accountant informed her that she owed capital gains tax and something called "depreciation recapture," totaling $800,000.

Meanwhile, the children had already used their money to pay off mortgages and debts and to finance the college expenses of their own children, so Rose could not ask them to share the tax bill. She had to pay it herself. After the hefty tax bill, Rose's income potential dropped to $45,000 per year. Her lifestyle would need to be greatly altered; she would have to leave the family home; and she would not have extra money to invest or to pass on to her children.

---

6. *If you don't know, calculate how much you owe and how much you spend.* In Chapter 6, "Goal Setting," you will learn that the expense assumption is the variable that has the greatest impact on long-term projections. If the amount of support of your Sudden Money is modest, your Reality Check will determine what your spending *limitation* will be. It will be up to you to design a lifestyle that fits within these limitations. If the amount is high, your Reality Check will show you the *range of income* you can consider and will give you an upper limit on spending.

Cyndi did not want to go to work after her divorce. She felt irreparably drained, first by the years of abuse she suffered at the hands of her ex-husband, and then by over a year of grueling divorce proceedings. She was determined to live off the assets she was left with. After selling the house, collecting all other assets, and paying the necessary taxes, she had $700,000. She had to make a plan to live on investment income.

Using the recommended assumption of the Reality Check, Cyndi had to limit her expenses to $26,000 a year until she was eligible for social security. The social security was estimated to be $12,000 a year, but would not become available for six years. Her desire to not work was strong enough that she accepted these limitations, grateful just to have the opportunity to not work.

Expenses, or Where Did All of My Money Go?

How much you spend each year will have a major impact on how long your money lasts. Unfortunately, most people do not have an accurate idea of how much they spend. To reach an estimate that is as realistic as possible, start by doing a trial budget using the income expense schedules in the back of this book. Use your credit card statements, checkbook registry, and any bills you have kept over the years to fill in the amounts spent on each category.

Most people will spend more than their list of expenses calls for, which is called *discretionary spending*. The funding of discretionary spending (sometimes called *mall money* or *mad money*) usually comes from visits to the ATM machine. These visits occur more frequently than most people estimate. It is so easy today to just go get some cash and to forget to enter the withdrawal in your checkbook. Being a semiconscious consumer is not an unusual state of existence, especially if you are in a fragile emotional state.

Even if you have so much money you couldn't possibly spend it all, it is still better to be aware of where your money goes. Remember that your money is an extension of you, and you get to use it as you want to. Spend your money with purpose; don't let it just evaporate into the unknown. If buying clothes is a priority, make the shopping intentional; otherwise, in the closet you will have clothes that you have never worn with the price tags still on them.

How Much Are You Spending?

If you do not already have a budget for yourself and you are unable to quantify how much you are spending, begin with your family bank statements. Sort your canceled checks into piles for food, housing, auto expenses, department store expenses, and so on. This is not hard to do, and it is necessary to determine how much you need each month. In addition, if you have dependent children, you will need to calculate anticipated expenses such as education, and you will want to factor in the cost of life insurance for yourself.

Or . . . The Alternative–The Cash Flow Exercise

Another way to find out where all of your money is going, starting today, is this simple cash flow exercise:

- Pay your bills twice a month and, in addition to listing them in your check registry, make a separate list that you will keep for several months, or start a spiral notebook with a page for each month for a year. If you are computer comfortable, use Quicken or another cash management system you like. What is important is that you can see on a piece of paper or on a computer screen where your money is going.

- Pay for everything else that is not a bill with cash.

- Give yourself an allowance by writing a check for the same amount each week. Buy your food, entertainment, and every-thing else with this cash. Don't go to the ATM machine—just use the allotted cash and see how you do.

You'll see right away what you are really spending if you are not using the credit cards, checks, or the ATM machine.

Cash Flow Watch

It will always be important to keep an eye on your cash flow. When Sudden Money recipients get into financial trouble, it is caused by either bad investments, overspending, or both. Just like the meteo-rologist keeps track of the weather each day, you should have a way to know that your cash flow is okay. When a hurricane is spot-ted way off in the ocean, meteorologists keep an eye on it. If it con-tinues to move toward land, they post a hurricane watch, meaning potential but not imminent danger. When you sense that things are out of control financially, you should go on *cash flow watch*.

If you have an aversion to any kind of budgeting, you will need to develop some way to check your spending before you get too far out of control. The following is a three-account *cash management system* that I recommend to every one of my clients.

1. *Emergency account.* One of these three accounts should be designated as an emergency fund. The income should be placed in an interest-paying account to be used for emergency expenses. It is good to use a money market account or a short-term CD or T-bill. This money should be easily available without large surrender charges. If you have an unexpected cash need, it is better to have an emergency fund than be forced to sell an investment.

   This account should initially be funded with one lump sum. Your advisor can help you determine how much should be held in the emergency account. If you do need this money at some point in the future, be sure to replace it as soon as possible.

2. *Holding account.* The remainder of the money should go into an interest-bearing holding account (e.g., a brokerage account). After that first time, rather than having numerous checks sent to you each month, keep your life simple by having all the interest, dividends, and any other investment distributions put into one money market account. Many brokerage firms automatically sweep all investment income into an interest-paying money market account, sometimes referred to as a *sweep account*. Use your month-by-month chart to determine what amount should be available by the end of the month.

   At the beginning of each month, write a check from the holding account to cover one month's expenses. Deposit this check into an operating account at a local bank. You should have more money coming into the holding account each month than you are budgeted to spend. Therefore, there should be money left over after you write the check to the operating account. The excess building in the holding account is being collected for large, nonmonthly expenses (e.g., annual insurance premiums), or for small emergency expenses (e.g., car repair).

3. *Operating account.* Pay your bills and all your monthly expenses from the operating account.

If you are regularly making additional withdrawals from the holding account that are not to cover large bills or emergency expenses, then you are spending more than you have budgeted or more than your Reality Check calls for. The cash management holding fund is intentionally limited to receiving your income so you can see how much you are spending and on what, without doing much damage.

Jeffrey was using this system for everything but his credit card payments. He was paying his Visa card bills from another money market account that was part of his investment account, and not part of his cash management system. The money was coming from the money market account that was originally designated as his emergency fund. The emergency money should not be spent or invested so that it will always be available for unexpected mandatory expenses (e.g., to replace a car, to pay for medical treatment, or to cover a cost associated with the kids).

By paying Visa charges of $2,000 to $5,000 a month, Jeffrey was draining the emergency fund, leaving him no choice but to sell investments if an emergency came up.

Over time, this scenario means using principal invested to pay income, which ultimately lowers the income and begins a dangerous downward cycle. If you are paying all the bills from your cash management account and there isn't enough in it, cut back your spending or rework your investment plan, don't just let it go.

If you are on a cash flow watch, go back to the cash flow system outlined above. I say go back because if your spending is getting out of control, you are not following the system.

7. *Know when a decision is irreversible. Irreversible* means you cannot change your mind. You cannot say, "*I didn't really mean that. Can I have my money back?*" When you enter into venture capital deals or other kinds of joint ventures, you are usually making an irreversible decision. The same is true when you give money to charities. And while real estate investments are not irreversible, they usually take a long time to get out of and may be costly to try to sell soon after your purchase.

When researching any investment, one of the fundamental questions you should ask is, *How do I get my money back?* With most stocks, bonds, and mutual funds, cashing out the investment is not a big deal, and it should take anywhere from 1 to 10 days. If you insist on making an investment decision while in your DFZ, these are the appropriate ones. Just remember that cashing out does not mean you necessarily get your money back; it means you get whatever the *market value* is at the time you sell.

When you buy life insurance, limited partnerships, or private offering investments, you will not have easy access to your money, whatever the value is. Insurance policies may not have much cash value for the first few years, and they have hefty surrender charges. Meanwhile, limited partnerships can lock your money up for many years, and since private offerings do not have a public market, you are not likely to have immediate buyers for your shares. While none of these investments is inherently bad, none is appropriate for purchase during your DFZ.

Yet another irreversible decision is the *irrevocable trust*. As the name suggests, when you put money into an irrevocable trust, in most cases, you have given the money away, and you no longer have access to it (although you may have access to the income it produces). While this may be an appropriate part of your financial and estate plan, it is important to work through the details with your planner, your attorney, and your accountant before you make a decision.

8. *Hold off on buying or starting a new business.*　Buying a business is always a serious decision. The old saying, "Everything costs five times more than you think and takes five times longer than you expect," applies especially to business ownership. This means you'll most likely have less income from the business; it may cost more to get it off the ground; and you may end up with an asset that you have trouble selling. Owning a new business or purchasing a franchise may be right for you, but it behooves you to allow yourself plenty of time to get a Reality Check on your finances and income needs and to do a thorough study of the potential of the business before you make a move.

9. *Review your insurance needs.*　Your new money creates a need to review your insurance needs. Because you might be considered rich, you might become a target for lawsuits. You can protect yourself and pay for the legal costs by purchasing a personal liability policy. Most people buy this kind of coverage as part of their homeowner's and auto insurance; it's called an *umbrella policy.* Buying a couple of million dollars' worth of this coverage is not expensive when it is purchased in conjunction with a homeowner's and auto insurance policy.

If you buy new homes, boats, and cars, be sure to increase your coverage for replacement and liability. If you are buying expensive jewelry, art, or antiques, be sure to have your purchases authenticated, appraised, and then insured, in that order. Many people skip the authentication step and just get an appraisal. If you have very expensive items, you might have trouble collecting from an insurance company if these items are lost or stolen.

When hurricane Andrew hit south Florida, many families lost art and jewelry collections. The insurance companies were trying to cut their losses anyway they could, and lack of authentication became their excuse for not paying claims. Many court battles were waged costing much money, time, and peace of mind before the claims were paid. The insurance companies said they had no way of knowing if the items in question were authentic, despite their appraisal value. One expert witness who appraised and insured the items recommends setting up an audit every two years to keep your records up to date.

In addition, you may need to increase your life insurance coverage. Most people would think that Sudden Money eliminates the need for life insurance. However, if you are now in a high estate tax bracket or if your money is received as guaranteed future payments, you'll need to do some estate planning. Life insurance is one way of creating the estate liquidity your heirs might need to pay estate taxes.

10. *Don't neglect your emotions.* Allowing yourself adequate time and space to experience the emotions associated with your windfall is so important that I have devoted an entire chapter to it (Chapter 4, "The Chute of Emotions"). For now, suffice it to say that I know of hundreds of people, some whom you have heard of, who have lost millions of dollars because their emotional state clouded their judgment. On the flip side, there is nothing as rewarding as achieving the mental and emotional clarity that enables you to create the kind of financial plan that will nourish your family and your community for years to come (see Chapter 14, "Giving and Sharing").

Following the guidelines of the DFZ will help keep you safe during the most delicate part of your Sudden Money Process. With time and the proper guidance, you will emerge from your DFZ as a more confident person, ready to become a good manager of your money. The first payoff is the dissolution of the stress that was associated with the initial receipt of the money. Then, as your situation becomes clear and understandable, you can begin to enjoy your life, no longer consumed with the worry, doubt, and fear that the money seemed to have brought with it.

But first, you have to deal with your emotions . . .

Feeling Your Windfall
The Chute of Emotions

During Phase One of the windfall experience, what frequently happens is that you experience a range of emotions that has been described as similar to going down a chute. You may feel elation, fear, depression, anger, grief, and distrust, all while you careen down this chute. This process is necessary, and you should not make any major decisions until you have taken the time to absorb what has happened and what it can mean to you. This is what the Decision Free Zone (DFZ) is all about.

Many emotions and their impact can be subtle and can go undetected until they have wreaked havoc on your financial life. This chapter will help you identify emotions—and combinations of emotions—that can play an important role in how you view and ultimately handle your new money.

You Can Ignore Them, but They *Won't* Go Away

It is not a good idea to ignore or deny any of your emotions, because they will only resurface at a later date. And when they do, they might be disguised as some other issue, making them that much more difficult to resolve. For instance, they might show up within the context of your investment decisions or in how you regard and treat the people in your life.

Ultimately, the degree of enjoyment and security you get from your Sudden Money event will be impacted by your emotions. Emotions can take many shapes, and most people benefit from enlisting the aid of a therapist who can help them understand the stages of complex emotions such as grief. Countless people have found that once they understood they were in the grieving process, which has stages that are relatively predictable, the anxiety associated with the experience lessened. They still felt the anger or hopelessness appropriate for where they were at emotionally, but they also understood that their pain would keep diminishing and that there were specific actions they could take to move through the experience more quickly.

Don't Try to Do It All Yourself

Just as it is difficult to be your own advisor in other areas, it is difficult to be your own psychotherapist. Even people who are trained in psychology, psychotherapy, or psychiatry have difficulty effectively treating themselves. A highly regarded therapist from Boston reports that he has a network of other therapists to work with when he gets stuck dealing with one of his life's many challenges.

Most of us do not have such a network. In fact, many families have a built-in bias against admitting they need professional help. Somehow, the concept of needing help translates into admitting weakness. Your DFZ is the perfect opportunity to get over this resistance and make sorting out your feelings a crucial part of being a responsible steward of your Sudden Money.

Don't Expect Anyone Else to Do It All, Either

It is difficult for you to be your own therapist; likewise, you shouldn't expect anyone else who is not trained in that area to do it either. I'm referring to your financial planner, your accountant, your attorney, and anyone else whom you trust and like enough to open up to. All of these other professionals have specific jobs that they are educated and paid to do. Let them do their jobs, and hire a therapist to help you with your emotional issues.

As professionals, your other advisors will understand that you must deal with your feelings before you make life-altering decisions, and they will be supportive. In fact, if they have experience with Sudden Money clients, they most likely know of a local therapist trained to deal with money issues.

You might also find a local support group to be comforting and healing. Many communities have groups for widows and accident victims, and most large corporations offer counseling for downsized employees. There are even groups that were formed to deal with the unique burdens of inherited wealth, and I know of at least one support group that was formed solely for lottery winners. I recently developed Sudden Money Retreats, which are weeklong orientation courses for recipients of windfalls and include a day with a specialist in the psychology of money.

You might also find some insights and help from the dozens of books on the psychology of money and other money-related topics. Considering the study of how we react to money is more popular than ever; I anticipate more and more books on the subject in the future. Check with your local bookstore or do an online book search for other books on this topic.

You might also want to talk to your minister, priest, or rabbi. Though they may not be specifically trained in the psychology of money, they undoubtedly have dealt with many individuals and families in crisis. They understand the pain that emotions can cause and might be able to help you to see through your confusion and make sense of your experience. Many clergy members are also good sources for finding therapists, because they tend to know their own limitations and have used professionals over the years.

The Chute of Emotions

When you receive your Sudden Money, it may be tempting to immediately put an additional room on your house or take a world cruise. There will be plenty of time for that; neither your house nor the world is going anywhere. Your first order of business is your emotions.

Numbness

Immediately after something traumatic occurs, and that something could be good or bad, many people say that they feel nothing. There is no appropriate elation, grief, or even disbelief about what has happened. Instead, they feel numb.

While numbness isn't the worst thing that could happen, it unfortunately is most often accompanied by indifference. This could be a recipe for disaster because if you don't care what happens and if you aren't feeling anything anyway, you just might take someone up on their proposition to take all of your money and invest it in a new theme restaurant.

If you are numb, chances are you have a whole bunch of feelings lurking beneath the numbness that are screaming to get out. The numbness could be your defense against actually having to experience those feelings. The good news is that once you work through them you'll be in a much healthier, clearer place. The bad news is that in order to get to that place, you have to do get down to business, which might be painful, and should include some therapy.

Fear

The way most people work through their fears is to develop a system of identifying the fear, getting and facing the facts, and then determining if they can live with whatever the real risk is.

For example, many people without investment experience have a general fear of losing their money. Their real fear, however, is often more specifically of the stock market. Once the fear is known, it can be addressed. The planner's job is to explain the risk of the stock market by describing the cycles the stock market has gone through over the years. They can also identify what events seem to trigger the ups and the downs of the market and which types of stocks are riskier than others. They can show you what the worst loss in a particular investment's history was and how long it took to recover.

In the case of stock market fears, there is statistical information that will help the planner to quantify the potential risk of each kind of stock. For other fears there may not be statistical information. However, you still need to get an idea of how much risk you are facing or the likelihood of the worst case happening.

Once you have the information and know what the worst case would look like, you can decide whether you want to take the risk. Always try to use information and good judgment rather than emotions.

Even after working through initial fears, several people I have worked with continue to express fears each time they face an unfamiliar situation or decision. Over time they have learned how to dissolve their fear by gathering information and putting the facts into the context of their personal finances.

Fear of Loss

When you don't have money, you don't have any money to lose or to worry about. When you acquire money in a lump sum, it logically follows that you suddenly have something to lose. Perhaps this is the first time you have felt this potential for loss. Don't underestimate this fear, as it can be incapacitating both financially and emotionally. And don't deny or ignore it either, because it will just show up again and again until you acknowledge it and deal with it.

It is important to communicate this fear to your financial planner. Your planner will tell you that fear is a predictable reaction to Sudden Money. But while it is a natural response, that doesn't mean it doesn't need to be managed. Fear will influence investment decisions until it dissipates. This means that you need to monitor its intensity and be wary of making major decisions until you reach a point where your decisions *are not related to your fear.*

EDUCATION IS YOUR BEST WEAPON There are some basic principles of investing that everyone should know before investing a penny. One of these fundamentals is that all markets (i.e., stocks, bonds, international, and domestic) will have periods of time when they are declining. Being able to withstand normal market declines is essential for any investor. If you have a strong fear of losing money, you have a strong likelihood of doing just that—losing money. Over and over again, declining markets have come back and moved ahead of where they were before the decline. The losers are the people who bail out during the low points.

The conservative way to make money has historically been to invest for the long term, staying put even when the share price or bond value has declined. A fearful investor has great difficulty doing this, and therefore is at greater risk of losing money. Chapter 8, which explains risk tolerance (a close relative of fear), and the subsequent chapters describing the most popular investment types, are must-reads before you enter the world of investing for the first time.

Isolation

Most people need to be connected with their families, friends, or coworkers; however, that connection might be threatened or even lost when one person suddenly becomes wealthier than everyone else in the circle. Why? Think of it this way: When you and your circle of friends and family are similar, and you change in a way that they are envious of, *their perception* might be that you have lost your connection with them. They might *think* that you no longer know what it is like to be like them. They might minimize your problems because they think that your money can either buy you out of your problems, or that it is at least some form of consolation.

When the ones you have been most at ease with now treat you like someone else—maybe someone better than they—you have lost your home base. In some cases, this is only temporary, and if you talk about the situation rather than ignoring it, it is sometimes resolved. In many cases, however, it becomes a permanent part of the Sudden Money experience, and needless to say, it is not always the best part.

Unworthiness

Feelings of unworthiness often manifest themselves in the mishandling of money. This mishandling usually takes the form of making bad decisions that lack any discernible sign of logic. People who feel unworthy often try to rid themselves of their money because, consciously or otherwise, they don't think they deserve it. Squandering also occurs because newfound money challenges who the recipient is, and many people are not up to the challenge. These feelings are best dealt with in psychotherapy because they are not part of the investment decision process.

Feelings of inadequacy frequently have deep roots, and they probably existed long before the Sudden Money. Prior to the arrival of their Sudden Money, most people had developed ways to deal with these feeling so they did not show up on a regular basis. When new money arrives, however, feelings of unworthiness must be acknowledged and worked through. As with other emotions, if this feeling is not resolved, it will cloud your judgment and cause you to make inappropriate, hasty, or just plain bad decisions.

Resentment

If your Sudden Money came from a divorce settlement or a horrible accident, you might feel resentful of the person or the circumstances that brought the money. For example, some divorces are the result of years of abuse, which you cannot put a dollar value on. Any resentment may result in the money being lost or used in a negative way.

Since the money that has come to you is probably important to your future well-being, you must try to separate your feelings of resentment and to see the importance of managing the money for your future good. By letting the money go to waste, you subtly continue your own pain or abuse. The money does not have to represent the past; it is possible to let go of the past and to start the new life the money offers you.

Martha's 35-year marriage didn't survive a midlife crisis. Her physician husband chose to discard his marriage and family for a new life with a much younger woman. Not only had Martha lost her husband, she lost her lifestyle, her social structure, and her hope for her future.

The combination of settlement money and temporary alimony was not nearly enough to allow Martha to live as she had been living when she was married. Therefore, early on, she made the decision to make the best of her situation by moving out of the expensive community where her husband and new wife lived, and she bought a home she could afford. She realized from her first planning session that she would never live as she used to, but that she could live a comfortable life and never have to go back to work if she invested and spent wisely.

Resistance

Your Sudden Money might put you in a position where it is possible to significantly alter your lifestyle in a positive way. Naturally, that requires change. Unfortunately, many people are resistant to change because it means stepping into the unknown. It can also mean an end to relationships and routines that have become part of your life. Even problem areas of your life may be difficult to change when they are familiar and comfortable.

For instance, you may find you continue a relationship with a difficult person, or you continue to struggle with a situation that is no longer necessary. You continue because of your fear of loss: leaving routines and people behind. You may even have enough money to quit your job and to move to the tropical paradise that you have always dreamed of. Then, surprisingly, you find you cannot leave the people you work with, even though you have hated getting up every morning to go to work.

Resistance to change is common, and in most cases it is no cause for alarm. Many Sudden Money recipients combat resistance by simply taking their time and working through their new possibilities very slowly. This way, the decisions they make are deliberate and well thought out. For instance, that move to the ideal tropical climate comes only after they have determined that it is a financially comfortable decision. In addition, they have thoroughly contemplated what it means to start over in a new locale, including establishing new friends and new routines.

If you find the prospect of change overwhelming, inaction is better than action in the beginning. Allowing yourself to be overwhelmed by the fact that your life has changed dramatically and that you have oodles of new worries is hardly productive, but eventually you are going to have to deal with the details of your new life. Let your therapist and planner guide you during this time; they will tell you what you should be attending to.

Distrust

Distrust can undermine any relationship, regardless of how long it has existed and how good it has been in the past. Some people start to distrust others and wonder if the people in their life are maintaining or beginning a relationship just because of the newly acquired money. This emotion is common for windfall recipients, and it is especially prevalent among those whose windfall is well publicized. Characters of all sorts come out of the woodwork when you've suddenly acquired millions of dollars, but not all of the characters are bad.

One man had been a successful business professional prior to winning the lottery. When the newspapers carried the story of his new fortune, he felt invaded by all of the phone calls and solicitations from stockbrokers, insurance salespeople, real estate agents, and other strangers interested in him for his money. He exaggerated the situation until his perception was that everyone in his life wanted something from him. It did not take long for him to take his immediate family out of the country and withdraw from the rest of his family and friends.

He now lives the life of a reclusive rich man. His phone number is unlisted, his home is guarded, and his family and friends miss him and wish he had never won the lottery. According to his sister, he had plenty of income before the lottery, yet there was never a problem with any of his family members or friends. The reality was that none of his siblings needed or wanted any part of his wealth before or after he won the lottery. But his perception was colored by his experiences with intrusive outsiders, so he didn't see his friends and family realistically.

There is a fine line between being skeptical and distrustful. It is logical to question why someone who was never friendly before suddenly acts as though you are an old friend. It also makes sense to be suspicious of those who claim to have a deal you can't refuse or an investment you can't lose with. Remember the simple rule that while you are in your DFZ, your reaction to any sales pitch is the same—no thanks. Once you are further along in the DFZ and you are developing your financial plan, you will discover what you really want to buy and how much you can spend on investments, homes, and the deal of the century.

I suggest that you separate the new people from the ones who have been in your life all along. Give your real friends time to get used to your new money. Like you, they will be stymied at first, but they might settle back down and just be your friends after a short period. The new people are difficult to sort through, so my advice is to let them earn your trust and confidence over time. If you don't have an unlisted phone number already, get one so you at least have some control over who can get to you.

Lack of Confidence and Lack of Experience

You might be able to run a Fortune 500 company, but if you suddenly acquire a great deal of personal wealth, you might begin to doubt your ability to make decisions.

Most of us have a nasty habit of overgeneralizing when it comes to intelligence. We think that if someone is intelligent and successful in one area, they should exhibit those same characteristics in every area. This is particularly true of people who are involved in any kind of business management.

To begin with, business management is not synonymous with personal financial management. Managing the finances *of a company* of any size does not necessarily involve the same skills and knowledge that are needed to successfully manage *personal* finances. Nevertheless, many people will erroneously expect you to be well versed in the ways of the stock market just because you have been successful in corporate America.

One CEO of a large NYSE company invested only in guaranteed investments during his career years. He didn't feel he had the time to learn about or worry about the stock market. When he received his lump sum pension money, he was unprepared to invest in stocks. He understood that stocks are important as an inflation hedge but he hadn't had the experience of owning them. Through friends who had retired earlier than he, he found that you do the same thing in personal finance as you do in business when you are not trained in a specific area—you work the best professional you can find.

Exuberance

You may feel exuberant and empowered when you receive your windfall. That's good, and you should. You may also feel that you are immortal, capable of changing lives, and in a position to save the world. That's not so good. Exuberance gone awry has been responsible for many financial debacles.

Suddenly having money is a powerful experience, but it does not automatically make you smarter, better looking, or more sophisticated than you were before. In fact, be wary of people who treat you as though you've been completely transformed, especially if they suddenly express interest in you after years of ignoring you.

If you had ever thought that for some reason wealthy people had more value than you did, you are particularly vulnerable to fall into the ego trap, which can lead to poor decisions. "Don't get above your raisins" is an old southern saying that advises you to remember who you are and not to put on airs and act like someone or something else.

Furthermore, the arrogance that some Sudden Money recipients exude can be sensed by scam artists from miles away. Scam promoters seem to sense the weakness of people who are not able to admit they don't know what they are doing or who are unwilling to follow the advice of prudent professionals.

Because of your Sudden Money, you might be told that you are an accredited investor who is eligible for investments reserved only for the big-money people, such as private placements, limited partnerships, and venture capital deals. But there is more to being an accredited investor than the amount of money you have. You also must be an experienced investor. There is a reason why some deals require you to have lots of money and to be experienced—*because they have more risk and the organizers have the responsibility to be sure you know what you are doing and can afford to take the possible losses.*

Don't let anyone tell you that wealthy people don't invest in mutual funds, stocks, and bonds. These traditional investment categories are the backbone of most portfolios and, in many cases, they are the only assets wealthy people invest in. You have not outgrown stocks and bonds just because you have new money. Start with the basics, and work toward becoming a seasoned investor. Once you are comfortable with your investment knowledge and skills, you can start to diversify if you really are intrigued with what the local big boys are doing. Just never put your family's security at risk for the hope of a bonanza from these kinds of investments.

Guilt

When the receipt of money is the result of the death of a loved one, the insurance or inheritance money will often produce feelings of guilt. Even when the death represents an end to years of caregiving, guilt is the common, dominant emotion. Fortunately, while it may be an inevitable emotion, it is also one that usually passes with time.

However, while it is around, guilt is one of those emotions that can be difficult to detect. Meanwhile, its effects can creep into many areas of your life and be the seed of poor decisions. If the origin of your money was a death, be sure to read the section on grief that follows. I strongly suggest that you deal with your feelings of guilt in psychotherapy with a grief specialist.

When Ann lost her husband, her children did not intrude on her financial decisions. Their reasoning was that she was a physician who was well educated and able to make her own choices. They did not realize that she had deep feelings of guilt because her husband, also a physician, did not get to enjoy the money they had saved for their entire lives. She also felt guilty about the insurance money she received.

Within three years she had gone through most of the money. She traveled incessantly and even brought friends and family along with her. Her trips were all first class, and when her family would ask if she could afford such an expense, her response was, "Of course, Daddy left me very well off." Ann also was generous with her grandchildren; she paid for their college educations and helped them get started with their lives after college. She was equally generous with the local charities, fully endowing her favorite one.

By the end of year four, the amount in her mutual funds dropped so low that she realized she wouldn't have enough to maintain her house. She was forced to sell her house immediately and buy a condo.

Her children finally figured it all out when her condominium board announced an assessment of $15,000 for each owner, and Ann asked her children for the money. Today, she is subsidized by her children just to make ends meet.

Grief

Grief is a universal emotion that psychologists, sociologists, and anthropologists have found has a profound impact on individual survivors as well as entire cultures. Its stages include shock, anger, depression, and isolation, and the progression culminates with acceptance. Each of the stages can last from weeks to years, and while there is a general order to them, stages can be repeated and even skipped. Not everyone gets through the process to the end.

Regardless of the details of your particular process, your grief can easily cause you to lose interest in your own well-being and to view the future as painful darkness. However, what might feel like a lifelong sentence to heartache might be a stage that must be experienced before you can successfully move on. Many times we want to get as far away from pain as possible, in which case discussing it with someone is threatening because that will bring up the precise feelings we do not want to address. But researchers tell us that not dealing with the pain of grief only makes it worse and makes it last longer.

When you are grieving, it is especially important that you avoid making unnecessary decisions. No one makes good financial decisions while they are feeling hopeless. There are more important things that you need to take care of—like yourself. You must understand that while you are grieving, particularly in the beginning, you are in a fragile state. You need to take care of yourself physically and emotionally. Unfortunately, taking care of yourself is often the last thing on your mind. This is why I strongly suggest joining a support group or meeting with a therapist.

If you insist on keeping your grief to yourself, I urge you to at least read one of the books on the grieving process, or visit one of the web sites or chatrooms for grievers. This will reinforce that you are going through the same stages that millions before you have passed through. While no one has been in your shoes and you might think that no one knows how you feel, there are thousands of people who have their own tragic stories to tell and whose experiences can help you move through your grief.

Mark and Janet were both in their 50s, and they had started to travel and to enjoy life after the last of their kids moved out. They were packing to go on vacation when Mark suddenly experienced chest pains and died of a heart attack. Janet described the pain she felt as unimaginable: a word like *grief* just didn't begin to describe it. Janet spent the first six months after Mark's death in a daze, and while her children and friends were there for her, she couldn't feel or do anything. She just wanted to die.

A buyer came along for the house, which had not even been put on the market. Janet had not thought about selling the house, but she did think about getting as far away from it as possible, because it reminded her of her husband. She sold the house, and to this day, she deeply regrets that decision.

Janet was not open to discussing her feelings with too many people, but she knew she had to pull herself together and to go on with her life. As she read various books, she began to get a clearer picture of what she was going through. She took the actions she could handle: She hired a financial planner and spent time with the accountant who had always handled her taxes. After several meetings and planning sessions, she began to make decisions.

Her first decision was that she wanted only guaranteed investments—she did not want to worry about losing money, and she wanted a predictable income. Then she worked with her accountant to sell the commercial building where Mark had his office. That deal was structured to give her income and added security.

Today, Janet goes to monthly meetings that her financial planner has for women in situations similar to hers. She is now ready to begin to learn more about investing, and she is taking a look at her long-term future. Although she made some classic mistakes that cannot be reversed, she is making all the right moves now. Janet knows the pain will never go away entirely. But she also knows that her life is in her hands, and she can, and will, continue to move forward step by step.

THE URGE TO GIVE IT ALL AWAY In extreme cases, some Sudden Money recipients will try to get rid of all of their money to avoid change or because they feel guilty or unworthy. If this is your experience, try to concentrate on the productive elements of the windfall, such as the ability to give more money to charities, fund someone's education, or start your own charitable foundation. All of these can be achieved without calling attention to yourself if you wish to remain anonymous.

Give yourself some time to process your emotions and to work with your Bliss List and Reality Check. Then, if you really do want to give it all away, at least make certain it goes to an organization that has not only a plan to use the money effectively, but also a track record of accomplishment. It will be wise to take a long time—like years—with this kind of gifting plan, to make sure your money goes to the right places.

Once you (and your therapist) feel that you have successfully worked through your feelings, you will be ready to begin thinking about what you want from your new money. To do this, you have to search your heart about what money means to you and where you want it to take you. A seasoned financial planner will help to guide you through your thinking about money, so that you are in the optimal position to chart your financial course. The following chapter will help you find that person.

Search for the Right Financial Planner

No matter how helpful this book is to you, it is not a replacement for a personal financial planner. I believe that all recipients of Sudden Money—even Certified Financial Planners—need to work with a financial planner for some period of time. The issue is not whether you need a financial planner, but how you will find the right one for your particular situation.

This chapter will describe the various types of financial advisors, explain why I recommend that you use a Certified Financial Planner, and take you step-by-step through your search for the right person to help you manage your Sudden Money.

It has never been my intention to give you specific financial planning advice. Although this book covers the most common Sudden Money scenarios, it could not possibly account for the many variables that make each person's situation unique and deserving of its own planning. The only publication that *can* address your unique goals, emotions, and family requirements is your own personal financial plan.

To create that customized financial plan, you should work with a financial planner who has experience advising people in similar Sudden Money situations. The right planner can minimize your chances of blowing the opportunity your money presents. The wrong planner—or no planner—can send you on the road to financial ruin. To get the full benefit from your Sudden Money, your optimal situation would be to work with the right personal financial planner from the beginning. Fortunately, there is no rush to make decisions about investing, so you can take your time searching for the right person.

I have warned against turning control of your money over to another person. It is your money and your livelihood, and no one will care as much about it as you do. But I have also explained that working with a financial planner does not mean that you have given up control or responsibility. The planner's job is to help you formulate your goals, understand your ability to handle risk, and prepare you to make your own decisions. Their long-term job is to help you respond to changes: in your life, in the economy, and in tax law.

Who Is Getting Help

According to various studies and surveys, the vast majority of people whom most would consider affluent do not do their own investing or their own financial planning. Instead, they prefer to hire highly trained professionals, much as a corporate CEO would hire a consultant to study an issue and report back on all the options and give recommendations. A report by Phoenix Duff & Phelps, entitled "The American Dream Reconsidered" (1997), used several studies and surveys to reach the following conclusions:*

- That advice giving is on the rise
- That affluent investors own mutual funds
- That affluent investors have reservations about investing on their own
- That the more money people have, the more likely they are to rely on professional advisors

As the financial services industry continues to study the savings and investing habits of high-income and high-net-worth individuals, it finds these investors to be less interested in financial products or shopping at financial supermarkets and more interested in developing and maintaining good chemistry with a financial advisor. In fact, trust was considered by the majority of investors sur-

---

* Phoenix Duff & Phelps, "The American Dream Reconsidered" (1997).

veyed to be the most important element in the investor-advisor relationship.

What's in a Name

As you begin looking for an advisor, you will find many different titles used by financial services professionals. Some titles signify important qualifications, while others can be used by just about anyone wanting to pass themselves off as financial services professionals. Just remember that you are not trying to hire a title; you are trying to hire a person. When a title indicates intensive education and ethical requirements, it is no longer just a title—it is a credential. The most recognized financial planning credential is the Certified Financial Planner (CFP) designation.

I am a CFP, and I believe it is an important credential that you should look for as you interview candidates. However, there are people who are exceptions to the rule: I know people who are not CFPs, whom I would not hesitate to refer to my family and to friends. Their clients benefit greatly from their expertise, their caring, and their ethics. If you are referred to someone who is not a CFP, by all means, interview that person. If a candidate offers all of the other qualifications that you are looking for, the absence of the CFP designation should not matter.

What Exactly Is Financial Planning?

As a profession, financial planning is somewhat new. The College for Financial Planning presented its first CFP designation in 1979. As the profession has matured and evolved, it has built a reputation for holding its members to high ethical standards. They must conform to state and federal regulations and participate in a rigorous continuing education program.

Financial planners are trained as generalists, but many specialize in a particular financial discipline, such as estate planning, retirement planning, investment planning, risk management, or tax planning. Other specialties include divorce planning, planning for family-owned businesses, and planning exclusively for women.

The process of financial planning is different from tax preparation or the kind of investing that most stockbrokers do. It involves viewing your finances as a whole and making decisions with this big picture in mind. A good accountant can help you find ways to minimize your taxes, and a stockbroker can give you good advice on stocks and bonds. If neither the accountant nor the broker knows your overall financial picture, including your goals and family needs, their advice will be of limited use. When new money comes into your life, the tax and investment decisions you have to make will be easier and more appropriate if they are based on your entire financial landscape rather than on parts of it.

Financial planners first help you focus on your personal goals and objectives, and then they help you develop an in-depth plan tailored to meet your needs. They are trained to understand your overall financial picture and *to help you to understand it better, too.*

Throughout the relationship, your advisor should constantly keep you on the course that you both set, making adjustments to accommodate your life changes. It is quite common to get emotionally caught up in a stock market buying frenzy, or to want to sell investments that are going through a down cycle. Knee-jerk reactions to financial news, though quite human, are usually a mistake. Calling your planner and discussing an investment decision within the context of your financial plan can save you from many unfortunate and regrettable investment mishaps.

For some people, working with a planner may be limited to an hourly basis. The planner discusses the initial financial plan, and the client implements the accompanying investment plan without the aid of the planner. This kind of relationship is effective for individuals with the time, temperament, and training to make and monitor their own investments and keep current with the tax law changes. For the majority of people though, an ongoing relationship with the right planner is the most effective way to go.

What You Should Be Looking For

The goal of your search is to find a seasoned professional with whom you can develop a relationship. This relationship may be more personal than most of your other professional relationships, because money is a very personal matter. When you discuss your money, you are discussing your hopes and your fears, your dreams and your disappointments.

Many people ordinarily do not discuss their personal finances with their friends, family, or business partners. When they do, the conversation is not easy. Good planners will encourage you to learn how to discuss this very personal matter because it will help them get to know you better. The better they know you, the better they can advise you.

A financial planner told me the following story:

The first time I heard an elderly male client discuss his impotence and his incontinence, I was embarrassed and uncomfortable. That was until I realized he was telling me of his fear of aging and dying without having provided properly for his family. He could have just said, "I'd like to go over my estate plan to make sure everything is in order." Without his very personal disclosure, I might not have understood his urgency and his sadness. I discovered that I was one of three people who knew of his physical difficulties. He told me because I already knew about the most private part of his life—his money. His health was actually less of a personal issue for him.

That's the kind of relationship all planners should be developing. That's how comfortable you should feel with your financial advisor. This highly personal side of the relationship between a planner and client develops over time, as trust and confidence build. No one expects you to reveal your innermost secrets when you first begin the relationship. What matters at the beginning is looking for someone with whom you feel safe and with whom you *think* you could build that kind of relationship.

Conducting the Search

Conducting the search for the right financial planner may take time. Because the right planner is one of the elements for successfully managing your Sudden Money, take the search seriously and be systematic. Start by making a list of what you want from the planner and a list of interview questions. Be prepared to check references and credentials. If your search will involve interviews with several planners, take notes immediately after each interview. Don't be in a hurry to make your decision. Remember, you are looking for someone to have a long-term relationship with.

What Are My Criteria?

Ideally, you are looking for someone who regularly works with people like yourself and who will understand your unique Sudden

Money–related needs. Your friend's brother-in-law may be a great life insurance salesman, but unless he also has years of experience as a financial planner working with clients with financial circumstances similar to yours, he is probably not a good candidate. Likewise, your sister may be a successful stockbroker, and eventually you may enlist her for her expertise, but in the beginning of your Sudden Money experience, you don't need investment advice. While you are in the Decision Free Zone (DFZ) of Phase One, you need to focus on planning, not investing.

Minimum Requirements

When sorting through the list of potential candidates, look for these minimum requirements:

- Experience in dealing with clients who have similar needs
- Experience (no less than five years) as a full-time financial planner
- History free of infractions with state or federal regulators
- Someone with whom you feel comfortable communicating

What you are *not* looking for is someone who is more interested in what they can sell you than what your needs are. For this reason, interviewing a stockbroker, or some other advisor compensated solely by commission, might not be a good idea. After all, most brokers are compensated when they buy or sell securities, and during your DFZ, you don't want to buy anything. Your best interest should be the reason for any recommendation by your financial advisor.

Where to Start Your Search

Choosing the right advisors will be important to present and future success. The search will take time, but it will be time well spent.

Recommendations from Others

Finding potential candidates may be easy if your friends and family use financial planners. Simply ask them if they know of anyone they would recommend to someone in your position. It is highly likely that your accountant and/or your lawyer will have worked with financial planners in your area. They can be a particularly good source of potential candidates. If you don't find someone you are comfortable with through these personal recommendations, you will have to broaden your search.

The Phone Book

Begin by looking in the Yellow Pages under "Financial Planners." Most independent planners will be listed along with the services they offer. When you call, ask if they offer a free initial visit to determine whether they can provide the necessary help. In the meantime, they will send you some information that should include a company brochure, a disclosure statement of the services they offer, the cost of the services, and the backgrounds of the professionals on staff.

Banks and Brokerage Firms

Many brokerage firms and some banks offer the kind of planning services you will need. When contacting these larger companies, I recommend that you speak with the manager and explain what kind of planning services you are looking for. You need to specify that you are looking for someone who specializes in comprehensive financial planning. If they don't have a qualified planner on staff at a location convenient for you, keep looking. Having your plan done by someone who is thousands of miles away at their home office is *not* what you are looking for.

Professional Organizations

There are several professional organizations that will give you names of financial planners who practice in your area. These organizations will not refer planners who have not kept up with their continuing education requirements, deviated from the organization's guidelines or regulations, or in any way violated their code of ethics. It is unlikely that these organizations will be able to narrow your search for you by specialty; that is up to you. Such organizations include the following:

Institute of Certified Financial Planners (ICFP)
7600 E. Eastman Ave., Ste. 301
Denver, CO 80231
(800) 282-7526
www.icfp.org
The ICFP is a professional association of CFPs and CFP candidates. It provides assistance and information to consumers who are thinking about enlisting the services of a CFP, and it helps CFPs maintain their continuing education requirements.

Certified Financial Planner Board of Standards

1700 Broadway, Ste. 2100
Denver, CO 80290-2101
(888) CFP-MARK
(303) 830-7500
www.cfp-board.org

The CFP Board of Standards grants the right to use individuals who embrace a code of ethics and rules of governance. It is the regulatory body that administers examinations to candidates, and it owns the CFP designation and has the power to revoke the designation.

National Association of Personal Financial Advisors (NAPFA)

1130 Lake Cook Rd., Ste. 150
Buffalo Grove, IL 60089
(888) FEE-ONLY
(800) 366-2732
www.napfa.org

This organization provides consumers with a list of financial advisors who offer comprehensive financial planning for a fee. Fee-only planners do not receive commissions for the sale of any product.

The Securities and Exchange Commission

450 Fifth St., NW
Washington, DC 20549
(800) 732-0330
www.sec.gov

This government organization can tell you if a financial planner is registered with the SEC as an investment advisor. It also provides educational materials.

Attend Seminars and Classes

You will find a variety of financial and investment-related classes and seminars in your area. They are typically advertised in the local newspaper, community center newsletters, and through class schedules at the local college. Some colleges offer classes as part of their curriculum, while others offer them as continuing education classes. Often, these classes are taught by financial services professionals as a way to prospect for new clients. Sometimes there is a fee, but most often there isn't.

There is nothing wrong with this practice, but it is very important that the "instructors" disclose what type of financial services professionals they are. These classes can be taught by brokers and insurance salespeople as well as financial planners. The orientation of the instructor will likely influence how the course will be taught and how the students will invest. If you desire to work with a CFP, only attend courses or seminars that are given by CFPs.

The Interview

Once you have gathered a list of candidates, you can use the interview process to narrow down your list. Just because someone was recommended by your attorney, or they psyched you up at a seminar, doesn't mean they are the planner for you. Meeting with each candidate and getting a feel for who they are and what they are about is how you begin to determine, for yourself, who you click with. To maximize the productivity of the interview, you must be able to articulate which services you are looking for and the kind of relationship you would like to create.

I understand that this may be difficult because you may now have a different set of needs than ever before, but it is a manageable process. First, think about what your needs are at this point. Many people feel so overwhelmed by the emotions they are experiencing that what they want most at this point is to bring some stability back into their lives. They can't even begin to articulate financial goals, and that's fine.

The Interview Process

These five steps will be useful in your interviews.

1. Before the interview, develop a list of questions that you will ask each candidate and write those questions down. If you write them down, you have one less thing to think about during the interviews, and you can concentrate on the responses of the candidates. You might want to use the following list of questions:

   - How long have you been in the financial planning business?
   - Do you have other clients in situations similar to mine? If so, how many?
   - What have they experienced with their Sudden Money?
   - What are your credentials?
   - How will you communicate with me? How often will I receive statements and have personal meetings with you?

- Will I be working with you or with your staff?
- How are you compensated?
- What kind of investments do you favor?
- What is your money management philosophy?

2. During the interview, you should expect to find someone interested in getting to know who you are and what your needs are. The planner should ask questions and listen carefully to your answers. Their questions should be objective and should center on your financial needs. They should be trying to determine how much experience you have had managing your money, and they should not neglect the emotional component of Sudden Money. It is important that they address the subjective side of your experience by asking you, "How are you feeling about your Sudden Money?" You should feel comfortable enough to look them in the eye and to tell them exactly what your feelings are.

3. During the interview, you should also be determining what the planner can offer you. The kinds of services most commonly offered are cash flow and budgeting, investment selection and ongoing investment management, retirement planning, education planning, insurance planning, estate planning, and tax planning. You might not need all of the services, and a planner might not offer all of them. This is why it is crucial that you know what you need in advance. *If you know what you need, you will know who has what you need.*

4. After the interview, you should take some time to write down a few paragraphs about the communication between you and the candidate. The initial interview will help you get a sense of whether the person has the desire and the ability to develop the kind of relationship you want to have with your financial advisor. Note whether the planner appeared to understand the challenges you are facing. Note also whether you feel like the candidate listened to your questions carefully and responded to them appropriately. Did you feel comfortable asking your questions and admitting when you didn't understand something? Were you able to tell the person what you thought in addition to how you felt?

5. After the interview, if you are looking for a relationship and not just someone to process transactions, you need to focus on both the objective facts as well as your subjective feelings. The objective considerations include which professional credentials the planner has earned, the type of designation and the amount of continuing education that they receive each year, and whether they have experience in the area in which you need help.

How Planners Are Compensated

There is no one right way for a financial planner to earn a living. You will find people who are clearly competent and ethical in each compensation category, and you might also find people whose integrity and ability are questionable. The reason you want to know how they are compensated is simply because, as the consumer, you have the right to know what you are paying for and how you are being charged.

By keeping this often-sensitive subject out in the open, you eliminate some questions that might otherwise arise regarding conflict of interest. You don't want to be sold investments or services that benefit your advisor more than you.

Financial advisors earn their living in one of five ways:

1. *Fee-only.* These are advisors who charge a fee but who don't earn commissions on the investments you make or the insurance you buy. The fee may be charged on an hourly basis, as a percentage of the money under their management, or on the amount of life insurance purchased. The fee schedule should be disclosed prior to the start of the relationship.

2. *Fee-based.* These are advisors who charge a fee and who may also earn commissions on the investments or insurance you purchase. The types of fees should be disclosed up front. Fees may be hourly for planning services, or they may be a percentage of the amount of money under management. Commissions should be disclosed on an ongoing basis. Quite often, commissions are used to offset the amount of the fee that is to be charged for management of a client's assets.

3. *Commissioned.* These are advisors who earn their living on the investments they sell. Though this kind of compensation

has come under pressure as the fee alternative has evolved, it may be a less expensive way to acquire the ongoing relationship you should be looking for. Don't necessarily eliminate an otherwise good candidate just because that person works on a commission basis.

4. *Salaried.*   These are advisors who usually work in the human resource department of large corporations or large planning firms. They are paid a salary regardless of what investments they sell.

5. *Hourly rates.*   These are charged by some advisors. In this case, it is necessary to get an estimate prior to enlisting the advisor. You should also ask what their billing policy is for ongoing services such as questions over the telephone.

The Right Match

Be sure to choose candidates who have the skills you need. It is best to find someone who has regular experience dealing with clients like you. If someone has worked only with people investing monthly for long-term goals such as retirement, they may not be as proficient at setting up an income portfolio for you to live on for the next 40 years.

Keeping Current

Asking about an advisor's continuing education experience will tell you something about how up-to-date they are and how committed they are to their profession. Laws change, the economy changes, and new investments are created every year. The better financial advisors read industry publications, attend conferences, and find other means of keeping up with their ever-changing profession.

Quality of Communication

Although credentials, competence, and education are all important, your relationship will succeed or fail based upon the quality of communication you have with your advisor. With each candidate, you should inquire about his or her availability for unscheduled phone conversations and if you will be provided with a memo of those conversations or any others.

In addition to verbal communication, your advisor will need to communicate with you in writing on a variety of issues. Do your candidates write plans in a professional and easy-to-understand way (ask to see samples)? How often are reports sent out?

Check References and Credentials

Ask for a list of clients with circumstances similar to yours, and *call the references* to ask how they feel about their relationships with the planner. Have their goals been met? Are they satisfied with the communication? Would they recommend the planner to someone in their family?

Goal Setting

Once you have identified and worked through your emotions and you have found a financial advisor, you are ready to begin creating your financial plan. The first step in that creation is figuring out what you want from your money. To make sound, appropriate investment decisions in Phase Two, you must first establish goals and their time-lines. This chapter is designed to help you through the goal-setting process so the plan you and your advisor create is appropriate for your unique circumstances.

I suggest that when you get to the actual calculation of your income needs, rather than simply listing the facts, try opening yourself up to possibilities you might not have considered before the money arrived. Once again, use your heart as well as your mind; your feelings are just as valid as any facts in this process.

You can do much of your goal-setting work by yourself, because this part of the process deals with your personal thoughts, feelings, and desires about money. You will use the list that you create in this chapter to do your Reality Checks (explained in Chapter 7) with the aid of your advisor.

Goal Setting: The Concept

Your new money may change how others perceive you, but it is up to you to define yourself by the choices you make and the relationships you develop. Who you are and who you want to be is up to you and you alone. While an increase in money requires you to make financial decisions, it also gives you the opportunity to decide if it is time to make some personal changes.

Before you reset your financial goals, step back and take a fresh look at yourself. Who have you become, what do you really want out of life, and who and what is important to you? Once you have a clear picture of who and what you want to be, you can create a financial plan to make your new visions, goals, and desires come alive. This may not be a new exercise for some of you. For others, however, such as the many people who live from paycheck to paycheck or who are completely absorbed in their families or careers, stopping to think about where they are and who they have become may be a luxury.

The goal-setting process presented here might have previously seemed like a hopeless waste of time because, for you to achieve your goals, your financial situation would have had to change drastically. Now that it has, you have the responsibility to think long and hard about your goals. This usually entails looking deep inside yourself and examining your past behavior, particularly regarding money. The outcome of such an examination might be that you redesign your entire life, or perhaps you'll find that you like everything the way it is. Whatever your conclusion, if you treat your deliberation process seriously and thoughtfully, your financial plan will reflect your deepest desires.

Goal Setting: The Process

You should commence the goal-setting part of Phase One as soon as you begin to feel your emotions settling down and you have found an advisor. Once you know how you *feel* about your Sudden Money, it is time to decide what you want to *do* with it. Remember that while it may be true that a huge sum of money will offer a wider range of possibilities than a more modest sum, each choice you make can have an enormous impact on who you will become and what you will be doing in the future.

There are five steps toward establishing your goals:

1. Create your personal Bliss List (a list of your goals and desires).

2. Prioritize the list according to importance rather than likelihood.

3. Separate the goals into short, intermediate, and long term.

4. Find out what you can afford by doing a Reality Check for each of the goals.

5. Prioritize again, adjusting your goals to conform to reality.

Life Goals versus Financial Goals

When you identify your goals, you are defining how you want to live and who and what are important to you. Some of your goals may be *life* goals, such as wanting to go to medical school. Other goals seem purely *financial*, such as wanting to be the richest person in your community. Life goals have a financial component (e.g., medical school costs money). Likewise, financial goals have personal components (e.g., maybe wanting to be very rich is your way of saying you want to have lots of money to pass on to your children).

Carmen said that her goal was not to accumulate wealth but to be a full-time volunteer for her favorite charity. At first, she didn't see the need to invest. As she worked through the goal-setting process, however, she realized that she had to take care of her money so she could support herself and be in a position to help her organization on a full-time basis. She found she needed to view her life goal from a financial perspective to make sure she could really fulfill her mission.

Step 1—Creating Your Bliss List

A Bliss List is a list of those things that—in a perfect world—you would have or do for yourself, your family, and others. In the initial stage of deciding what to put on your list, don't think as much about what you can afford; rather, think about what would make you happy and fulfilled. Use your heart, and pay attention to your feelings as you go through this exercise. Try to pinpoint the things you are passionate about and deeply believe are important. If you want to sail around the world, put that on your list. When you get to the Reality Check (step 4), you will establish the cost and whether your dream trip is feasible.

Cathy had the desire to travel and see the world. She was 42 years old, single, and had a management position in a large corporation when she inherited $250,000 from her grandmother. The amount was generous, but it was not enough to live on, and according to her family at least, it was most certainly not enough to support a life of world travel. Yet, travel was at the top of her Bliss List.

Cathy had never realized just how important traveling was to her, because she had not thought it was even a remote possibility. Her inheritance allowed her to stop and take stock of what her life was about and where she was going. It was then that she decided to stop ignoring what she had wanted more than anything.

Cathy was prepared to take some risks to fulfill her number one desire. She worked out a plan with her financial advisor to take $25,000 for travel money and invest the rest for at least 20 years. If Cathy could let the balance of the money stay invested and achieve an average stock market return, the inheritance money plus the money she had saved prior to her grandmother's death would be enough to provide a comfortable retirement. The catch was that she had to earn her way while traveling; she could not spend any of her retirement money.

Cathy put the money to work with her advisor, and she set up a communication system via the Internet to check on her investments and to e-mail her advisor. Her first adventure was as a deckhand on a boat sailing from Fort Lauderdale, Florida, to Australia. She spent one year working on a sheep farm in Australia, came back for a brief visit with her family, and then took off for the Swiss Alps. Her next adventure was living with a Swiss family interested in having their children learn English. The family paid for her airfare and gave her room, board, and a small stipend. Best of all, they paid for her travels with the family. Last I heard, she was enjoying taking the children on holidays throughout Europe. After two years of seeing the world, she still had $24,000 in her travel account.

When making your Bliss List, it helps if you ask yourself some key questions. Take some time and write down your answers. Let a few days go by and repeat the exercise. Some people find their answers change a little bit each time. You may want to continue to do this exercise over a longer period. Just remember to use your heart while compiling your list, no matter how many times you do it.

If you have a partner or spouse, you should each make separate lists and then compare notes. Ask yourselves questions such as:

- What is really important to me?

- Where do I want to be in 5 years? in 10 years? in 20 years?

- What do I want to be doing?

- What dreams do I have for my family?

- What have I always wanted to do but never had the opportunity to do?

- Whom do I want to help?

- If money were no object, what would I be doing?

- What is my perfect day? week? month? year?

- How would I like to look back on my life when I am dying?

Step 2—Prioritizing Your Bliss List

If you really let yourself go while doing the Bliss List, it will be a long list. When you feel the list is complete, you need to arrange it according to what is most important to you and what you can live without. If it seems impossible to determine which goal is *the* most important, group them. It's okay to have three goals occupying the number one spot. The Reality Check (described later) will help to establish further which ones are possible and which ones need to be modified or eliminated. Again, if you have a partner who is involved in this process, prioritize your items separately, and then combine them into one list.

The goal of prioritizing is to help you focus on what is most important to you, even if those items don't seem financially realistic. Many goals do not seem possible at first, and in my experience, it is often the *perception* of financial limitations that keeps dreams from becoming reality. If you discover a desire that would make you feel fulfilled and complete, why limit your thinking before you have determined whether you can find a way to make it happen? You might have to give up other desires or wait a while for your money to grow, but if your desire is strong enough, you'll be able to adjust.

Step 3—Separating the Goals into Short, Intermediate, and Long Term

The actual funding of each item on your final list will require you to know when you will need the money. For short-term goals, money is usually kept in a money market account, government bond, or bank certificate of deposit. For long-term goals, money is usually invested in stocks or stock mutual funds. Establishing the timetables for your goals while you are in Phase One will allow you to allocate your money properly in Phase Two. Appropriate investment selection in Phase Two is what will help you make relatively certain that you will have enough money available when it's time to achieve each of your goals. If you have difficulty quantifying any of your goals, ask your financial advisor for help.

The following begins to illustrate the relationship between the timetable for your goals and the general investment types you will choose to support them.

Short-Term Goals—Three Months to Three Years

Short-term goals require investments with very little risk to your principal. The investments appropriate for short-term goals usually have low interest rates (because they have very little or no risk) and no growth potential. The expression "parking your money" refers to leaving your money on the investment sidelines, out of the growth investment category, to accumulate interest and to be available when you need it.

However, there are no set rules regarding short-term investments. For instance, interest rates are not always predictable. Sometimes a money market account will pay more than a two-year certificate of deposit, so assume nothing and shop around. While you are shopping, you should be looking for safety, access to your money, and a reasonable rate of return. In addition, if possible, try to commit your short-term money for a year or two because you will probably get a higher interest rate than if you are planning on using it immediately. Be sure to read Phase Two to familiarize yourself with how interest rates affect investments. Investing money for short-term goals will be relatively easy once you understand how to make interest rate-based decisions. Some investments appropriate for the short term are

- Money market accounts
- Checking accounts

- Savings accounts
- Certificates of deposit
- U.S. Treasury bills
- Short-term municipal bonds

Intermediate Goals–Three to Six Years

When your goals fall into the intermediate time frame, you can afford to take slightly more risk by investing in conservative stocks and intermediate-term bonds. If you choose to use stocks for these goals, stick with stock mutual funds, which will give you the benefit of diversification and professional management. Look for funds that have a good history of doing well during previous stock market declines. You should consider mutual funds that are rated as having below-average risk. (See Chapter 11 for a complete discussion of issues related to mutual funds.)

When your time frame is from three to six years, you need to pay attention to possible investment-related costs. Some mutual funds will charge an up-front fee (called a sale charge, or *load*), while others will have surrender charges. Both up-front and back-end charges may reduce your overall investment return. Before you invest intermediate money, or any money for that matter, ask about all the charges involved.

In addition, pay attention to any possible tax consequences. Do not invest short- or intermediate-term money in retirement accounts if the money is going to be withdrawn before you reach age 59½. Money withdrawn from these accounts before age 59½ is considered an early withdrawal. This means you will owe income tax on this withdrawal and an additional 10% early-withdrawal penalty.

Long-Term Goals–Over Six Years

For goals exceeding six years, you can afford to take more risk. The more time you have to commit your money, the greater the risk you can afford to take. However, there is a limit, and it is dictated by your ability to handle the risk. Regardless of how wonderful the long-term stock market returns may look, there *will* still be down years. If you are not psychologically prepared for these downturns, there is a possibility that you will react emotionally and sell at the wrong time, creating a permanent loss of capital.

The whole point of taking more risk with your long-term money is that you have time to wait out the down cycles because you don't need the money. Historically, the stock market has always rebounded and achieved new highs. To share in this success, however, you must have the fortitude to stay with your investments during the bleak times. Before you make your long-term investment plans, be sure you understand stock market risk and how you feel about it. Spend time on Chapter 8, which will help you understand investment risk and your ability to deal with it.

Step 4—The Reality Check

Now that you know what you'd like to do with your money and when you would like to do it, the question is, what can you afford, and how far will your money stretch? As the name implies, the Reality Check is used to find out if a particular goal or set of goals is realistic. When a large sum of money comes into your life, it is difficult to know what its potential really is. Without understanding the limitations of your money, it is difficult to create an accurate financial plan. If your financial plan is off, when it comes time to choose investments, they too will not be on target.

The Reality Check can be used to determine how much income your new money can produce and how long that income will last. It can also help you to project the long-term consequences of spending large amounts of money on things like cars and houses. Use the Reality Check when you are grappling with questions such as: Can I afford to quit working forever, and does it really matter if I buy a boat instead of putting that money into long-term investments? The information you receive should give you enough insight into your finances to allow you to make clear decisions.

The following chapter continues to define the Reality Check and gives you examples of how this process has helped my clients. It provides you with the step-by-step process I use for determining the actual cost of the items on my clients' Bliss Lists and to help them make long-term projections. You should use the same process with your advisor.

The Reality Check

N ow that you have already prioritized your Bliss List and arranged it according to your preferred timetable, you need to establish the cost of each item. The cost, combined with variables such as inflation, investment return, and your age expectancy, is what will help you to determine which items are realistic for you. This is what the Reality Check process is all about: testing the financial viability of the items on your Bliss List.

The Reality Check is an important step because it helps you decide how to allocate your money when it comes time to invest during Phase Two. You will do this exercise with your advisor to ascertain which goals are affordable and which goals need to be adjusted or eliminated. You can also do it anytime you need to figure out how long your money will last under different circumstances.

This chapter will provide you with step-by-step instructions on how to perform a Reality Check, as well as sample Reality Checks that I worked through with my clients. Whether you are working on your original Bliss List or answering a what-if financial question years from now, the basic elements of the exercise will be the same.

The Bliss List and the Reality Check

To perform a Reality Check on an item from your Bliss List, you will need to do the following:

- *Establish the current cost of the item.* In other words, what would it take to purchase it or make it happen *today?* Be as realistic as possible, and do whatever homework is necessary to find an accurate number. If you have to estimate, use a higher number rather than a lower one.

- *Set a timetable.* Decide when you want to reach the goal or how long you will need the income for. The time frame of your goals will dictate how you save and invest for them. For short-term goals, the emphasis is on safety and availability; longer-term goals will allow you to take more risk. When you are looking for lifelong income, add 10 years to the average mortality assumption for your age. If your windfall has occurred at an earlier age and you're considering quitting your job, consider how long your windfall must last. If you are 40, you'll need income for at least 50 years! Running out of money in your old age is not a good thing.

- *Adjust the cost for inflation.* Once you have determined the current costs of the items on your Bliss List, they must be adjusted according to the time frame. Again, be conservative. The value of any currency will decline with the rate of inflation. Therefore, it is best to project a slightly higher rate than the current one.

  Not all goals will have the same inflation rate. Some costs will rise faster than inflation; some will rise more slowly. For instance, college education costs typically outpace inflation by a few percentage points. If you know the college or university you are interested in, call them to determine the rate at which their expenses have been increasing. If you don't know where your child will go to school, your advisor will be able to provide the average rate increase for the type of school that the child will most likely attend.

  In contrast, real estate may increase at a much slower rate than inflation. In some areas, the price of homes may be decreasing due to a problem within the local economy. Again, check on statistics relative to the area(s) where you may own real estate and be conservative with your assumptions.

  To build and maintain wealth and protect your lifestyle, the return on your investment portfolio must outpace inflation. For instance, today the inflation rate is 2%. I would run your Reality Check at 3% or 4% to create a more conservative projection. In other words, the future projections will indicate that you will have a smaller amount of "today's" dollars providing income in the future. It also means that you are creating a cushion for the unexpected.

As inflation changes, it is important that you redo the projections to confirm whether you need to make changes in your lifestyle. Table 7.1 shows an example of inflation.

- *When doing Reality Checks for future goals, make an interest rate assumption for short-term goals and an investment return assumption for longer-term goals.* Your investment return will depend upon your ability to assume risk and your ability to manage your investments wisely.

Guaranteed investments such as bonds offer lower returns, and they do not have a consistent history of outpacing inflation. Meanwhile, though stocks are not guaranteed investments and they involve risk, they do have a history of outpacing inflation. In most cases, it will be important to have a blend of guaranteed and nonguaranteed investments in order to achieve a rate of return that will keep your portfolio growing, and more important, *keep the income derived from the portfolio growing.*

It is okay to use historic rates of return for stocks and bonds when doing your Reality Checks. For 60 years, stocks have averaged 11%; bonds, 6% (according to Ibbotson). Therefore, a portfolio divided equally between stocks and bonds would produce a taxable return of 8.5%. If you are going to put more money in stocks, the assumed rate will be higher. If more than half of your money will go into bonds, make a lower assumption.

TABLE 7.1 Projections of Inflation for Present-Day Living Costs of $100,000

Inflation Rate	Time Period (in years)						
	5	10	15	20	25	30	35
3%	$115,933	$134,403	$155,815	$180,638	$209,414	$242,774	$281,447
4%	$121,671	$148,036	$180,114	$219,142	$266,625	$324,396	$394,683
5%	$127,634	$162,902	$207,914	$265,363	$338,683	$432,261	$551,692

■ *Don't forget about taxes.* Adjust your rates of return and your spendable income for taxes. Your Sudden Money could have pushed you into a new tax bracket. Explore this possibility and make your assumptions on an after-tax basis. Money growing inside qualified retirement accounts will be growing tax-deferred; money invested in municipal bonds will probably be tax-free; money earned from selling stocks held for more than 12 months will be taxed at the 20% capital gains rate. It is complicated to make all of these tax adjustments, but it is important. Your financial advisor will be able to make the tax adjustments so you can get a better projection of how long your money will last under different scenarios.

Variables That Affect Your Reality Check

Make Annual Spending Assumptions

Be realistic. Don't put yourself on a very tight budget leaving no room for unexpected expenses like car repair or replacement, medical costs, or tax increases. Be careful to create a lifestyle that you can easily afford, as scaling back can be costly and difficult. It is better to have a realistic plan from the beginning. If you've assumed that you'll spend more than you really do, you can either increase your standard of living or enjoy building more wealth and financial security by allowing your investments to reinvest and grow.

Lifestyle is one of the few variables over which you have control. The cost of goods, the performance of stocks and bonds, and your marginal tax rate are factors beyond your control, and certain expenses (e.g., mortgage payments and insurance) are generally fixed for you. What you purchase at the grocery store, how often you dine out, and how much you travel are decisions that you alone are responsible for.

Don't Underestimate These Variables

To really understand the importance of each of these variables, it is helpful to make a variety of assumptions. To see how the assumed portfolio rate of return impacts the projection, start by assuming you use only guaranteed investments that average a 5% annual return. Then, use an 8% return to illustrate a 50/50 blend of stocks and bonds. Finally, use a 10% return, which would be a growth portfolio consisting mostly of stocks.

Each variable has an impact; some will have more influence on the projected outcome than others. Use variables based on conservative assumptions first. For example, start with a low investment return, and if the projections are not looking good, make increasingly higher assumptions until the projection works. It is a good idea to begin by changing one variable, while keeping all the others the same, as follows:

- Portfolio valued at $1 million
- Expenses of $50,000 per year before taxes
- Inflation at 4%
- Investment return of 5%

Given a 5% investment return, you would begin to invade your principal in the second year. This is caused as expenses rise due to inflation. The result is that you need more money each year to maintain the same lifestyle. By the 24th year, you would have exhausted your investment portfolio. With an 8% investment return, you begin to invade principal in 13 years and the portfolio will be depleted in 33 years. At 10%, the portfolio would continue to grow and last.

In many Reality Checks you will want to test combinations of variables. Once you know how a projection works with different investment returns, your next step might be to determine the impact of lowering or decreasing the assumed annual expenses.

Continuing the above example, if the expenses are increased from $50,000 to $75,000, a portfolio with an average return of 5% will be depleted in less than 15 years, with a 7% return it lasts 18 years, and with a 10% return it lasts 29 years.

Of course, in the real world investments produce varying returns from year to year. Whether invested in bonds, banks, or stocks, a consistent annual return is unrealistic. The illustrations assume static rates of return and are for projection purposes only. Since most investors need a portfolio that is a mix of guaranteed and growth investments, a 10% return might be aggressive. Comparisons like these are used to demonstrate the range of possibilities.

For the person concerned with extending their money's longevity for their lifetime, there are two options:

1. Decrease expenses.
2. Increase the rate of return.

The easiest option may be to decrease your spending. The second option requires an increased tolerance for risk. You can combine the options and get a positive effect as well.

A Sample Reality Check: Teresa and Charles Martin

Teresa and Charles Martin won $14 million in the lottery. They chose to take the (reduced) lump sum, they paid all taxes, and they now have $4 million. The Martins are both 53 years old and they have three children: one about to begin medical school, one starting college, and one starting her junior year in high school. Teresa's parents are not in very good financial shape and are considered part of the immediate family.

Before they won the lottery, the Martins would have described themselves as an average middle income family. They both worked and Charles' income paid for their day-to-day living expenses, while Teresa's earnings were put toward education expenses. Now they feel rich; they are millionaires. The question was: Just how rich are they?

They wanted to retire immediately, buy a new house, give money to their kids, and help Teresa's parents. They also intended to start living more lavishly, including more vacations, new cars, new clothes, and jewelry. Table 7.2 shows the Martins' Bliss List.

This list is enviable but not achievable, at least not the way it is now. The short-term goals—new house, vacation house, boats, and gifts to the kids—would cost $1 million. To meet their education goal, it is estimated they will need to invest $390,000 now to make tuition payments for the next six years. After allocating money for the short-term goals and the education goal, they will have $2,610,000 left for income investing. Unfortunately, this remaining amount is not sufficient to produce the annual income they are hoping for.

To produce $250,000 a year for 45 years (10 years beyond their projected lifetime), Teresa and Charles will have to invest $5,950,000. This amount assumes they continue to be moderate risk investors, putting half the money in stocks and half the money in bonds, to receive an 8.5% return. To provide the $50,000 for Teresa's parents they will need $660,000, again assuming moderate investment risk.

They have a considerable amount of money to work with and many of their goals are achievable if they are willing to make some

TABLE 7.2 The Martins' Bliss List

Goal	How Much	When	Amount Allocated
Short term			
A new home	$500,000	Now	$500,000
A vacation home	$250,000	Now	$250,000
A boat	$100,000	Now	$100,000
Financial gifts to kids	$150,000	Now	$150,000
Intermediate term			
Education expenses	$500,000	For 6 years	$390,000
Long term			
Annual income from investments	$250,000 per year after tax	For 45 years at 3% inflation	$5,950,000
Income for parents	$50,000 per year after tax	For 20 years at 3% inflation	$660,000

adjustments. For instance, they could spend less on either of the home purchases they are anticipating. Taking a mortgage on either of the properties might work for some couples, but Charles and Teresa are adamant about not having any mortgage payments in retirement. An alternative solution would be to could forego the gifting to the kids and give them their education money only.

To make the income numbers work at 3% inflation, they will have to assume they can get more than a 16% average annual rate of return. This kind of assumption is unreasonable, even if they are willing to put all of their money into stocks and skip guaranteed bonds all together. They need either to put more money into the investment portfolio or to reduce the amount of income for themselves and for Teresa's parents.

To find their way through this part of the exercise, they need to answer some important questions. How much more money will the portfolio need? What kind of an income cut will work? What if they reduced the amount they gave the kids and reduced their income goal? To get the answers, they will have to keep testing the projections. The following is a flow of their what-ifs:

- What amount of money needs to be invested to produce $250,000 a year for 45 years at 3% inflation?

  6% Return $8,000,000   **8.5% Return** $5,950,000

  10% Return $4,900,000   **12% Return** $4,100,000

  14% Return $3,350,000

- What amount of money needs to be invested to produce $150,000 a year for 45 years at 3% inflation?

  6% Return $4,900,000   **8.5% Return** $3,750,000

  10% Return $2,950,000   **12% Return** $2,400,000

  14% Return $2,050,000

- How much will have to be invested to produce $50,000 a year for 20 years at 3% inflation for Teresa's parents?

  6% Return $795,000   **8.5% Return** $660,000

  10% Return $605,000   **12% Return** $550,000

  14% Return $495,000

- How much will have to be invested to produce $25,000 a year for 20 years at 3% inflation for Teresa's parents?

  6% Return $410,000   **8.5% Return** $350,000

  10% Return $325,000   **12% Return** $300,000

  14% Return $479,125   **16% Return** $428,914

The Martins are faced with making choices that many families will have to make with their Sudden Money. Their Reality Check showed them that even $4 million is not enough to achieve everything they want. They might be able to have many things on their list, but not everything on their list. It will be up to them to adjust some of the goals to make their list realistic.

If they cut their new home expenditure by $200,000 and eliminate giving each of the kids $50,000, they can pay for the education expenses but will still have to reduce their income expectations.

They can project an annual income of $150,000 after tax if they assume a 10% return rather than 8.5%. However, they still cannot afford to give Teresa's parents an income. They will have to cut another $140,000 from the initial purchases to give them just $10,000 per year for the projected 20 years.

The Martins can also choose to invest the entire amount for another seven years. This means they will continue to live as they always have, and wait until age 60 before they retire. Their $4 million might grow to $8 million if they average 10% a year, and then their Bliss List would be achievable.

Teresa and Charles agree that waiting 10 years to enjoy their new wealth is not acceptable. Some compromises are necessary, and this is what they are choosing to do:

- Buy the new home for $400,000, the vacation home for $200,000, and the boat.

- Fund the college expenses for the children, but refrain from giving them any cash. (After the homes, boat, and college funding, they have $2.9 million to invest.)

- Continue to work for another six or seven years, in which time their portfolio is projected to grow to $4 million. The only income they will take from the investment portfolio is $30,000 for Teresa's parents, everything else will be reinvested. Teresa's income, no longer needed for college savings, will go toward the added annual expenses of the new homes.

The delayed retirement was not a tough decision once they worked through the Reality Check exercise. There was no doubt in their minds that they would pay for the education of their children and help Teresa's parents. Once these goals were taken care of, they prioritized their goals. They didn't mind working for awhile longer as long as they could be enjoying their new homes. Once the plan was put into place, going to work was not a burden. They felt more fulfilled with their careers than they had before the big win.

Step 5—Prioritize Again

Remember that Reality Checks are projections based upon assumptions. The results of Reality Checks are not facts; they are indications of how your money will hold up under different scenarios. It is best if you and your advisor run these numbers once a year to be sure you are on the right track. When you have spent too much or your investments have not kept pace with your assumptions, you will have the chance to make adjustments in spending or investing. This way, the changes you will make will be more like fine-tuning than damage control.

As you complete the final step in setting your goals, you may have to be selective. Some goals may be easier to let go of than others, some may be postponed, and others may be reduced. Each individual will have their own views when it comes to prioritizing, so this can make merging your list with your partner's list challenging. Try to stay creative, as most goals can be altered rather than eliminated.

For instance, you might agree to work for a few more years before you retire, rather than to accept a retirement income that is lower than you would like. Another compromise that might be warranted occurs when one partner wants to live in the city while the other prefers the country. You might not be able to afford the kind of homes you like in both places, so the compromise would be to buy two smaller homes, or a large home in one location and a smaller home in the other.

Before you can complete your list of goals, you might have to try several different scenarios to find out what is possible. Deciding if you should make different assumptions, lower your expectations, or change your timetables will mean making various projections to understand the range of possibilities you have.

PHASE TWO

By the time you reach Phase Two, you should know how you feel about your Sudden Money, and you should have established what you want your Sudden Money to do. You should have found a financial planner with whom you are comfortable working. Your emotional state should be more stable after your stay in your Decision Free Zone, and you should be ready and able to make financial decisions, lifestyle changes, and begin to invest your money. Phase Two is the time to buy the new home, to stop working if you have determined you can afford to, and to start investing.

In Phase Two, you will be learning about yourself as an investor so that you can create an investment plan that will support your financial plan. This is the time to select the investments that are designed to produce the results you are expecting, combined with how much risk you are willing to take in order to fulfill your expectations. I have created a tool to help you categorize yourself so that you will be able to make optimal use of the section on the three basic investment vehicles. After you have assessed yourself, you will be positioned to consider stocks, bonds, and mutual funds in the context of your own goals and risk tolerance. At that point, you and your planner will be ready to invest your Sudden Money to support your life, lifestyle, and goals.

The Risk/Reward Relationship

Risk means different things to different people. It can mean the possibility of lower-than-expected returns, the possibility of losing some or all of your principal, and/or the loss of future purchasing power. The reality is that there are numerous types of risk, and every investment you make will involve at least one of them. Even investments that are considered "safe," such as CDs and U.S. Treasury bills, have some kind of risk.

Part of being a responsible steward of your money is learning about the various kinds of risk and deciding which ones you are willing to take. For Sudden Money people this is of paramount importance, as Sudden Money does not usually arrive with any regularity and, in most cases, is a once-in-a-lifetime event. If it is lost, it usually cannot be replaced.

This chapter explains the kinds of risk you will encounter and 10 effective ways to minimize your overall risk.

Risk/Reward

The relationship between risk and reward is the basis of investing. In general, the greater the potential reward, the greater the risk. If the payback for taking risk is the potential for reward, it would behoove you to have sufficient reward potential to compensate for all the risk you take. It makes sense then that low-risk investments (e.g., U.S. Treasury bills) have low return potential, or low interest rates. Meanwhile, higher-risk investments (e.g., common stocks) have higher return potential.

It is possible to find investments with lower-than-average risk and higher-than-average reward potential, but they are not the norm. What you want to avoid is buying investments with more risk than reward potential, and unfortunately, these investments are easy to find.

How to Measure Risk

Neither risk nor reward is absolute; how great each is depends on how great you perceive it to be. For instance, before you can judge the success or failure of an investment, you need to answer two questions: (1) has it met your investment objective, and (2) how has it performed compared with its peers? If you bought a corporate bond with the objective of receiving income, it probably will not have grown in value as much as a stock purchased for its growth potential. On the other hand, if the stock grew by 20% and the bond did not grow but paid you 8% income, the stock is not a better investment than the bond. The bond did what you wanted it to do: It sent you monthly interest payments.

Indexes

Each investment you own has a benchmark, called an *index*, which is a measure of the performance of a group of similar investments. The index is a tool that tells you the direction of either the stock market in general, or a specific segment of it, such as Internet stocks. You use it to help you determine whether the investments you own are doing well. The following chapters on the individual investment vehicles explain specific indexes.

Can I Avoid Risk?

No. Every investment involves some kind and degree of risk. As I have been advising, education is your best defense against common mistakes throughout your Sudden Money Process. Education helps you understand and plan for what is to come, but it cannot prevent all disappointments, particularly when it comes to matters that are out of your control. Much of the risk that can affect your investments *is* out of your control. What you do have control over, is whether you will take those risks.

Naturally, knowledge of the different kinds of risk will help you to be prepared and aid in your decision-making process. But the combination of knowing what risk to take *and when to take it* is critical. For instance, the stock market has a great long-term track record, but it can be very risky for short-term investing. If you have an important expense coming up within a few years, such as a down payment on a home or a tuition payment, you are better off using investments such as money market accounts and U.S. Treasury bills. When investing for the short term, you want to be sure that the money you need is available and not tied up in stocks that may be in a temporary decline.

Many times it is not a question of whether an investment is good, but whether it is *suitable.* To determine this, you will need to know your time frame, your objective, and the kind of risk you are willing to accept to accomplish your objective. Once you have completed the time frame and objectives exercises (i.e., The Bliss List and The Reality Check) in Chapters 6 and 7, you are ready to establish what kind of tolerance you have for risk.

Your first step is to understand what kinds of risk you are likely to encounter. The seven most prevalent are:

1. Market risk (risk of principal)
2. Inflation risk
3. Interest rate risk
4. Reinvestment risk
5. Liquidity risk
6. Political risk
7. Credit risk

Market Risk

Market risk is the risk that the value of your investment may decline. It is the risk most people focus on because it is so obvious. When an investment is worth less than what you originally put into it, you will tend to feel uncomfortable and your instinct may be to sell that investment. Just being aware of this possibility before you invest, and perhaps anticipating a coming market decline, will help you stay committed to your investment during tough times.

Understanding how market risk may affect your stocks or bonds will help you remain rational when you might otherwise panic and sell. Market risk can occur because of a decline in the overall stock or bond markets or because of something particular to the investment itself. When the loss is due to general market conditions, wise investors will hold on to their investment until the market recovers. When the problem is with the individual investment, then there is some investigating to do.

At times, a mutual fund or an individual stock will not be doing well, even when the market of which it is part is climbing upward. There could be any number of reasons for this, such as a change in management or a change in public perception resulting from media coverage. Your investigation should include checking with your advisor and keeping a close eye on the news. In the case of a mutual fund, you should call the fund company directly, as their shareholder service representatives will probably have something to report.

Investments that have market risk are considered long term (five years or longer), and the best way to manage this risk is to leave your money in the investment until the market cycles back up. Understanding market cycles positions you to take advantage of how others will react to market risk. For instance, during a down cycle of the stock market, not only do you want to stay in, but you might also take this opportunity to buy a few good-quality investments on sale.

Inflation Risk

Inflation risk is also referred to as *purchasing power risk.* As you may have noticed, inflation slowly but surely erodes the purchasing power of the dollar. From 1970 to 1997, the purchasing power of a dollar decreased by 75%. Let's assume you had retired in 1970 with a guaranteed (not to go up or down) income of $100,000. You probably would have felt secure in developing a lifestyle that cost $100,000 a year. By 1997, however, the cost of living increased to the point that you would need $175,000 to afford what $100,000 bought you 27 years earlier.

If inflation continues to average 5%, as it has for the last 30 years, costs will double every 14 years. Many everyday costs have increased and will continue to increase. Look at the following examples of prices in 1970 compared with 1997:

	1970	**1997**
Postage stamp	$0.05	$0.32
Luxury car	$2,800	$36,000
Movie ticket	$1.00	$7.50

The way to combat inflation is to make certain your investment portfolio earns more than inflation. The real rate of return on an investment is what is left after subtracting the rate of inflation and cost of taxes.

Historically, stocks have outperformed inflation more often than bonds or money markets and savings accounts. Most people wishing to support themselves from their investment earnings need to add stocks to their mix of investments. If the stock portion outpaces inflation, it is possible that the portfolio as a whole should at least keep pace with inflation.

To manage long-term inflation, you can add enough stocks to the portfolio to keep up with inflation. If you want to own only bonds, however, you must be willing to reinvest and not spend some of the interest income your bonds produce. Depending on the level of interest rates and the size of your portfolio, you may find a portfolio invested solely in bonds will not be able to meet all of your financial needs. One way or another, your investment portfolio must keep growing to ensure your purchasing power.

Interest Rate Risk

Interest rate risk is the risk that your bonds or other interest-sensitive investments will decrease in value when interest rates go up. If you buy a bond that is paying 6% interest and a year later the same kind of bond is paying 7%, your bond will be worth less than what you paid for it. In order to make your bond appealing to a potential buyer who could buy a 7% bond rather than your 6% bond, you will have to lower your price. However, in most cases, if you hold your bond until it matures, your principal will be safe.

Conservative investors hold their bonds until they mature. This way they know exactly what they will receive and when, even though the value may fluctuate over the years. Experienced bond buyers lower their interest rate risk by buying bonds of varying maturities, which is a technique called *laddering*. If interest rates go up, the shorter-term bonds will be able to be reinvested into new bonds at higher rates. If interest rates go down, the longer-term bonds will still receive the higher interest rates as the shorter-term bonds must be reinvested at the lower rate.

Reinvestment Risk

Reinvestment risk is the risk of interest rates declining while you are holding on to higher-interest-paying bonds. As a result, when your bonds come due, your income will drop because the available bonds are paying less interest.

In 1982, Joe and Martha inherited a large sum of money from Joe's family, and the couple retired immediately. Tax-free municipal bonds were paying 9%, so they put all of their investment money in 15- and 20-year bonds because they didn't want to have to worry about the stock market. Twelve years later, the bonds were beginning to be called (if a bond is callable, the issuer has the right to pay back your money earlier than the maturity date of the bond) and the new rates were 5% rather than the original 9%. By 1998, most of their bonds had come due or were called, and their income dropped by almost 50%. And the bad news didn't end there.

Their guaranteed investment plan was upset by inflation as well. Inflation had averaged 4% since they retired; consequently, their cost of living had gone up by 90%. It is easy to figure out that a 50% reduction in income and a 90% increase in expenses either requires an entirely different approach to investing or a drastic change in lifestyle. In their case, they chose to change both.

Reinvestment risk is best managed by laddering, or buying bonds of various maturities, and diversification, a technique that is discussed in detail later in this chapter and then again in the chapter devoted to bonds.

Liquidity Risk

Liquidity risk is the risk of not being able to turn your investment into cash when you want to. Some investments, such as limited partnerships and real estate, do not have well-established daily markets. This means there may not be any buyers willing to buy your investment when you want to sell it.

Stocks, bonds, and mutual funds may also be considered illiquid even though they have well-established markets. In their case, the illiquidity comes in the form of market risk. If your need for cash comes at a time when the stock or bond market is in a decline, your impulse may be to sell. But there are very few instances when that is a good idea. You are almost always better off keeping the money in place until the markets improve and the prices go back up.

The best way to manage liquidity risk is to make sure you have sufficient money set aside in a very liquid place such as a money market account. You also could have other money earmarked for cash flow needs in higher-paying investments (e.g., U.S. Treasury bills are a little less liquid but usually pay more than money markets).

Political Risk

Political risk enters the picture anytime you invest outside the United States. When there is political unrest in any country, the stocks and bonds issued from there will decrease in value. This is particularly common for investments in less-developed countries where the political climate is volatile at times. You can lower this kind of political risk by diversifying.

International investing can be an important part of your investment strategy because international markets offer opportunities not found here. Investing outside the United States allows you to take advantage of strong economies in other regions, and those investments can be used as a way of protecting against downturns in the domestic market.

Most advisors will agree that you should do some international investing, but recommend that you spread your international investing across the globe. The reason is that if you invest in countries that are at different stages of development, you are diversifying your risk and reward potential. For example, in 1999, emerging markets such as Brazil had less political stability than some developed European countries. Therefore, investments based in Brazil had higher risk and higher reward potential.

Political risk may also arise with your domestic investments. For example, when there is talk of rising taxes—income, sales, or social security—it is perceived as a detriment to the financial markets. Furthermore, Wall Street typically has an opinion on presidential elections, and that opinion may make the financial markets quiver during election years. The domestic political risk is easier to foresee and to plan for than international political risk, and it can be managed by staying current with the news coming out of Washington.

Credit Risk

Each time you buy an investment with a stated interest or dividend rate, you should research the reliability of the payor. You can determine this by checking their credit rating with one of the rating agencies, such as Standard & Poor's, Moody's, or Duff and Phelps. Corporations and governments receiving high ratings are considered to be more financially stable and able to make their interest and dividend payments. When financial stability goes down, so do the ratings. When ratings decline, value declines.

Ten Ways to Minimize Risk

1. *Know your investments.* Each kind of investment has its own set of risk factors, so if you know your investments, you'll know what kind(s) of risk you are taking. For instance, bonds are subject to interest rate risk, credit risk, and purchasing power risk. When interest rates increase, the value of bonds decreases; when interest rates decrease, the value of bonds increases. When Wall Street judges a company, government, or government agency that issues bonds to be less reliable and less able to pay the interest and return the principal, the credit rating of that organization is lowered. This means that the bond's rating is lowered. When a bond's rating is lowered, it is less desirable and its price drops. As for the effects of inflation, bonds are not designed as growth investments—the principal value is guaranteed to be the same at maturity—therefore, there is little chance they will keep pace with inflation.

2. *Diversify.* The point of diversification is to create a balanced portfolio that will help you achieve your income needs and your growth needs while lowering the risk presented by any one investment. There is no single investment that will do everything you will need, and there is an art, and a science, to combining investments to suit your individual needs.

Your investment strategy will probably call for a portion of your money to go into growth investments and another portion into fixed investments. The growth portion will be composed of different kinds of stocks or stock mutual funds, including stocks from large, medium, and small companies in the United States, as well as those from countries outside the United States.

The percentage that goes into each will depend on your ability to take the accompanying risk, your investment objective, and where you see future potential. For instance, small company stocks in the United States and stocks of small companies located outside the United States present the highest risk and the highest potential return. Even if you are a moderate risk taker, you can add a small percentage of small company stocks to your portfolio without making the entire portfolio too risky. By diversifying your risk over several kinds of stocks, you lower the potential risk of the portfolio as a whole. If one stock goes down there is a chance that another will maintain its value or go up.

The same principle holds true for the fixed investments. Your instinct may be to own mostly high-quality bonds, but with proper diversification you may have room to buy a high-interest-paying, low-rated bond or a bond mutual fund if the opportunity presents itself. You can do this because the risk of the low-rated bond is offset by all of the other high-rated ones held in the portfolio.

3. *Keep enough money for emergency needs.* Always try to position yourself so you won't have to sell any investments in a hurry to cover a need for cash. Though most stocks, bonds, and mutual funds can be sold quickly, the decision to sell an investment should be just that—an investment decision—not a cash flow decision. You should sell an investment only if it no longer meets your objectives, if it is not performing up to your expectations, or if you have a better place to invest your money. The last thing you want is to have to sell an investment at a time when the price is down and you feel it has great future possibilities.

4. *Stay with investments you understand.* Keeping your investment portfolio simple is the best plan for most investors. You will be able to accomplish all of your investment and income goals by sticking with stocks, bonds, and mutual funds. But the greater accomplishment is to understand what you are doing with your money and to know what to expect from your investments. As many advisors tell their clients: "If you can't explain an investment to your 12-year-old, you shouldn't own it."

Over the course of time, you will come across investments that offer either very high returns or very appealing tax advantages. These esoteric investments will have complications not usually found with basic investments, and you should understand all of their implications before you take the plunge. Complications will ultimately mean more risk—possibly more risk than you would take if you truly understood what you were getting into.

5. *If it sounds too good to be true, say no thank you.* There are very few new investment discoveries, yet unscrupulous people invent new ways to swindle money from naive investors every day. They conjure up seemingly fantastic phony investments and know they will appeal to the greed, fear, and misplaced trust of those who do not do their homework. If your Sudden Money was well publicized, your name may be on the list of the kinds of people you never want to do business with. When approached by phone, through the mail, or in person, you should follow these rules:

- Never invest over the phone.
- Don't give any information about yourself, your credit card number, or your bank account.
- Explain to solicitors that they should contact your advisor—not you personally—and give them the names of your financial advisor, CPA, or attorney. If you show an interest in knowing more, you will be pursued tenaciously. Your advisors will probably check with you before they start to investigate the offer to make sure you want to spend the money to pay for their fees. Unscrupulous promoters are counting on you wanting to save the fees involved in investigating the offer, thereby never discovering that you are being taken advantage of. If the fees involved in investigating an offer seem too high, that is another reason to pass.
- Trust your instincts. It's okay to *not* invest because something does not feel right. When you are new to investing or you are still under the influence of the suddenness of your new money, many investments may not feel right. Lack of experience may also be responsible for your reluctance. Regardless, go with your feelings even though you may miss some good opportunities. It takes time to develop your discrimination and become comfortable with your decisions. Erring on the side of caution is always preferable to taking unnecessary risks for Sudden Money recipients.

6. *Commitment.* Another requirement to minimize your risk is commitment to your investment plan and to the individual investments that compose that plan. Being committed is much easier when you have anticipated what could happen to make you panic and want to sell.

Some advisors like to put their clients through what they call a "lifeboat drill." If you have ever been on a cruise, you know that before the ship leaves port every passenger is required to go to a pre-assigned lifeboat and receive instructions on what to do in the event of an emergency. A short time later, all the passengers are back to enjoying their cruise vacation and feeling confident that they know more about the ship and what to do if an alarm is sounded. This kind of drill is the cruise line's way of lowering the panic level and increasing the success of the emergency procedures if the ship actually experiences problems.

You would begin a lifeboat drill with your investment plan by going through some worst-case scenarios based on the past history of the investments and trying to project what the future might hold. Then, you would apply these projections to your investment plan and goals.

Next, determine if you would be better off holding or selling during these hypothetical events. Assuming this exercise indicates holding is the better plan, try to determine if you think you will have the emotional ability to stick with it. If you have the intellectual knowledge and the emotional strength to withstand the worst-case scenarios, then you will be (better) able to have the kind of real-life commitment you need to minimize the possibility of selling at the wrong times.

7. *Understand investment cycles.* Understanding investment cycles will not only make it easier to know when to buy and when to sell, but it will build your resilience and commitment during down cycles. Since the stock and bond markets both have over 100 years of history, it is possible to forecast, in a general way, how they will react in the future.

When your investments are going down with their respective markets, it is easier to stay committed when you are aware of the historical fact that they will eventually cycle back up. New investors are at a higher risk of making the mistake of selling during a down-market cycle simply because they have never been through the experience before, and they tend to not believe the research until they have personal experience to support it.

There once was a mutual fund that was considered to be "the" best stock mutual fund in the world. This fund had the best returns of any mutual fund during the 1980s and was known and owned by investors around the world. The financial press was so fond of this fund that, for a while, it seemed like every story about stock mutual funds referred to it as the best.

As a result of all the publicity, more and more new investors were signing up. For many of them, this was their first investment, as the mutual fund industry was just becoming popular. Yet even with all its popularity, great returns, and skilled management, roughly half of the people who invested in this fund during the 1980s lost money. The fund, like the stock market it invested in, had some down cycles during the 10-year period. New investors as well as some seasoned investors lost confidence and sold, fearing either the fund or the stock market itself.

As the down cycles gave way to the next up cycle, "the" best fund in the world once again made great returns for its investors. Those who had dumped the fund were left standing on the sidelines, having to decide whether to buy back in at a much higher price or to move on in search of another fund.

---

8. *Don't get greedy.* There is an old saying on Wall Street: "Pigs get fat but hogs get slaughtered." Another saying is: "Fast cash doesn't last." Most wealth is built over time rather than overnight. You are in an unusual position if you have received Sudden Money, and one of your biggest challenges is to find the right way to use your new money to build solid, dependable financial security.

Stretching for unrealistically high returns is more likely to return you to where you were before your Sudden Money than it is to make you even richer. We humans all seem to have some greed within us. Try to recognize yours, and pay special attention to when you are making an investment decision based mostly upon greed, as this is usually a sign that you are on thin investment ice.

9. *Don't borrow money to invest.* If you borrow to invest, you can lose control of when to sell your investment, increase the cost of the

investment, and possibly lose more than the money you invested. Need I say more?

10. *Don't* chase *yield.* This advice is aimed at the conservative income investor who typically buys bonds or CDs for safety and income. The interest rate that a bond pays is referred to as its *yield.* When interest rates drop, people with all or most of their money in bonds have less income to live on as their bonds come due. If they are unwilling or unable to lower their expenses, then they must buy lower-rated bonds that pay higher interest rates. As they continue to *chase* a higher yield, they are taking on more and more risk to their principal.

The lower the bond rating, the higher the risk that the bond may default. By buying low-rated bonds, the yield-chasing investor becomes exposed to precisely the risk of principal they were trying avoid. If you are going to invest all or most of your Sudden Money in bonds or CDs, you must have a plan for dealing with changing interest rates.

How Much Risk Can You, and Should You, Take?

If you have never invested before or have never had the responsibility for so much money all at once, knowing what kinds of investments to choose is difficult. The planning you did in Phase One should have helped establish what you want from your Sudden Money: your goals, income needs, time frames, and overall financial plan. In Phase Two, you are about to put the plan into action, which requires you to make investment decisions.

Examining your *tolerance for risk* will tell you *what kinds* of risk you can take and *how much* risk you should be taking. The following risk tolerance indicator is designed to help you understand yourself as an investor. It takes into consideration your goals, your income needs, and your time frame, and it helps you to clarify your expectations and feelings about taking risks with your Sudden Money. At the end of the exercise, your total number of points will identify you as a conservative, a moderate, or an aggressive investor.

Note: This tool was designed as a guide, not as the final judgment. The results you come up with are not absolutes, and your tolerance for risk may change with knowledge, experience, and time. After you read each question, circle the answer that is closest to how you feel right now.

Risk Tolerance Exercise for Sudden Money Recipients

Investment Objective

What do you want from your Sudden Money?

a.	Income	1 POINT
b.	Income with some growth of principal	2 POINTS
c.	More growth than income	3 POINTS
d.	No income, just growth	4 POINTS

To what extent will you rely upon your Sudden Money for income?

a. I will stop working and live off my investments entirely.   **1 POINT**

b. I plan to continue working and take a small amount of income from my investments.   **2 POINTS**

c. My Sudden Money is all the money I have. I plan to let it grow until I have enough to live on forever.   **3 POINTS**

d. I have other income and will use the Sudden Money to build a financial dynasty for my family and for generations to come.   **4 POINTS**

What percentage rate of income will you need from your investment portfolio? Multiply the amount you have by 4%. Use the amount you will have after paying taxes and setting money aside for large one-time expenses.

a.	This amount is less than I need to live on.	1 POINT
b.	This amount is enough to meet all of my living expenses.	2 POINTS
c.	This amount is more than I will need to live on.	4 POINTS
d.	This amount is much more than I need to live on.	6 POINTS

INVESTMENT OBJECTIVE TOTAL _____

Time Horizon

What age range do you fit into? Typically, the older you are, the fewer the number of years you will need to rely on this money for.

This list assumes that if you are 75, you will live for another 10 to 12 years and will not need the inflation protection that a 30- or even a 60-year-old would need. If your family has a history of longevity, then adjust your answer accordingly.

a. Over 75   1 POINT

b. 65 to 75   2 POINTS

c. 55 to 65   3 POINTS

d. 45 to 55   5 POINTS

e. 30 to 45   6 POINTS

f. Under 30   7 POINTS

How long will the money be able to grow before it is needed?

a. I will need income right away.   1 POINT

b. Five to 10 years.   3 POINTS

c. More than 10 years.   5 POINTS

TIME HORIZON TOTAL _____

Expectations

Ten years from now, how do you expect your standard of living and your income to have changed?

a. I expect no change—same income, same standard
of living.   2 POINTS

b. I expect a moderate increase in income.   3 POINTS

c. I expect a substantial increase.   5 POINTS

Five years from now, what do you expect your portfolio value to be?

a. About the same as now   2 POINTS

b. A small increase   3 POINTS

c. Much larger than now   4 POINTS

What average annual investment return do you feel is reasonable to expect?

a. 4% to 6%   1 POINT

b. 7% to 10%   2 POINTS

    c. 10% to 13%   **4 POINTS**

    d. Over 14%   **6 POINTS**

What rate of inflation do you anticipate over the next 10 years?

    a. 5% to 6%   **1 POINT**

    b. 3% to 4%   **2 POINTS**

    c. 2% to 3%   **3 POINTS**

    d. 1% to 2%   **4 POINTS**

    e. Less than 1%   **5 POINTS**

What impact do you anticipate your Sudden Money will have over your lifetime?

    a. It will give me some more income to enjoy myself with.   **1 POINT**

    b. It will give me the secure feeling of financial freedom.   **2 POINTS**

    c. I expect this money to grow and to be used and enjoyed for generations.   **4 POINTS**

    d. I will use some of it to fund or support causes important to me.   **5 POINTS**

               EXPECTATIONS TOTAL _____

Investment Experience

Have you invested in stocks, bonds, or mutual funds prior to receiving your Sudden Money?

    a. No, I have never invested before.   **1 POINT**

    b. Yes, I invested a few thousand in stock that went belly-up.   **2 POINTS**

    c. Yes, I invest regularly in my company saving plan [e.g., 401(k), 403b, etc.].   **3 POINTS**

    d. I have made personal investments in stocks and mutual funds.   **5 POINTS**

How would you rate your knowledge of investing?

    a. I am a beginner, unfamiliar with most investment terminology.   **1 POINT**

b. I have moderate experience, and I read regularly
   about personal money management and investing.   **3 POINTS**

c. I am very experienced, and I have a solid grasp of
   investment strategies and their risks.   **5 POINTS**

If you ever lost money investing, how did you feel?

a. I felt stupid and angry, and I sold the investment.   **1 POINT**

b. I regretted the loss but stayed with the investment.   **4 POINTS**

c. I felt it was a good opportunity to invest
   more at a lower price.   **5 POINTS**

EXPERIENCE TOTAL _____

Risk Tolerance

Which of the following statements would best describe your reaction if the value of your investment portfolio declined 20%?

a. I would be very concerned because I cannot
   accept fluctuations in the value of my portfolio.   **1 POINT**

b. I invest for long-term growth but would be
   concerned about even a temporary decline.   **2 POINTS**

c. I invest for long-term growth and accept
   temporary fluctuations due to market influences.   **4 POINTS**

Which investments do you feel most comfortable owning?

a. Bank certificates of deposit   **1 POINT**

b. U.S. government securities   **1 POINT**

c. Stocks of well-known, established companies   **3 POINTS**

d. Stocks of smaller, growing companies   **4 POINTS**

Assuming you have a well-diversified portfolio, how would you react if one of your investments lost more than 25% while the market was doing well?

a. I would sell it immediately and fire my advisor.   **1 POINT**

b. I would be very concerned, try to find out what
   the problem was, and determine if the investment
   had the potential to recover.   **2 POINTS**

c. I understand that occasionally there will be investment disappointments, this is why I diversify. **3 POINTS**

d. If there was a good reason to hold on to the investment, I would do so. **4 POINTS**

RISK TOLERANCE TOTAL _____

Total Points

Your score will identify you as a conservative, moderate, or aggressive investor. If your self-perception is not in alignment with the category your score indicates, go over the questions again and discuss the discrepancy with your advisor.

Conservative Investor

From 17 to 25 points means that you are a conservative investor. At least for now, you should concentrate on fixed, guaranteed investments. You could invest 10% to 20% of your Sudden Money in dividend-paying, blue chip stock or stock mutual funds if you'd like to get used to the ups and downs of the stock market.

Stocks	10% to 15%
Bonds	80% to 85%
Cash	5% to 10%

Moderate Risk Investor

From 26 to 50 means that you fall into the moderate risk category. You should be comfortable owning stocks and stock mutual funds as long as you have some money in fixed, guaranteed investments. The bulk of your stock investments should be divided between large-capitalization U.S. stocks and midcapitalization U.S. stocks, with a minor portion in some small company stocks and international stocks.

Stocks	40% to 60%
Bonds	55% to 35%
Cash	5%

Aggressive Investor

From 51 to 75 means that you are able to tolerate a high degree of volatility within your investment portfolio. You are willing to accept the ups and downs of the stock market in return for the potential of high returns. Your stocks and/or mutual funds should be diversified between large-, medium-, and small-company stocks in the United States as well as internationally.

Stocks	65% to 90%
Bonds	30% to 5%
Cash	5%

Summary

At this point, my Phase Two discussion has introduced you to the main types of risk, explained how to manage your overall risk, and given you a general sense of how much risk you are most likely to be able to sustain. In the next three chapters, you will be introduced to the three basic investment vehicles—stocks, bonds, and mutual funds—and you will begin to personalize the information and see your financial plan begin to transform into an investment plan.

Stocks

The American stock market has worked well for both individual investors and the corporations they invest in. As an individual, you have the opportunity to invest your money in well-known companies, such as Disney, IBM, and General Electric, or in new start-up companies that might be the next Microsoft. By becoming a shareholder in a variety of companies, you are investing in the economic development of America.

In this chapter, I will explain the basics of stocks, including what kind of risks accompany each kind of stock. You'll learn how to make stocks a part of your portfolio, even if you are risk averse. If you are not risk averse, you'll learn some strategies to maximize your profit potential without adding unnecessary risk. Regardless of risk tolerance, everyone should invest at least a small percentage of money in stocks because history tells us it will pay off in the long run.

What Does It Mean to Own Stocks?

As a shareholder, you are an owner of the company. As an owner, you are entitled to share in the earnings of the company (i.e., the money remaining after the company has paid its expenses and income taxes). Your share in the earnings may come either in the form of *dividends* or the increase in the value of the stock (also called *capital appreciation*). As an owner, you also have the right to vote, one vote per share, and the right to attend annual meetings.

The Performance of Stocks

Historically, stocks have been the most rewarding type of investment. Looking back through time it is easy to see the long-term resilience of the stock market. From 1966 to 1998, in spite of depressions and recessions, wars, presidential assassinations, and political turmoil, the stock has averaged 11%. Bonds, meanwhile, increased an average of 6%. Though the difference between stocks and bonds is only 4%, over time that translates into an enormous difference. Ten thousand dollars invested in bonds for 38 years would have grown to $90,000, while the same amount invested in stocks for 38 years would have grown to $527,000.

Types of Stocks

Blue Chip Stocks

These are the stocks of the largest companies with a history of

- Good earning and dividends
- Leading their industry
- Growth potential

You will recognize the names of most blue chip stocks because they are strong, well-established companies. Companies like General Electric, General Motors, and Procter & Gamble are examples of blue chip companies. Sometimes these stocks are referred to as *large-capitalization stocks*.

Blue chips are bought for their stability, although their prices may go down with market conditions and industry cycles. They also make sense if your objective calls for income from your growth investments, because blue chips usually pay a dividend. The amount they pay is less than what you would get from a bond, but you have the potential for superior growth along with your dividend income.

Growth Stocks

These are companies whose earnings are increasing above the average rate. Rather than paying a large dividend, they choose to reinvest their earnings into the growth of the company. People who invest in growth companies are looking for increases in share price rather than income. These shareholders would prefer to see the company buy new equipment, build factories, or open new markets with the hope of increasing the value of the company and the price per share.

Growth stocks can be blue chip stocks, or they can be stocks of newer, less well-known companies. They are bought for their future potential growth instead of current income. Investors buying this kind of stock should pay close attention to the company's progress while they hold the stock.

Cyclical Stocks

The general business cycle in America has somewhat predictable expansions, contractions, and recessions. Certain industries follow that general business cycle (e.g., automobiles, steel, some manufacturing, and heavy machinery). It makes sense, then, that the most important factor when considering the purchase of a cyclical stock is timing of the purchase. Their stock prices will generally go up when the economy is expanding, and they will go down when the economy is contracting. Long-term investors who study cyclical stocks buy when the prices go down; when the share prices go back up, they stop buying and hold what they have bought.

New Company Stocks

Newer companies that have not had time to build a consistent history of above-average earnings are difficult to follow and can have large swings in share price. These companies offer both higher risk and higher return potential, so investing in them is considered more speculative and should be done with a smaller portion of your money.

Though it is difficult for a large, established company like Exxon to double in price, a small company can double or triple its value in one year, and sometimes in less than a year. However, it is important to understand that it is also more likely for a new company stock to drop in value by 50 or 70 percent in one year than it would be for Exxon's stock to plummet. Some new companies that thrive and grow will be blue chips 20 years from now, but many more will fail.

Income Stocks

These companies concentrate on paying high and steady dividends. Typically, companies that pay high dividends do not grow in value as much as those that pay only moderate or low dividends. If a company is paying high dividends, it is using most of its earnings to accomplish this goal. Therefore, the money that goes to paying the dividend is not available to be reinvested for future growth.

Investors who buy income stocks, such as utilities, which are known for their dividends, are at least as concerned with income as with growth. Look for a company that has a long track record of increasing its dividends every year so you have a good chance of keeping pace with the inflation rate.

Recap

Each kind of stock has both strengths and weaknesses. It makes sense to concentrate on the types that meet your tolerance for price fluctuation and your need for income. At the same time, you may want to own a small amount of the other types of stocks as well.

Type of Stock	Stability	Income	Long-Term Growth Potential	Long-Term Risk
Blue chip	Good	Good	Good	Low
Growth	Fair	Poor	Excellent	Moderate
Cyclical	Poor	Fair	Good	Moderate
Income	Good	Excellent	Fair	Low
Newer	Poor	Poor	Excellent	High

Following the Stock Market

The easiest and most accessible way to follow the direction of stock prices is to pay attention to the daily quotes of the most popular *indexes* and *averages:*

- The *Dow Jones Industrial Average* (DJIA) tracks the movement of the general stock market and is based on 30 widely held stocks listed on the New York Stock Exchange.

- The *National Association of Securities Dealers Automated Quotations System* composite index (Nasdaq) gives you the direction of prices for approximately 5,000 stocks that are traded over the counter.

- The *Standard & Poor's 500 Index* (S&P 500) includes 500 stocks (mostly industrial corporations) and is a general measure of the stock market movement.

Foreign Stocks

Investing in companies outside of the United States by purchasing individual stocks diversifies your portfolio in a unique way because the political and economic forces that affect those investments are different from the ones that affect companies based here. However, that same factor is the biggest drawback to foreign stocks: The information about those political and economic forces is tougher to get. In addition, you might run into special taxes, currency problems, or transfer difficulties.

One way around these potential problems is to buy foreign stock mutual funds, which allow you to achieve diversification that would be difficult for you to get on your own without a lot of time spent researching. The delicate area here is making certain that the fund managers are skilled and experienced in researching the stocks of foreign companies and the potential glitches that accompany them.

Diversification

An important rule to follow when investing in stocks is to never bet the ranch on only one stock. The concept of diversification goes further, however, and it is important for you to understand it and adhere to it. I like to describe diversification as a 4-part strategy that *every* investor should be using.

Part 1. *Own shares of many different companies.*   The idea is that if one company is going through a tough time that results in a decrease in their stock price, other companies in your portfolio may be doing well. It is unlikely that all your stocks will go up or down in lock step. If Merck is struggling, Microsoft, GE, and Home Depot may be charging ahead, allowing your portfolio to continue to grow while Merck is down.

Part 2. *Invest in companies of different sizes.*   Corporations are categorized by the total value of their outstanding stock (commonly known as their *market capitalization*) as either large-capitalization, midcapitalization, or small-capitalization. Generally speaking, large-cap stocks, such as blue chip stocks, are shares in America's largest and most established companies; midcap stocks are shares in smaller companies; and small-cap stocks are issued by more local and/or young companies.

Part 3. *Investing in different industries.* While Ford, General Motors, and Chrysler are different companies, they are still in the same industry, and a cyclical industry at that. If the economy goes into a recession and people slow down the rate at which they buy cars, all three of your companies will be in trouble at once. It makes sense to buy stock in several different industries (e.g., technology, consumer goods, utilities, and transportation) to avoid such a problem.

Part 4. *Invest in several different economies.* The U.S. stock market is no longer the biggest or the highest performer in the global marketplace. When the U.S. market is strong, other markets may be weak, and vice versa. As a group, stock markets abroad have outperformed the U.S. stock market 17 out of the last 30 years.

Though diversification is crucial, there is such a thing as being overdiversified. This occurs when investors buy small amounts of many different stocks. You can avoid overdiversification by concentrating on your goals and by investing only in the companies that you feel have the best chance of meeting those goals.

Advantages of Stocks

- Most investors buy stock because they want *growth* (i.e., appreciation in the value of the stock). While building wealth has its appeal and great fortunes have been made in the stock market, many people see the stock market as their vehicle to keep their wealth from eroding due to inflation. It is this desire for inflation protection that creates the need for and interest in buying stocks. Stocks are the only major asset class that has historically outperformed inflation.

- Investing in corporate America has been the path to financial security and wealth for many people who otherwise would not have had the opportunity to acquire large sums of money.

A Greek immigrant worked day and night to get enough money to buy a chicken farm. He and his wife raised chickens and children. The money they earned by selling chickens was used to buy more chickens, and the money from selling eggs was put into mayonnaise jars until they had enough to buy stocks. For a while, they did well with their stock investments, then suddenly they lost more than half of their hard-earned money when the stock market crashed. He wanted to go right back to saving money and buying stocks, but she wanted nothing to do with taking a risk ever again.

The story goes that he would put most of the money into the mayo jars, but he had begun a secret savings jar of his own hidden under the porch. Once again, he began to buy stocks—stocks of companies that he had heard of and that made products he used. He kept buying until he had earned back all that was lost, plus some extra. Only then did he tell his wife that they were back in the stock market.

They continued to stay invested in stocks, earning enough to send their four children to excellent private colleges where they earned impressive degrees and became successful professionals. When he died, he left his children an estate worth hundreds of thousands of dollars and a legacy of confidence in the American capitalist system.

- There are *tax advantages* of stock ownership. When you have owned a stock for at least 12 months and you sell it for more than you paid for it, your profits are taxed as capital gains. The maximum capital gains rate of 20% is almost one-half of the highest ordinary income tax rate of 39.6%. The lower capital gains rate is one way the government encourages investments in American corporations. You can keep it for decades and you won't owe taxes until you sell the stock. Stock *dividends* are taxed at the ordinary income tax rates.

The Greek chicken farmer sold stocks only when he needed money to pay for big items like tuition, and eventually for his nursing home care. At the time of his death, he had owned most of the stocks for more than 30 years.

His children received these stocks with a great advantage called a step-up in basis. This means they received the stocks as though they had bought them on the day of his death. In other words, all of the gains over all those years were not subject to capital gains taxes.

For instance, if he had purchased 1,000 shares of AT&T 30 years ago for $8,000 and had sold those shares for $95,000 before his death, he would have owed capital gains on the $83,000 profit. However, because he owned the stocks at the time of his death, his children inherited the stocks as though they had paid $95,000. The cost basis of $8,000 was stepped up to $95,000, which virtually eliminated the capital gains tax on the investment.

- Common stocks are considered to be *liquid* investments because they are easily bought and sold. Stocks sold on any of the major stock exchanges can typically be sold on any day that the exchange is open. Now it is possible to put in orders to buy or sell stock at all times of the day on the Internet.

- Stocks are *easy to follow.* You can get prices in most local newspapers, from your broker or advisor, and from the Internet. Information on the companies you own and what different experts are saying about them can also be found in the media, over the Internet, and from the companies themselves.

- Historically, investors have been rewarded for staying with their investments during the down market cycles. Once you make your initial purchases under advisement, you and your advisor should monitor them closely, but you will probably want to sell only rarely and for good reasons in order to minimize taxes. Again, a market downturn, which causes most stocks to drop, is generally not a good reason to sell.

Disadvantages of Stocks

- Stocks are *not guaranteed.* If the company does well, you do well, and if the company does not do well, you may lose some money. If the company goes out of business, you lose your investment.

- Though some stocks do have a history of paying dividends, most do not pay high dividends and those *dividends are not guaranteed.* Most companies take all of their earnings and put them back into the company, hoping to increase its profitability for shareholders.

- Stock *prices are volatile and unpredictable.* The goal of buying low and selling high can be tough to achieve in the short run. The steep drops that can occur in the stock market often cause unprepared investors to panic and sell their investments at the wrong time. If you do not understand that the stock market moves in cycles, it is easy to think that you may never recover your lost money and that you should sell immediately following a decline to save what you can. But time is your friend in stock investing.

The S&P 500 has lost money 50% of the time in a one-year period, but it has never lost money over a 20-year period.

My Recommendation

I am not a big fan of complicated strategies for buying stocks; very few of such plans have produced consistent results over long periods of time. For instance, many people claim that they are able to time when you should get out of the market and when you should reenter to achieve maximum financial benefit. This strategy sounds great but has no history of working. In fact, while many would like to think they are minimizing their risk by trying to find the right time to buy and sell their stocks, they in fact can be seriously increasing their risk of losing money. Markets tend to move in short bursts. The biggest risk with investing in stocks is being out of the stock market during these powerful moves.

My first words of wisdom are to *keep it simple.* If you are buying individual stocks, develop a strategy for buying and establish the point at which you will sell. Work with your financial advisor on a logical allocation of your stock money (i.e., how much will be put into blue chip, growth, and income stocks).

There are only two strategies I consistently favor, because they are the two that have proven to be beneficial over and over again, no matter what changes have taken place in our economy:

1. *Buy and hold.* Buy the stock of good solid companies and never sell it unless you need the money or the company becomes fatally flawed. This is the strategy the Greek chicken farmer used so successfully. It has yet to go out of fashion and is still the best long-term approach. It does, however, become a challenging strategy to adhere to when the stock market is going through a prolonged down period.

   For those of you who just might want to believe someone who claims to be a market-timer, consider the following before you sell a single share: If you were in the market every day from 1982 to 1990, the return on your investments would have been about 18%. But if you were out of the market for the 10 best days during that time period, your rate of return would have been cut by one-third, leaving it at 12%. And if you were out for the 10 next best days—a total of 20 days—your return would have been 8.3%, according to Cambridge Associates.

2. *Buy on sale.*   When the stock market cycles down, you may be able to buy your favorite stocks at bargain prices. Even the best-quality stocks will go down with an overall stock market correction. A drop in share price in this scenario creates a good buying opportunity. If a quality suit you liked went on sale, it would be a more appealing purchase opportunity than if you had to pay full price. The same is true for stocks.

Bonds

onds are like IOUs: When you purchase them you are lending money to the institution that issues them in exchange for the promise that your money will be returned to you on a specified date in the future. In the meantime, that institution agrees to pay you income periodically, until the bond's maturity date. Bonds, therefore, are purchased for their income, as they typically do not appreciate.

Although their worth is set at the beginning and they don't have the potential to skyrocket for any reason like stocks do, bonds likewise don't have the potential to plummet. Because they are guaranteed, the return on bonds is generally low, as you are not taking much risk when you purchase them.

If you have determined that your tolerance for risk is low, your investment plan will probably be composed of a large percentage of bonds. If your tolerance for risk is high, you should not avoid bonds altogether, as they can be a great source of income and they are the perfect vehicles for ensuring you have a certain lump sum years from now.

Just like stocks, there are advantages and disadvantages to owning bonds, and it takes an educated investor to figure out how to best incorporate them.

Before you learn about the types of bonds and why you would purchase them, you need to understand some terms and the way they affect one another.

Face value, or par value. The value that is printed on the front of the document.

Bid price. The amount a broker pays for a bond (not face value).

Asking price, or selling price. The amount a bond sells for (again, it is not equivalent to face value).

Spread. The difference between the bid price and the asking price.

Premium. The amount by which the selling price exceeds the face value. A *premium bond* has a market price that is higher than its face value. You would purchase such a bond if you need a higher current income. The additional income, over the time you own the bond, usually offsets the premium. A bond sells at a premium because, when it was originally issued, interest rates were higher than they currently are.

Discount bond. A discount bond has a market price that is below its face value. This means you will get more back for it than you paid, yet your income while you own it will be less. A bond sells at a discount because, when it was originally issued, interest rates were lower than they currently are.

Maturity. The date at which a bond issuer agrees to repay the principal (face value), and at which any accompanying risk ends.

Interest rate. The interest rate (also called *coupon rate*) of a bond is your income. It is the percentage of the face value that you are paid, usually semiannually, but in some cases monthly. Therefore, if you have purchased a $5,000 bond at 8%, you will probably receive two payments of $200 each year until the bond's maturity.

Reinvestment risk. The risk that when your bond matures, rates will be lower and you will have to reinvest your money in a bond that pays less interest. This causes your income to decline.

Yield, or return. The percentage return that the income stream represents. It is a percentage of the amount you have invested in a bond.

Call features. If a bond is *callable,* that means the issuing institution can redeem it (usually at a premium) prior to its maturity date. Bonds with interest rates that are higher than the current interest rate are most likely to be called in because the creditor (the bondholder, *you*) is receiving a higher yield than necessary. The issuer will repay you, then replace your bond with a new one that offers a lower yield. This means the issuer's cost of borrowing drops.

Laddering. Laddering is a technique used to create diversification with bonds. It is achieved by purchasing bonds of varying maturities. This accomplishes two important goals of financial planning. First, it means that only a small part of your bond portfolio comes due in any one year, giving you protection against reinvestment risk if rates decline. By the time other bonds in the portfolio mature, rates may be higher again. Second, if you have planned efficiently for large, future expenses, you can invest now to have the money when you need it down the road. For instance, if you know you will need tuition money in nine years for your eight-year-old, you might purchase four Treasury notes that will come due prior to each year a tuition payment is due, starting in nine years.

Diversification. You can diversify your bond portfolio by laddering your bonds, as explained above, and by purchasing bonds of different issuers and ratings.

How the Interest Rate and Ratings Affect Bonds

Between the time you purchase a bond and its maturity, its price will fluctuate due to changes in the interest rate and the rating of the bond. The interest rate of bonds is directly related to their maturity. In general, bonds with shorter maturities have lower interest rates because the amount of *interest rate risk* that you assume is less. The longer the time for which you are lending your money, the higher the probability that the interest rate will change, so the higher the risk you are taking.

When interest rates rise, the bond value falls. The inverse happens, as well. For this reason, interest rate risk is the most important risk for bondholders.

When purchasing bonds, you will enlist the help of the two best-known rating services, Moody's and Standard & Poor's. In general, the higher a bond is rated, the lower the risk you assume when you buy it, so the lower the yield. The bond rating scales are as follows:

	High	Low
Moody's	Aaa, Aa, A, Baa, Ba, B, Caa, Ca, C	
Standard & Poor's	AAA, AA, A, BBB, BB, B, CCC, CC, C	

Bonds with ratings of BBB/Baa or higher are known as *investment-grade* bonds; those below are referred to as *high-yield* bonds, or *junk* bonds. The latter have much more risk and should be investigated thoroughly prior to purchase.

If an issuer's rating falls, that issuer must pay higher interest payments in order to sell bonds to compensate investors for the greater risk. This causes the market price of its outstanding bonds to fall. If, on the other hand, the issuer moves up the rating scale, the interest rate that investors require will fall, and the market price of its outstanding bonds will rise.

Perhaps the safest bonds with the lowest risk are those that are *insured* by a third party who will take over the timely payment of interest and principal if the issuing agency runs into problems. Because of the safety of insured bonds, the yield will be a bit lower.

Types of Bonds

Bonds are issued by U.S. government agencies, state and local municipalities, and corporations. When you invest in bonds:

- You lend the issuer money in return for a promise to have it repaid by a specific date (its maturity date).
- You are paid a stream of income (a percentage of the face value of the bond), periodically, until that date.

U.S. Treasuries

The United States Treasury Department is responsible for funding the federal government. Much of the money raised to fulfill this financial obligation comes from the sale of securities called *Treasury obligations,* which come in three forms: Treasury bills (T-bills), notes, and bonds. They are all backed by the full faith and credit of the United States. All are state tax–exempt, low-risk investments that offer a lower yield because of these benefits. They can be purchased from the Federal Reserve, for no fee, or from your financial advisor, for a fee, which is tax-deductible.

TREASURY BILLS Treasury bills are issued with maturities of 3, 6, and 12 months. The minimum amount for a T-bill is $10,000, and they are sold at a discount. This means that the interest is immediately yours (e.g., if you were to purchase a $20,000, one-year T-bill at 8%, you would get a check for $1,600), so your net cost (in this case, $18,400) is less than face value. The amount of the discount is not considered ordinary income until the T-bill matures, at which point it must be declared for tax purposes.

TREASURY NOTES Treasury notes can be sold at a discount, at par, or at a premium, and they pay their interest every six months. In addition, they have a much longer life span (up to 10 years), and their minimum investment is lower ($5,000 for those maturing in less than four years and $1,000 for those maturing in four years or more).

TREASURY BONDS Treasury bonds are very much like Treasury notes with longer life spans (their maturity periods are from 10 to 30 years). Some include a call provision, which allows the Treasury Department the right to redeem them before they mature.

Municipal Bonds

Our state and local governments are responsible for the construction and maintenance of our roads, water facilities, bridges, and public schools, among other things. Unfortunately, those institutions don't always have the up-front resources necessary for such often-expensive and time-consuming tasks.

For this reason, they borrow money from individuals and other institutions, in quantities of $5,000. In return, investors get a stream of income that is not subject to federal income tax. If you live in the state that issued the bond, you are free of state and local taxes, as well. In addition, that income is guaranteed, and you can use it as collateral to borrow up to 90 percent of its market value. The trade-off for these benefits is that municipal bonds usually carry a lower interest rate than bonds that are taxable, such as corporate bonds. Further, many municipal bonds are callable, so be sure to ask your advisor about this factor.

There are two types of municipal bonds: *general obligation* (GO) bonds and *revenue* bonds, which are repaid in different ways. The GO bond is considered the safest because it is backed by the taxing authority of the issuing municipality. Therefore, the municipality that issues the bond will actually raise taxes if it has to in order to repay you. Revenue bonds, however, are usually sold in order to finance a project that will receive income upon completion. Relying on the revenue-generating ability of the project, be it a stadium, a sewage treatment plant, or a hospital, is obviously riskier than relying on the complete taxing authority of a municipality or state. This is why revenue bonds usually offer you a higher yield than GO bonds.

Corporate Bonds

Corporate bonds usually offer a higher interest rate than other issuers, and the income paid on them is fully taxable on all levels. They are issued by industrial, utility, finance, and transportation companies to finance special projects and expansions.

When you purchase a corporate bond, you do *not* become a shareholder of the company. Therefore, the profits of the corporation do not affect the income you receive. On the upside, the bond is a safer investment than stock in a company because the interest on bonds is paid out before dividends are paid to stockholders.

Some corporations issue *convertible* bonds, which permit the bondholder the option of exchanging them for shares of the corporation's common stock. This combines the best of both investment worlds, although there is usually a lower interest yield for such bonds.

Corporate bonds can be purchased in denominations of $1,000 and may or may not be *callable.* If the market interest rate falls below what it was when you purchased the bond, your bond might be called.

To research corporate bonds, you'll once again look to Moody's and Standard and Poor's. As you might imagine, the bonds with the lowest risk get the highest ratings, because the ability of the corporation to pay interest and principal is strong. But those are also the bonds with the lowest yield. If a bond has a particularly high yield, that yield is your inducement to take the accompanying high risk.

Foreign Bonds

Foreign bonds are just like bonds issued in the United States, except they are subject to different economies and political situations. Those differences create different types of risk, such as when the value of the foreign currency declines in relation to our dollar. Meanwhile, including foreign bonds in your portfolio is a good way to diversify *because* of the differences in economies and political situations.

Zero Coupon Bonds

As the name suggests, zero coupon bonds do not pay any coupon interest. They are issued at a discount and the bondholder is paid face value at maturity. Naturally, the higher the interest rate is, the larger the discount becomes. They are issued by the U.S. government, municipal authorities, and corporations.

What makes these bonds attractive is that they have a *compounded* rate of return. This means that from the start, the interest is added to the principal (increasing the principal), and the next interest amount is calculated *using the increased principal*. If you do not need the current income and you are planning to meet a future need, particularly one far in the future (e.g., your toddler's college tuition), the discount from zero coupon bonds can save you a considerable amount of money. The absence of a stream of income from them eliminates the possibility of *reinvestment risk* for that income. Your interest is locked in and is compounding, and you don't have to make any decisions.

Advantages of Bonds

- Dependable stream of income that may be tax-exempt.
- Safety—your investment is backed by the full faith and credit of the issuer.
- Certainty of investment return—At the moment you purchase a bond, you know exactly what your return will be if you hold it to maturity.

Disadvantages of Bonds

- Your investment does not usually appreciate, so your principal loses purchasing power over time due to inflation.
- Your investment loses value if interest rates rise after you buy a bond.
- You are exposed to reinvestment risk when your bond is called or matures.

- Your bond's rating could possibly be lowered, thereby decreasing its market value, but not its maturity value.

- Your bond's interest payments might be suspended if the issuing entity encounters financial problems. Your principal repayment might be delayed, or in the case of a bankruptcy, it might never occur at all.

Mutual Funds

Mutual funds give investors an affordable way to invest in a large number of companies within several industries. In addition, they remove the guesswork from the selection process by enlisting the help of experts whose sole responsibility is to manage the fund and whose income often depends on the success of the fund. Mutual funds have become popular because they allow investors to participate in the stock and bond markets without having to pick the individual investments.

There are thousands of mutual funds. In fact, there are more mutual funds than individual stocks. If you do your research, you'll discover that there is at least one that is appropriate for your needs. This is the one investment no one should ignore.

What Is a Mutual Fund?

A mutual fund is a collection of investments, managed by a knowledgeable professional, that is owned by a large number of investors. It has an objective and its holdings are chosen because they have been deemed to be the best to fulfill that objective. They can be composed of stocks, bonds, and other securities, or a combination thereof, and the percentage of each is contingent upon what the fund's manager is trying to achieve (i.e., the fund's *objective*).

The net asset value (NAV) is the value of all of the assets owned by a fund once its liabilities are subtracted.

The price of a share of the mutual fund is contingent upon the value of the investments that compose the fund. When the overall value of the fund increases, the value of each share increases, and vice versa. As the investments in a fund are sold, gains and losses are realized. These are passed on to shareholders every year. As the investments in a fund pay interest and dividends, these too are passed on to shareholders. Therefore, it is important to pay attention to the tax consequences of owning a mutual fund and how those taxes may impact your net total return.

The investment advisor or fund company is required to provide you with a *prospectus*, which is a disclosure document that explains a particular fund's objective and that tells you about the fund's manager, the fees you will be charged, and the performance history of the fund. It will also note that "past performance is no guarantee of future results." In other words, you cannot invest in a fund's history, although you will use that history as an indication of its attractiveness as an investment vehicle for you.

The prospectus will also give you an idea of how often there is turnover in management, how long the current manager has been working with it, and what the exact management fees are.

What Fees?

Some mutual funds charge a sales fee, which is known as a *load*. Funds that do not charge a sales fee are known as *no-load* funds. In addition, all funds have administrative, management, and regulatory expenses, which are deducted from the share to arrive at the net asset value. These vary with the fund family and the size and type of fund. There are three basic kinds of mutual fund products:

1. *Open-end.* As the name suggests, this type of fund remains *open*. When investors buy shares, their investment is added to the fund portfolio. When they sell shares, their investment is pulled out of the fund portfolio. Therefore, the size of the fund fluctuates as money flows in and out of it, as well as when its holdings fluctuate. Open-end funds will always sell at net asset value (plus sales fees if it is a load fund).

2. *Closed-end.* In contrast, a closed-end fund has a predetermined number of shares, and once those shares are purchased,

it *closes* itself to new money. These funds can sell at a premium or discount to net asset value.

3. *Unit investment trust (UIT).* The shares in UITs are called *units*, and there are a fixed number of them, as in a closed-end fund. However, unlike closed- and open-end funds, the investments in UITs are fixed, and they have a preset date by which all of their assets will be liquidated. In other words, the trust purchases certain securities and holds them, distributing any interest or dividends earned.

Unit investment trusts are not actively managed. If a security is sold for some reason, it is not replaced. Further, as the holdings mature, they are not replaced either, so the size of the fund decreases until it is completely liquidated.

Find the Fund That's Right for You— Match Your Risk Tolerance and Objective

One of the most appealing things about the mutual fund industry is that there is a place for everyone. No matter what your tolerance for risk is, how long your time horizons are, and how much money you have, you will be able to find a product that suits your needs.

Selecting a suitable type of mutual fund is not that different from deciding if your portfolio should consist of more stocks than bonds. If stocks are the better investment for you, then growth funds, which are stock based, will be where you'd want to look. Your choice will be based on your objective.

Growth Funds

The objective, as the name suggests, is growth, or *capital appreciation*. These funds are less concerned with income. They tend to invest in larger, more established blue chip and growth stocks.

Aggressive Growth Funds

The objective of these stock-intensive funds is *high capital appreciation*. Their holdings usually consist of stock in newer companies, growth companies, and industries that are out of favor.

Growth-and-Income Funds

The objective of these funds is *income as well as capital appreciation*. They invest in large, well-established companies (e.g., blue chip companies) that have the ability to pay larger dividends than smaller and newer companies do. If you recall the discussion about blue chip stock, you'll know that whenever there are larger dividends involved, there is less risk involved.

Balanced Funds

Balanced funds invest in both stock and bonds. Shareholders get income from the high-yielding stocks as well as from the bonds, and they also enjoy the capital appreciation that comes from the stocks.

Income Funds

Income funds invest in both stocks and bonds that pay high dividends, but due to their income objective, they may own more bonds than a balanced fund would.

Index Funds

Index funds are designed to mirror the performance of one of the benchmarks I described earlier, such as the S&P 500. If the S&P rises 15% this year, index funds will rise about that much as well. (I say "about" because management fees prevent the funds from precisely matching the rise or fall.)

Bond Funds

Naturally, these funds consist of different types of bonds, depending on the fund's objective. Contrary to what you might think, these are not all safe investments. There are bond funds for more aggressive investors, and there are bond funds for conservative investors whose main purpose is to protect their principal.

Bond funds are designed to pay income. They can range from conservative, short-term funds that pay modest interest, to high-yield funds that invest in lower-rated, higher-risk bonds. Bond funds should not be confused with individual bonds, because mutual funds do not have fixed interest rates or set maturity dates. Both the value of your investment and the income you receive from a bond fund can change.

Overseas Mutual Funds

Global funds invest in both the U.S. and the overseas stock markets. Meanwhile, *international funds* do not include U.S. securities. These funds are a great way to diversify your portfolio because they spread your risk across other markets.

Sector Funds

These specialized funds concentrate on specific market sectors (e.g., technology, financial, real estate, natural resources). Because all of their holdings are from one sector, these funds have little diversification. If your fund's sector is doing well in the overall market, your fund is likely to be doing well, and vice versa.

Advantages of Mutual Funds

- *Professional management.*   Most people do not have the time, energy, or inclination to research enough investments to create a diversified portfolio that meets their objective. Hiring someone to do that is usually worth the small fee you pay, and a mutual fund is one way to hire a professional manager.

- *Diversification.*   The diversification achieved by fund managers would take far more time for an individual; it involves an expertise that most people do not possess, because it takes time to cultivate.

- *Liquidity.*   If you choose to sell your shares, you can do so and have your money within one week.

- *Convenience.*   Mutual funds allow you to invest in companies that you might not otherwise have been able to invest in, because there are a lot of other people pooling their money with you to make the investments possible. Further, once you determine what your objective is, someone else is going to do all of the hard work for you.

- *Availability and reliability of information.*   Mutual fund information is available in most daily newspapers throughout the country. The funds are listed alphabetically, and their NAVs, changes in NAV from the previous day, and the year-to-date total returns are usually listed as well. Some papers, like the *Wall Street Journal* and *USA Today,* will give more information and will rate the funds on particular days of the week.

    Most business magazines and all of the personal finance magazines will have monthly stories on funds. Many magazines will do in-depth quarterly reviews on mutual funds. For instance, *Morningstar Mutual Fund Research* has excellent information available at public libraries and over the Internet (www.morningstar.com).

Mutual fund information is highly regulated by the Securities and Exchange Commission (SEC), so it is also highly reliable. The SEC must approve all information on funds before that information can be released.

Disadvantages of Mutual Funds

- *Taxation of capital gains.* Mutual funds are required, by law, to pay out 90% of their capital gains by the end of each year. Unless you own the fund inside a tax-deferred retirement account, this requirement means you may be paying taxes on profits you have not really earned. It is possible to have gains within the mutual fund portfolio in the same year you have lost money on that investment.

  The gains may have been achieved by selling stocks within the portfolio during the first half of the year while stock prices were high. If the stock market took a steep downturn during the second half of the year, the price of your shares may be down, showing a loss for the year. The fund will have to distribute the gains to you before the end of the year. You will most likely reinvest these distributions and buy more shares, perhaps at a favorable lower price.

  Ideally, you want to control when you pay tax on your investments. In most cases, this means delaying taxation until you sell the investments. When you buy growth mutual funds outside of tax-deferred accounts, look for funds that have a history of only minor capital gains distributions each year. Some funds state their commitment to tax efficiency by calling themselves tax managed or tax-efficient funds.

- *False diversification.* If you own five mutual funds, each of which holds 100 stocks in its portfolio, you probably do not own stock in 500 different companies; there is likely to be some overlap. If you do not want to duplicate any holdings, make that kind of review a part of your mutual fund research. If your advisor subscribes to *Morningstar Mutual Fund Research*, the review can be done quickly and easily.

- *Overdiversification.* Considering that there are over 7,000 mutual funds and that new ones are introduced each month, it is possible to own too many funds and be overdiversified. Try to find the top couple of funds for each of your objectives, and stay current on how those funds are performing. A small but well-selected portfolio of mutual funds is much easier to keep track of and manage than a portfolio filled with a wide variety of funds.

PHASE THREE

Once you have completed Phase Two by putting your money to work, you automatically enter Phase Three, which lasts for the rest of your life. You will manage your money, find meaningful ways to share it with others, and ultimately transfer it to your heirs. During Phase Three, you will continue to learn about yourself and your attitudes toward investing, spending, and gifting your money. Your knowledge and confidence will continue to grow, and you should derive increasing joy from the life you have created with your Sudden Money.

In Phase Three, you will concentrate your energy on maintaining your chosen lifestyle and achieving your long-range goals. To do this most effectively, you will need to develop a system to make sure your investments stay on the right track. This does not have to mean daily rituals of checking all of your investments, but it does mean finding a system to periodically review your progress and make the small adjustments that will keep you moving in the right direction.

Once you have set up a monitoring system, you will begin to consider matters that pertain to estate planning. As you begin to have estate planning discussions with your family and your advisor, you will find it is not just about money—it is about people, causes, and future generations. You may find the process helps you define what is, and what is not, important to you. Your estate plan, like your investment plan, may change over time due to changes within your family, changes in tax laws, and changes within yourself.

When you are comfortable with your finances and you know you have created a sustainable, as well as an enjoyable lifestyle, you may want to find ways to share your money and/or your time with others beyond your family. The sharing and giving of your time and money can bring greater meaning and fulfillment to your life than you previously imagined. During Phase Three, you will be able to explore how and where you would like to direct your energy and money in order to make the most significant impact.

Staying on Track

n Phases One and Two you defined the "track" you need to stay on to fulfill the desires and dreams you have for your life as a result of your Sudden Money. You should now know what kinds of investment returns you should be expecting and about how much you can spend each year. Phase Three begins the moment you implement your investment plan. Throughout Phase Three, which will last for the rest of your life, you will need to make adjustments and refinements within your plan and your portfolio to accommodate changes.

This chapter will help you establish a system for keeping track of your investments so that you can remain informed of exactly what your Sudden Money is doing. Remember that you are always heading to some specific destination; however, unless you periodically examine your path and your intentions, *you might be surprised by what that destination is.*

Watching the Numbers and Being Flexible

Staying on track means that you are monitoring your investment returns and your spending so that they will match the assumptions you made when your financial plan was first created. But staying on track is more personal than watching the numbers; it means being flexible enough to accommodate the personal changes within your life. Despite having spent considerable time going through the exercises of Phase One and finding out what you truly want from your Sudden Money, your examination of yourself and your money is not over.

Life is not stagnant, and some say the only thing we can count on is change. Some of those changes are radical, but don't worry. As your life begins to move in a different direction or take a new shape, simply revise your financial plan to address these changes. You do not have an obligation to maintain the investment and life plans you made when you first received your Sudden Money. Your focus should be on using your Sudden Money as a tool to help you attain the highest possible fulfillment from life, whatever that means to you.

Along with changes you may experience personally, the economy will certainly change, tax laws will be rewritten, and the stock and bond markets will go through their cycles. These are all changes to which you will have to learn to adjust each year. The only way you can adjust and not get caught in the downdrafts is to have a system of monitoring your investments, your cash flow, and yourself each year. The following system will allow you to take advantage of change rather than get clobbered by it.

Monitoring System

In order to know when you need to adjust your investment plan, you will need a system that allows you to stay current and informed. There will be several areas of your new life that need to be kept track of: home, investments, insurance coverage, and life events such as divorce, retirement, estate settlements, or the sale of a business. You will receive legal documents, contracts, and account applications, as well as monthly statements. All this paperwork may seem overwhelming and unnecessary; however, all of it should be saved and organized efficiently so it can be retrieved when needed.

Your financial advisor, your attorney, and your accountant will keep records as well, but you need to have your own set. Your advisors are mortal, and they too will be gone someday, perhaps making your records difficult to find. Furthermore, over the years you may change advisors, and your new advisor will need to have some history of what was done before. Most of all, you should keep your own set of records because it gives you more control over your financial affairs.

Monthly Statements

Take some time each month to read your monthly statements, even if there are several and they are confusing at first. You will have a separate statement for each brokerage account and each bank account you own. Get into the habit of checking the starting and ending balance of each account, as well as the monthly activities and the values of the assets listed. Keep the monthly statements in a file or create an investment binder for them.

By doing this each month you will become familiar with your investments, your income, and your spending habits. Even if you have numerous accounts and it all appears complicated and over-whelming at first, you will feel empowered by your increasing sense of control over your financial situation.

Perhaps the most effective way to quickly gain control of your finances is to create a consolidated statement showing the following:

- Name of each account
- Earnings made on each investment
- Investment income taken in
- Amount of cash in the account

The consolidated statement can be done monthly or quarterly. Either you can set this system up yourself, or you can ask your advisor to do it for you.

Quarterly Review Meetings with Your Advisor

Your advisor will most likely be available throughout the year to answer questions either over the phone or by e-mail. However, it is important to have regular meetings scheduled to do more in-depth reviews of your financial position. These review meetings can be held quarterly or semiannually; annual review meetings are usually too infrequent, as a lot can happen over 12 months.

During these meetings, you should:

- Go over the investments you hold. Find out if they are keeping pace with their benchmarks, if there have been any changes in management, ratings, or earning expectations. Discuss what you should hold, sell, or buy, and why.

- Discuss any changes in your life, pending changes in marital status, children's needs, any major expenses coming up, and health concerns.

- Review your tax position: Estimate capital gains taxes on buys and sells; determine whether you are better off in tax-free municipal bonds; and determine if you have an opportunity to lower your taxes for the present year.

- Review, for estate planning purposes, what and how much is in your partner's name.

- Express concerns about anything having to do with your money, including how your advisor is doing his or her job.

Check Your Reality Checks

Most of the work you did in the Reality Checks of Phase One were long-term projections based upon assumptions of what the inflation rate would be, what your annual investment returns would average, and how much annual income you would need. Any and all of these assumptions can change in any given year. Even slight changes over a long period of time make a difference.

It is a good idea to rerun your Reality Checks each year using the current information and making conservative long-term projections. If things are not working out the way you had originally planned, you will have the opportunity to make necessary adjustments well before any real trouble occurs.

If your expenses are higher than you had anticipated, you will need to try to either increase the rate of return on your investments or cut back on your spending. Sometimes, you will need to do both. Without the Reality Check exercise to give a glimpse of the future, you might continue to spend too much and not catch the problem until you are experiencing serious financial difficulties. Rerunning the Reality Check will force you to look at your reality, and it might prevent you from wasting time in denial when changes need to be made.

Annual Meeting with Yourself

At least once a year, schedule time to be alone with yourself. Conduct a State of My Life Review. You can use the Bliss List exercise to examine what is important to you as time goes by and to make adjustments in your priorities, as well as your future hopes and dreams. Your evolving Bliss List is a reminder of the fact that you create your life by the decisions you make each day.

I recommend that you keep a journal so you can look back on what was important to you last year and the year before. This journal should include your Bliss Lists as well as your major personal and financial decisions and actions. This helps you to see just how much you influence all the aspects of your own life. Life does not just happen to you—you create it.

The Binder System

Over the years of keeping track of my clients' information, I have found that using a system of three-ring binders works best. I prefer to keep two sets of binders so my clients have the same information at home that I keep in the office. It may be possible to keep all the information in one binder at first, but over the years you will need several to hold all of it. Eventually you will want a separate binder for your home, your investments, and your insurance. It is a good idea to have a separate binder for important life events such as retirement, divorce, the sale of a business, and estate settlement.

The Contents of Your Binders

You will need a three-ring hole punch, dividers, and tabs, all of which can be found at any office supply or stationery store.

Some information should be kept for a long time, some for a year, and some should not be kept at all. Try to avoid the hassle of keeping more than you need; it can quickly become confusing and overwhelming.

HOME RECORDS BINDER

- *For capital gains tax purposes.*   Keep your closing documents from the purchase of your house, records of the cost of all improvements, and the closing documents when you sell the house. These records will help you determine if there will be capital gains taxes owed when you sell, and if so, how much.

- *For income tax purposes.*   The interest that you pay on your mortgage and on your home equity line of credit may be deductible from your taxable income. Your local property taxes may also be deductible. Keep copies of the statements you receive as proof of the amount you paid. Keep this information for at least three years.

■ *For insurance purposes.* You should insure any expensive items you acquire or inherit. In addition to a homeowner's policy, you may need to have separate policies or riders added to the main policy to cover jewelry, antiques, and other collectibles. Keep the actual policies, the records of authentication, appraisals, and riders that provide coverage for specific items. If the amount of money you have invested in these kinds of items is large, you should have an audit done every few years so you can obtain new appraisals and any necessary increases in coverage. If you do have a loss or a theft, it will be easier to collect from the insurance company if there isn't any question regarding authenticity, appraised value, or whether you still owned the items at the time of the reported loss.

INVESTMENT BINDER The investment binder is for keeping track of your investment income, the value of your individual investments, the progress of your investment plan, and the history of your investment transactions.

CASH FLOW If you are depending upon your investments to provide the majority of your income, you absolutely need to have an investment income plan. In Phase One, you will have worked out an investment income plan detailing where your money will come from each month. The amount may vary from month to month because some investments pay monthly, some pay quarterly, and yet others pay semiannually. Your investment income will also vary from year to year as interest rates change and as your stocks increase in value.

Create a projected cash flow chart showing what you expect your income to be for each month for the coming 12 months. Update the chart every 6 months. Use the chart to check the receipt of the income.

MONTHLY STATEMENTS Each month you may receive several statements: perhaps an IRA account, trust accounts, joint accounts, and maybe IRA rollover accounts. Create a separate section in your binder for each account; otherwise, it will get very confusing. Keep all the statements throughout the year, and at the end of the year throw out all but the year-end statements.

CONFIRMATIONS OF TRANSACTIONS The year-end statement will have most of the information that you will need to keep; however, it may not show all of the changes that were made during the year. You will want to keep track of when each investment is purchased and/or sold. Keeping this information will help you remember where the money was reinvested when investments were sold. If the changes take place in a taxable account, these records will help you determine the cost basis for capital gains tax purposes.

CONSOLIDATED UPDATES Periodically (I do it quarterly), you should prepare a consolidated investment update. This statement should list the investments from all your accounts: retirement, trust, joint, and so on. I have found it useful to have the following information on these consolidated reviews:

- The name of the investment
- The name the investment is held in
- The date the investment was purchased
- The original purchase amount
- The number of shares owned
- The current price per share
- The market value on the last update
- The current market value
- The percentage gain or loss since the original purchase

I also like to have a column for comments such as any withdrawals or additions made to the investment, or if it was sold, where the money went.

The consolidated statement should be organized by type of investment. Therefore, all municipal bonds, regardless of what account they are owned in, should be listed together. The same should be done for all growth stocks, international mutual funds, and so forth. This way, you can see at a glance what your asset allocation is and how each allocation is performing. It is much easier to judge your success and progress when you are looking at one big picture rather than several different pieces.

CORRESPONDENCE Keep communications between you and your advisor in one section of the binder. If you wanted to find out why one thing or another was recommended or reinvested several years ago, chances are you would have had some correspondence on the subject that may contain the information you are looking for.

MEETING NOTES Many things will be discussed during your meetings with your advisor. You or your advisor should list each item discussed, the action you agreed to take, and what you will discuss during the next meeting.

Each Investment Should Have Its Own Section

You will receive more paperwork than you will want or need to keep. The following are my recommendations for how to handle what could quickly become mounds of confusing documents.

INVESTMENT PLAN Keep a copy of your original investment plan that lays out your objectives and how they will be accomplished. As new plans are written, add them to this section.

ACCOUNT APPLICATIONS Each time you sign an account application, keep a copy. You may have accounts in various names: your name, trust names, joint accounts with others. You will have separate applications for qualified retirement accounts that should include the names of your beneficiaries. When you sign an account application form, you are agreeing to the terms of the account, which are usually listed on the back of that form.

PHONE NUMBERS AND NAMES OF CONTACT PEOPLE This list should include your financial advisor, your banker, your tax expert, your attorneys, your insurance broker, your real estate agent, and anyone else you rely on for financial information, services, and/or advice.

ACCOUNT TRANSFERS When you move money from one brokerage account or money manager to another, keep the transfer paperwork. This includes the last statement of the account you are transferring.

RETIREMENT ACCOUNT TRANSFER RECORDS Each time you roll over a qualified plan or transfer from one custodian to another, keep all of the related paperwork. You may need to prove that you made the 60-day rollover deadline or that you made a direct transfer rather than a rollover.

TAX RETURNS Your investment binder is a good place to keep your tax records. However, if your tax filings are complicated each year, you might be better off with a separate tax binder.

Insurance Binder

Keeping track of the documentation for your various insurance needs can easily become an overwhelming task. This simple system will make information well organized, accessible, and easy to maintain.

LIFE INSURANCE When you buy life insurance coverage, you should keep the illustration that was shown to you when you bought the coverage and the contract you receive from the company. In addition, you should keep records of any changes you make in the policy, beneficiaries, face amount, or amounts or frequencies of premium payments.

INFORCE LEDGERS If you own universal life or whole life insurance, you will want to request an inforce ledger every four or five years. The ledger will tell you how your policy is performing, if the assumptions originally made are on track, if it is possible to stop making premium payments, and if you should make adjustments to the policy. Keep all inforce ledgers in a separate section of the binder.

LIST OF POLICIES If you own several policies, make a simple chart to help you keep track of how much insurance you have, who owns each policy, who is insured with each policy, who the beneficiaries are of each policy, and the annual premium amounts owed. Identify each policy by the insurance company name and the policy number.

OTHER INSURANCE COVERAGE The insurance binder should also be the place to keep the information and policies for your disability income insurance, your long-term care insurance, and your health insurance. Each should have its own section with the policy and records of any changes made.

In addition, make a separate list of all your non–life insurance coverage. The list should include the name of the company, policy number, amount and frequency of premium payments, and who is covered.

Technology

Though technology will save you time and will help you easily keep an eye on your cash flow, your investments, and your insurance coverage, it does not take the place of the binder system or any other paper system you use. Some original records and documents must be kept. Paper files may be easier for a spouse or other family member when it is time to settle your affairs. Also keep in mind that technology becomes obsolete rather quickly, so if you are going to use your computer as your main tracking system, make sure you have a way of keeping up with the changes in technology. Make sure you can transfer your previous records to any new system you adopt.

If you are comfortable with technology, you can keep most of your records on your home computer. Even your brokerage and bank statements can be sent and stored electronically. You can pay your bills over the Internet, and you can keep track of your income and expenses by having your bank account and credit card charges sent directly to your personal Quicken files. Because computers can experience a host of different problems, be sure to keep your information stored on discs, or better yet, keep printouts of the current and year-end statements.

Become Your Own Visionary

Once you become comfortable with monitoring your progress, it will become effortless. At this point, you should be receptive to reexamining who you are, for the reality is that Sudden Money will change the way you look at your life. Do justice to yourself and to your new circumstances by developing a long-term vision of how you would like your life to look, of whom you would like to become, and of how you would like to pass your intentions and your money to the people and causes you hold dearest.

Estate Planning
Transferring Your Wealth to the Ones You Care Most About

Now that the planning of Phase One and the investing of Phase Two have been completed, you have the privilege of deciding how your Sudden Money will extend beyond your life to influence the lives of others. Estate planning is about transferring what you own to the people you care about. It is a loving and responsible act that can make a huge difference in the lives of others.

Many people want to put off their estate planning discussion because it involves talking about death. Anyone who has had to settle the estate of someone who died without having had their estate in order will tell you that it can be a nightmare to clean up. When the estate is settled, often the nightmare isn't over. Lives can be permanently, negatively altered, and family relationships can be destroyed. Money, homes, and other assets can go to unintended beneficiaries.

However, it is quite easy to avoid such undesirable scenarios and create exactly what you would most want to happen. There are many different strategies you can use, and in most cases you can accomplish what you want without using complicated techniques. This chapter provides an overview of estate planning basics and some of the more common challenges Sudden Money recipients are confronted with.

Work with an Estate Planning Attorney

I strongly recommend that you work with an attorney who specializes in estate planning because estate tax law is a complicated area
of law that changes frequently on both the federal and state levels.
Over the years, I have seen many otherwise competent general
practice attorneys give awful estate planning advice. Estate tax
laws are different in each state, so it is important to have an attorney familiar with the laws in the state you consider your domicile.

It is a good idea to meet with your estate planning attorney every
few years to review your estate plan. In addition to changes in the
law, there may be changes in your life that need to be addressed.
Like your financial plan, your estate plan should be an organic document that reflects changes within your life.

Your financial planner should also be part of your estate planning
team. Many of your decisions will have an impact on your cash
flow—present and future. Your planner will have a clear view of your
assets, particularly your investments. Before you sell, gift, or transfer
assets to trusts or to other people, have your planner run a Reality
Check to determine the long-term impact of the proposed change.

Write It out in English First

It is not unusual for estate planning documents to be written in
legalese and never clearly understood by anyone but attorneys. To
be sure that you have accomplished what you really intend, write
out what you think you have created in your own language. Ask
your attorney to tell you how each item on your list has been represented and achieved. A family's list may include something like the
following:

- We want each other to be taken care of financially. The surviving
  spouse should have access to all the income and control it until he
  or she dies or is unable to make decisions.

- We want to limit the amount of estate taxes owed.

- The children will each receive an equal share of the estate after the
  second spouse dies. If one of our children should die while one of
  us is still alive, their share of our estate will ultimately go to their
  children. We want the family money to stay within our bloodline.

- If the surviving spouse remarries, our family assets will go to our
  children—not the new spouse or the new spouse's family.

Your Plan or the State's Plan

There is always an estate plan, either yours or the state's. If you die without a will or other legal documents, the state you live in will determine who gets your money, your home, your investments, and everything else you own. The state's plan may be the opposite of what you would have wanted, and once you are gone, there is nothing you can do about it. Your loved ones are at the mercy of the civil servants that carry out the laws. Each state has different rules, but most give a surviving spouse only a percentage of the estate, and the children would each get an equal share of the rest, to be received at the age of majority (usually age 18).

Probate

Probate is the legal process of making sure that the deceased's assets go to the proper heirs. This is what happens:

- If you have not named a guardian or personal representative in your will or trusts, the probate judge will make these appointments. The personal representative is responsible for administering the estate, paying bills, making inventory lists, and maintaining the lives of the dependent heirs during the probate process. The guardian and the personal representative therefore have significant influence over the family while the probate court is settling the estate. The people appointed by a probate judge may or may not be people you trust or who, from your perspective, are the right people for the job. If, however, you have not named these people beforehand, at this point it is the state's decision.

- The entire estate settlement process becomes public record, and often the result is that there is no privacy for your family and loved ones. Some salespeople make their living by reading court records to get their sales leads. Your family could be subjected to the aggressive tactics of people trained to take advantage of others during times of confusion and grief.

The reality is that when you die, everything will not necessarily be okay just because that is your wish; you have to make decisions and take action. If you don't, life for those you leave behind may become threatening, confusing, and costly. You can make arrangements to create almost any scenario you want, but you must plan in advance to achieve the desired results.

How Your Assets Are Owned Matters

The manner in which you own your assets determines the control you have over them during your life and where they will go when you die. You either own assets by yourself, jointly, or with others.

Sole Ownership

Sometimes the term *fee simple* is used to describe sole ownership. As the sole owner of an asset, you alone have control over whether you sell it or give it away and where it goes when you die. Anything owned solely by you at your death will be part of your estate and may be subject to estate tax.

Joint Owners with Rights of Survivorship

When you are a *joint owner with rights of survivorship,* you own all of the asset with another person. This is a common form of ownership with married couples, but it is not limited to married couples, nor is it limited to only two owners.

During your lifetime you can sell or give away your proportional share with the permission of the other owner or owners. When you die, your share automatically goes to the surviving owners; however, your share may be subject to estate tax.

It is the survivor part of this form of ownership that makes it a complicated and unique way to share ownership. Between spouses it may make sense if the intention is to have the surviving spouse become the automatic owner of the asset when the first spouse dies. It is more complicated and troublesome for nonmarried persons, because it is possible for your heirs to lose the rights to an asset that you own with a partner or a sibling. It can also cause problems when a parent owns a home or brokerage account with one child with rights of survivorship.

Marge had three grown, responsible children, and her intention was to treat them all equally when her estate was distributed. Her daughter Sara lived close by, and the others lived out of state. Marge put Sara's name on all her bank and brokerage accounts, which totaled $1.5 million dollars. She reasoned that if she was unable to look after her money and pay her bills, Sara could easily take over. The other children also liked the fact that Sara was willing to take on this responsibility.

What none of them realized was that during Marge's lifetime, her assets held with Sara were subject to Sara's creditors. If Sara was sued for any reason, say an accident she caused, Marge's assets could be at risk because the law would see them as Sara's assets as well. No one could picture an event like this, but then again, no one foresees random acts of misfortune.

The other complication that was sure to occur was upon Marge's death. All the assets held as joint tenants with rights of survivorship with Sara would belong to Sara—they would not be divided among the three children. Even if Sara were kind, fair, and willing to give her siblings their share, this would complicate her own estate planning. Giving $500,000 to each of them would mean she would be using $1 million of her unified credit. Depending upon when Marge died, this would mean paying some gift taxes. If the gifting transpires after 2006, when the amount we can give free of gift and estate taxes is scheduled to increase to $1 million, Sara's entire unified credit would be used up, leaving her children to pay hefty estate taxes upon her death.

Marge could accomplish what she wanted and save everyone the confusion, expense, and possible misunderstandings by putting these accounts in a revocable living trust. The trust could name Sara as the person who takes over the finances when Marge is unable to continue, and it could name each of the children as equal beneficiaries. The assets would clearly remain under Marge's control and ownership, and Sara could not be construed as an owner.

Joint Tenants in Common

When you own an asset with others as a joint tenant in common, you own your specific share. Each owner has control of their percentage share: They can sell it or give it away without the consent of the other owners. There is no limit to the number of owners, although multiple owners can be confusing. You name the beneficiary of your share so that the other owners will have no claim to your portion unless you want them to have it.

Joint Owners by the Entirety

This is a form of ownership reserved for married couples. Neither person can sell or give away their ownership without the permission of the other. The law interprets this ownership to mean that each spouse owns the entire asset. Upon the death of one spouse, the surviving spouse automatically owns the entire asset, and the value of the deceased spouse's share is included in their estate.

Stan and Nancy were companions for 20 years. They lived as though they were married, but Stan felt so burned by his first marriage that he chose to never marry again, even after his former spouse died. Being 15 years older than Nancy, he wanted to make sure she would be provided for if he died first. They shared a home, owned cars, and lived off of his $2 million investment portfolio. He met with his stockbroker to discuss how to title his investment account so that the money would transfer directly to Nancy and would not go to his daughter who had had nothing to do with her father for the last 25 years.

Stan's concern was admirable, but his mistake was to try to save the fees of an estate planning attorney and to get advice from his trusted broker. The broker advised him to put the investment account in both of their names as tenants by the entirety. In the state in which they resided, *tenants by the entirety* means that both owners own 100%; at death, the surviving owner would own 100% automatically.

What the broker did not know was that this form of ownership was only available to married couples. At Stan's death, Nancy had no legal claim to his estate, the home they had lived in, the car she drove, or the income from his investments. Nancy had to hire an estate planning attorney to try to establish a common-law marriage and her ownership of the assets that Stan intended to leave her. Otherwise, the state would give all of Stan's assets to his estranged daughter, who had not spoken to him for most of her adult life.

Trusts

Trusts are useful as estate planning tools. They can be used to take care of people you love and to disinherit people whom you don't want to have any of your estate. They can be used to settle your estate efficiently and privately because assets held inside of trusts are not subject to probate. Properly structured trusts can save both income and estate taxes, but improperly structured trusts can increase taxes and cause other unintended problems.

Types of Trusts

Living trusts are set up during your lifetime. Testamentary trusts are set up at your death. Living trusts are either revocable or irrevocable. The two major differences between revocable and irrevocable trusts are control and taxes. First, I'll give you some general information about how trusts work, and then I'll get into the specifics of each type.

There are differences in the rules on how to properly set up and fund trusts. Work with an attorney specializing in estate planning to ensure that your goals are accomplished.

Revocable Trusts—You Have Control, You Pay the Taxes

A revocable trust gives the creator of the trust control over what goes in and out of it and the power to eliminate the trust altogether. As the creator of the trust, you have all the control, you set up the terms, and you decide if the terms should be adhered to or changed. In addition, you pay the taxes on the income the trust generates at the same rate you pay income taxes on your other income.

Revocable trusts are usually set up to help make estate settlement more efficient, private, and free from the probate system. But they are also helpful for your lifetime needs. For instance, within the trust, you may appoint a person to take over your financial affairs if you are unable to act for yourself. This eliminates the need for a court-appointed guardian should you become disabled. This kind of appointment is what Sara needed in the preceding example. You may also appoint a different person to handle your investments and yet another to make health care decisions.

When you fund a trust, you change the title of the assets you would like to be part of the trust. For example, if you have a brokerage account that you want to be governed by the trust, you would change the name on the account from your name to the trust's name. The account would then be owned by the Michael James revocable living trust, dated June 2, 1994, rather than by Michael James.

Only assets that are held inside the trust are governed by the trust, so be careful to fund it with only the assets you want to be controlled by it. There are no income tax consequences in this kind of transfer of ownership, nor will this create a gift tax.

Revocable living trusts do not save on estate taxes, because you are still considered the owner of the assets held in the trust. You are the owner because you have retained the power to control the assets and income.

Irrevocable Trusts: You Give Up Control, You Eliminate Estate Taxes

When you create an irrevocable trust, you are usually giving up control of the assets you placed in the trust. In general, you do not have the right to make investment decisions, take income, change the beneficiary, or dissolve the trust. Some states, such as Alaska, have state trusts that allow more control than others; however, the control is still very limited. The most common estate planning reason to set up this kind of trust is to get the assets placed in the trust out of your taxable estate. The general IRS thinking is that if you don't control it, you don't own it; your estate pays taxes only on what you own when you die. You may owe gift taxes when you transfer assets to an irrevocable trust.

Because you don't own the assets, you will not owe taxes on the income they generate. However, the trust will owe taxes and at a rate that quickly accelerates to the highest tax rate, which is 39.6% at this time. Even though you may personally be in the 28% tax bracket, your irrevocable trust may be in the 39.6% bracket! This is why when you are investing the money held inside an irrevocable trust, it is necessary to address tax consequences. Tax-free municipal bonds and capital gains assets are examples of investments that are well suited for irrevocable trusts.

The Unified Gift and Estate Tax Credit

Each person is allowed to give away a limited amount of money or property without incurring any gift or estate tax. The gifts can be made while you are alive or at your death. The amount is called the *unified credit*, and the limit is scheduled to increase until it reaches $1 million per person in 2006. At this writing, the amount is $675,000 per person. Therefore, estates with taxable assets totaling less than $675,000 will not have to pay any federal estate taxes.

ESTATE TAX BRACKETS ARE HIGHER THAN INCOME TAX BRACKETS The amount of the estate above the unified credit will be taxed starting at 37% and go up to 55%. Because estate taxes are higher than personal income taxes, it makes sense to use the entire unified credit in addition to any other applicable estate planning strategy to avoid or reduce estate taxes. Most strategies are designed to either remove assets from your taxable estate or to somehow reduce the value of the assets that remain in your taxable estate.

ANNUAL GIFTING AMOUNTS In addition to the unified credit, you can give away up to $10,000 to as many people as you'd like each year. The money or property you give under this amount is free of any gift taxes and is not subject to income tax by the recipient. You are not required to file a gift tax return when you give $10,000 or less, but it may be recommended by your estate planning attorney to help keep your records straight.

Annual gifting is one way to reduce your taxable estate, and it is done most effectively by gifting assets that are appreciating or by purchasing life insurance. In both cases, the $10,000 you give today may be worth much more at the time of your death. Using this type of strategy allows you to magnify your unified credit. Each spouse has $10,000 to give. Therefore, together they may make joint gifts of $20,000.

If you give any one person more than the allowable annual amount, you will be using up your unified credit. For example, if together you wanted to give each of your five children $30,000, you would have exceeded the annual limit by $20,000 for each child for an excess total of $50,000. You would be required to file a gift tax return and your unified credit would be reduced from $675,000 to $625,000. If you did this each year you would eventually use up your unified credit during your lifetime. At your death, your heirs would not have any credit to apply to the estate taxes.

Gifting may be a good way to decrease the amount of your taxable estate, but be sure you can afford to make the gifts before you start giving money away. Go back to the Reality Check with your financial advisor. Do some long-term income projections assuming the annual gifting you'd like to do before you start giving.

The Unlimited Marital Deduction

Married couples can pass an unlimited amount from one spouse to the other as long as the surviving spouse is an American citizen. Because of this liberal, unlimited marital deduction, many couples simply leave everything to each other and miss the opportunity to use both of their unified credits. This year, the combined credit for a married couple is $1.35 million. If the credit is increased as planned by 2006, the combined credit will be $2 million. If the entire estate is passed to the surviving spouse at the first spouse's death, only one spouse uses the unified credit. This could cost the estate an extra $250,000 in estate taxes, assuming the entire estate is valued at $1.3 million dollars.

Marital Trusts

It makes sense to take full advantage of the unified credit because estate tax rates are high and can deplete the estate you envision passing on to your heirs. If you are married, you should take full advantage of the unlimited marital deduction by dividing your assets in such a way that each of you has at least the unified credit amount in your name.

Couples will commonly create two revocable living trusts, each funded with enough assets to equal the unified credit. When the first spouse dies, the money in their trust will go into an irrevocable trust. The surviving spouse will have access to the income from this irrevocable trust and limited rights to the principal, but this new trust will technically not belong to the surviving spouse. Other beneficiaries will be named as the principal owners, and they will receive the contents of the trust when the surviving spouse dies.

Because the surviving spouse has neither the ability to name the other beneficiaries nor unlimited use of the principal, the assets in this trust are not part of the surviving spouse's estate. Therefore, regardless of the amount this trust has grown to, it is not taxed at the second spouse's death. The entire amount goes to the heirs without tax.

Life Insurance Policies

Life insurance is traditionally used to provide for dependents if the breadwinner of the family dies. There is, however, another use that could save your estate a lot of money. The death benefit from a life insurance policy is not subject to income taxes, but it may be subject to estate tax if the estate is over the unified credit amount ($675,000 in 1999). With some foresight and planning, you can keep the death benefit from being subject to estate tax. This is accomplished if you do not own the policy that insures your life.

Because of your Sudden Money, it is likely that you will have an estate large enough to be subject to estate taxes. One of the most common ways of planning to pay the tax is to buy a life insurance policy and then have someone else, or an irrevocable trust, own the policy and pay the premiums. (See "Great Estate Assets," later in this chapter, for details.)

Taking Inventory of Your Estate

An estate is made up of everything that you both own and owe. It may include items that are not at first obvious, such as:

- Real estate
- Stocks, bonds, and mutual funds
- Bank accounts
- Life insurance policies you own
- Annuity payments or other contractual payments
- Retirement accounts
- Income tax refunds
- Business interests
- Custodial accounts (if you created them) for underage children of whom you are custodian
- Cars, furniture, jewelry, and art collections

When you take inventory of everything you own, list the value and how you own it if you own with someone else. This list may change each year, so it is a good idea to make an estate inventory part of your annual financial review. Without an annual update, your estate may grow larger than you had thought and may require some additional estate planning. It is possible for your estate to become lopsided with too much money in one spouse's name or too much in heavily taxed estate assets such as IRA accounts.

Evaluating assets from an estate planning point of view is different from viewing them from a lifetime-use point of view. Assets like IRAs are great lifetime assets because they allow you to defer taxes. From an estate planning point of view, however, they become difficult because all the deferred income tax is due along with estate taxes. Meanwhile, some assets that are not very useful during your lifetime, such as life insurance, can become great for estate purposes. Let's look into how to qualify your assets so you can get a better idea of the value and impact of your estate.

Difficult Estate Assets

Assets that are hard to liquidate or that are subject to income as well as estate taxes are difficult estate assets. Real estate, closely held businesses, illiquid stock, and future income payments are examples of assets that will be subject to estate tax but may be hard to liquidate to get the money to pay the estate taxes.

IRAs, 401(k) plans, and other qualified pension plans will be subject to income taxes as well as estate taxes. The surviving spouse may be able to roll the retirement plans over into his or her own name and defer taxes, but at their death, taxes might be due immediately unless advanced planning creates further deferral options.

Tax-deferred annuities are subject to income and possibly estate taxes. For the spouse to not pay income taxes, they must be a joint owner of the annuity. Nonspouse beneficiaries will owe taxes on the gains within the annuity as well as possible estate taxes. Many estate planning advisors recommend that their clients use up their annuities during their lifetime to avoid a tax problem for their heirs.

Good Estate Assets

Stocks, bonds, mutual funds, and other assets that would be subject to capital gains taxes are favorable estate assets. When these assets are sold, the amount of capital gains tax due is calculated by subtracting the basis (the cost) from the current value. When these assets pass as part of an estate, the basis is stepped up to the value at the date of death.

For example, stock that you bought 20 years before your death for $10,000 may have grown to $200,000 by the time you die. If you sold it before you died, you would have to pay capital gains tax on $190,000, the difference between your basis and the fair market value. The tax would probably be at the maximum 20% capital gains rate, (20% × 190,000 is $38,000). However, if you still owned the stock at the time of your death, your heirs would get a step up in basis. Their basis would be $200,000, rather than $10,000. When they sold the stock for $200,000, they would not owe any capital gains tax.

Great Estate Assets

Life insurance is, in many ways, the ultimate estate planning asset. If owned properly, it can increase an estate like no other asset can. "Owned properly" usually means that it is not owned by the deceased person. Instead, the spouse or one of the children own it, or an irrevocable trust is set up specifically to own the policy. When life insurance is owned this way, the death benefit can be both income and estate tax–free, regardless of the size of the policy. For many large estates, it is the most reasonable solution to paying the estate taxes as long as the owner of the estate is insurable.

Policies you already own may be transferred into an irrevocable trust, but you must survive for three years after the transfer for the policy to be officially out of your estate. It is worth it to set up the trust, as life insurance may be the answer to providing the money to pay estate taxes and to increase the amount of money that your heirs receive.

A Final Note

This chapter has introduced you to an important but complex financial planning discipline. As you work your way through your estate plan, stay focused on the people side of the equation. It is great to find ways to pass more money on to your loved ones and less on to Uncle Sam, but don't let reducing estate settlement cost rule your planning. Before you accept any estate planning strategy, ask yourself and your advisors how it will affect you during your life and your heirs after you are gone. Plan to use your Sudden Money wisely during your life and transfer it as a gift from your heart when you are gone. Keep it as easy and as simple as possible for them to settle your affairs.

Your Sudden Money may someday become someone else's Sudden Money. As you do your estate planning, think about how you can help your heirs with their Sudden Money experience. Help them learn from your experience and find opportunities to increase their financial literacy. Help them become confident with their own finances, but most of all, help them develop healthy attitudes about money. Teach them the joy of giving and sharing the money they have, so that they will be better prepared to manage, enjoy, and pass on the assets they inherit from you.

Consider an annual family retreat that focuses on the psychology of money, the philosophy of wealth, and how other families have dealt with their wealth. There is more than enough evidence that inheriting a large amount of money is challenging and can be disastrous. Seek out ways to meet the challenge, prepare your heirs, and help them prepare their heirs. Start a family tradition of discussing money issues; make this a part of your family legacy.

Giving and Sharing

If you want happiness for an hour—take a nap
If you want happiness for a day—go fishing
If you want happiness for a month—get married
If you want happiness for a year—inherit a fortune
If you want happiness for a lifetime—help someone else
—CHINESE PROVERB

There is an ancient life-enhancing technique that is reputed to increase your well-being, make you healthier, enrich your relationships, and help you live a long and fulfilling life. This technique can also dissolve the emptiness and isolation that may have come with your Sudden Money. The technique is so powerful that medical doctors think it may reverse heart disease, lower your blood pressure, and strengthen your immune system. It reduces your anxiety level, increases your sense of self-worth, and usually includes the much-needed spread of gratitude. Today, this ancient technique is known as it has been for centuries—the act of giving.

The ancients knew that giving and sharing produced powerful inner results. They didn't know why or how, but they observed what we observe today: Cultures from around the globe notice that

The quotes in this chapter were found in *Give to Love*, by Douglas Lawson, Ph.D. (San Diego, Alti Publishing, 1991).

when you connect with your community and put your time and resources into a project or cause that you believe in, it makes you feel better. In fact, it actually makes you better.

At this point in your Sudden Money experience, you know that money does not buy love, health, respect, or appreciation. They are not commodities and they cannot be purchased at any price—they must be earned. Unfortunately, they may also be lost when Sudden Money arrives. There are many stories of friends, family, and coworkers becoming uncomfortable enough that they break the relationship with a Sudden Money recipient.

If you have experienced a loss of belonging and now feel lonely and isolated, you know you need to make some changes. If you followed the steps of Phase One and Phase Two, you should feel confident that you have handled your money responsibly and have avoided the classic Sudden Money mistakes. Now, it is time to turn your attention to the world around you and to connect with the people and organizations that need you, just as you may need them.

Why Philanthropy Is for Everyone

This chapter has been included to encourage you to extend beyond yourself and your family and to experience the amazing feeling of fulfillment that comes from giving. Rather than emphasizing the tax benefits of charitable giving, I choose to spend most of the space in this chapter to inspire you to open yourself up to the tremendous personal benefits that simply come with the act of giving. I am not saying that charitable giving should be done for better health or spiritual fulfillment, although studies have suggested both are a result.

> It is one of the most beautiful compensations of this life that no man can sincerely try to help another without helping himself.
> —RALPH WALDO EMERSON

The key word in Emerson's quote is *sincerely*. You can't buy the positive effects of giving just by writing a check to get a tax break. The greatest benefits come from being personally connected and really caring about the mission of the nonprofit organization that you support or create. Try to have some face-to-face contact as well as offering financial support. For instance, volunteer to work at a soup kitchen, help homeless people fill out job applications, sign people in for a walk/run to raise money for a cure for cancer, help build a house, hold babies confined to long stays in the hospital, or teach someone how to read.

A Plan for Giving

Your Sudden Money may have given you either more resources to share and/or more free time to volunteer. If you went through the recommended steps of Phase One, you have had the opportunity to rethink your life goals and priorities. If you went through the entire recommended Sudden Money Process, you have invested your money, set up a system for staying on track, and done some estate planning. With you and your loved ones provided for, it is a good time to add a Plan for Giving to the other planning that you have done.

Step 1—Identify Your Passions

The Plan for Giving is a tool to help you clarify your core beliefs, concerns, and life passions. It will help keep you from giving to too many non-profit organizations and from not being committed to any one. Many people report that they respond to mail solicitations they get from hundreds of nonprofit organizations, and they give each $100. While this is certainly generous, it really does not give you the chance to be involved with any one of them. When your resources are diluted, the personal rewards of knowing you have made a difference are also diluted.

You don't have to limit yourself to existing organizations. Think about changes you feel should be made, people you would like to help, and opportunities you want to be made available. Great things have been accomplished by ordinary people who cared enough and were passionate enough to make changes in their communities. As a result, they have saved the lives and spirits of people they never knew.

For example, a well-known fact that you probably know is that grants from the Carnegie Corporation were responsible for creating the library system we have today. But do you know that Carnegie also contributed to research that led to the use of television for preschool research (does *Sesame Street* ring a bell?)? Furthermore, do you know that foundation grants were also responsible for developing the white line along the shoulders of the highway (to keep drivers from hugging the center lines)? Likewise, the region-alized, systematic approach we use to respond to emergencies, known as *911*, was also made possible with grant money to regular people who saw a need and tried to find a way to fill it.

Your passion and commitment to the mission of the organization or to the project, like the 911 number, is what makes giving so deeply satisfying. Everyone is different and has their own ideas of what will satisfy them most. For some it is helping their religion. For others it could be the arts, animals, the environment, education, women's causes, the homeless—the list goes on and on. It is okay to feel strongly about more than one cause; you can have a primary and a secondary commitment. Just be sure to prioritize your list, stating clearly your primary and secondary commitments. This will be important when you are allocating your resources, both finan-cial and time.

Step 2—Involve Others

If you are married or have a life partner, do two separate lists and then compare them. Many families have enjoyed selecting one or two causes as their group focus. However, it is not necessary to reach a consensus, it is okay to have your individual focus. This is about you, your heart and soul, no one else's.

If you have children or grandchildren, nieces and nephews, it is good to involve them in the giving plan. Let them be part of the planning, they may want to help more than you think. A 1989 sur-vey by the Independent Sector found that 58% of teenagers volun-teered their time to help others. They also found that 90% lent a hand when asked. Teenage volunteers get the same benefits that adults get, and they learn early on that they can make a difference in the world.

If it is appropriate, give them some resources that they can share with an organization they feel strongly about. Give them an amount of money or perhaps arrange transportation for them to volunteer. If they're old enough, let them use the family car to do some community work like Meals on Wheels. Teaching children good giving habits at an early age will serve them well throughout their lives. The earlier they discover the personal satisfaction that comes from being involved in community causes, the more natural it will be for them to continue this activity as an adult.

If you are alone in life, consider taking on a volunteer job with a friend. Make it part of your social contact for the week, go together and maybe have lunch or dinner together after your shift. If you don't have a friend to go with, be open to meeting people while you are volunteering. People who like to be part of the community are usually interesting and positive people, the kind of people that may be missing from your life now.

Step 3–Use the Reality Check

At this point, you should check your generosity with your present and future cash flow. This is when you do a Reality Check for your desired giving. Work with your financial planner to set the financial guidelines, and find out what you can afford to give by using the Reality Check exercise. If you are planning to give a large single sum, run the future income Reality Check to see what the long-term effect will be without the money you are about to give away.

If you will be gifting each year, make sure that each year's gift is affordable, and plan to review your finances on a set annual schedule to determine what amount to give each year. Because of changing market conditions and unexpected expenses, you may be able to give more or less than the previous year. When the stock market does well, many individuals give more than during years when they have lost money in their investments.

Step 4–Review and Journal

Life changes and so may your giving. You may have helped to find a cure or to accomplish a mission, and then it will be time to go to the next mission.

Your wealth may increase or decrease, your family needs may change, and you'll need to respond to the changes with flexibility. You can only commit to what you can do now. Your passions may lead you in a number of directions over time. Pay attention to how you feel—if you are getting the good feelings even when times are tough for your cause, keep going; however, when the giving becomes a burden, you must make changes.

Keep a journal to chronicle your journey on the giving path. This exercise may be, in the end, your most important Sudden Money Document. It will tell your heirs how you used and how you felt about your money. More than that, it will tell anyone who reads it about your commitment to humanity—it will become your legacy of giving. Two generations from now, you may have become a myth, a legend, or just the relative who had lots of money. When someone takes the time to read your giving journal, they will see into your heart, and they may be inspired also to journey down the Path of Giving. What a great gift to pass along to your future generations.

> Wealth is a means to an end, it is not an end in itself. As a synonym for health and happiness, it has had a fair trial and failed miserably.
>
> —JOHN GALSWORTHY

Decide How You Will Give

Once you have decided to give, the next step is to determine how you will initially participate. Will you give money, investments, real estate, or art? Will you volunteer or provide professional services? Quantify the amount you will give and the time you will offer. Make sure you can afford to make both the desired financial and time commitments. Again, if you are sharing resources and a life with someone else, make sure that your Giving Plan and theirs are both affordable. Here, you may need to make some compromises and adjustments to try to stretch your resources to cover the most ground.

There are various ways to make financial gifts. The following are some basics you will want to know as you refine your Giving Plan.

Outright Gifts

Gifts such as money and some investments are easy to donate to a nonprofit organization. If the investment is traded on any of the major exchanges, the value is easy to establish. The nonprofit organization will be able to liquidate the investments and to have immediate use of the money. Nonprofit organizations do not have to pay capital gains taxes; therefore, some investments will be more advantageous than others from your tax point of view.

Capital Gains Assets

The ideal gift from a tax point of view is a highly appreciated asset. For example, when you donate to a qualified nonprofit organization a stock that has grown in value, that you owned for 12 months or longer, you get to deduct the current market value of the gift (though there are limitations to the amount you can deduct). In addition, you do not have to pay capital gains taxes on the profits you made while owning the stock. The big mistake would be to sell the stock first and then to donate the proceeds of the sale. Then, you would owe capital gains taxes unnecessarily. Once the qualified nonprofit organization receives the stock, *they* can sell it and not have to pay the capital gains tax.

Short-Term Capital Gains Assets

Assets you have owned for less than 12 months are known as short-term capital gains assets. If you donate a short-term capital gains asset, you will only be able to deduct your basis—the price you paid. You will not get credit for the fair market value as you would with a long-term capital gains asset. When you are considering which assets to donate, it makes sense to donate long-term assets.

Capital Loss Assets

If you want to donate a stock that has lost value while you owned it, you should sell it before you make the donation. When you sell an investment that has lost money, you get to take a capital loss deduction either against your capital gains or against your income (again, there are limits on how much of a deduction you would get against your income each year). If the nonprofit organization were to receive the stock and sell it, they would not get the benefit of the deduction.

Annual Charitable Deduction Limits

Each year, there will be limits on the amount of charitable deduction you can take. The limit is set by your adjusted gross income, the kind of nonprofit organization receiving the donation, and what the donation is. If the donation is to a public nonprofit organization, you may deduct up to 50% of your adjusted gross income. If your income is not high enough to use the full deduction, you may carry over the excess amount each year for five years.

If the gift is to a private foundation, you may deduct up to 30% of your adjusted gross income, and the same carryforward applies. At times, the IRS has only allowed you to deduct the amount you paid for the asset when the donation went to a private foundation. At this writing, the IRS allows the full fair market value deduction for private foundation gifts, but that may change.

Before you make a donation of money, investment assets, real estate, or art, talk to your accountant. You may want to have an annual meeting with your financial planner and your accountant to discuss your donation intentions. They will be in a good position to help you stretch your gift while receiving the best tax breaks available.

Hard-to-Value Assets

Real estate, art, and antiques are more difficult assets for nonprofit donations. Their value is not readily accessible, and buyers may or may not be easy to find. Before accepting donations of real estate, nonprofit organizations will want to make sure that there are no environmental complications, that there are no problems with the deed, and that there is a reasonable market for the property.

Art and antiques must be authenticated and appraised to establish their value. Because they are perceived as difficult assets to liquidate and value, the tax deduction you will receive will be less than for real estate and investments.

Charitable Trusts

There are two forms of charitable trusts that you may find intriguing and useful: (1) the *charitable remainder trust* (CRT) and (2) the *charitable lead trust* (CLT). The CRT is designed to pay income to the income beneficiary or beneficiaries, then at the end of the trust's term, the remaining amount goes to the principal beneficiary (the nonprofit organization). When you make a donation to a CRT, you name the income beneficiaries (typically you and a spouse). You also set the length of the trust (usually for both of your lives). Once you are both deceased, whatever is left in the CRT goes to the nonprofit organization that you have named.

The benefit of a CRT is the income stream; the drawback is that the tax deduction is less than for an outright gift. Because the nonprofit organization does not get the money for a potentially long time, your donation is considered an incomplete gift (i.e., there are income strings attached). Before you create a CRT, discuss your motives with your financial advisor; there are a few variations, each with its specific advantages. If you want income now and if you would like the income to have the potential of increasing over the years, a *charitable remainder unitrust* (CRUT) works best. These trusts pay out a set percentage of the value of the investment within the trust. If the investments go up, you receive an increase in income; if the investments have a bad year and lose money, you will have less income.

If you want a fixed income without the possible fluctuations, a *charitable remainder annuity trust* (CRAT) is best. Sometimes referred to as a gift trust, a CRAT pays out a specified amount of income each year, regardless if the investments go up or down. You trade the reliability of income for the possibility of an income that keeps pace with inflation.

If you want to make the donation now but don't want income until a future date, or if you plan to take a small income now and want more income in the future, a *net income with makeup provisions charitable remainder unitrust* (NIMCRUT) allows that flexibility.

Each trust has advantages and disadvantages. The financial planning possibilities are numerous with CRTs, particularly with highly appreciated assets that do not have much income potential. If you sell the assets, you will pay the capital gains tax and have the after-tax amount to invest for income. By donating it, the nonprofit organization sells it without the shrinkage of the capital gains tax. You will end up with more money invested for income.

The drawback of a CRT is your heirs do not receive this money upon your death. For some families this is fine, for others it is troublesome. In some cases, a replacement trust funded with a life insurance policy will make sense. If the policy is owned by an irrevocable trust, the death benefit may pass free of estate and income taxes. Though this may seem to be a perfect solution, you need to consider the cost of the life insurance, and your insurability. In some family situations, it is better to use a CLT than the life insurance trust.

The CLT is the opposite of a CRT: The income goes to the non-profit organization, and the remaining amount goes to your named beneficiaries. The use of charitable trusts opens up some very interesting planning opportunities for you, for your family, and for the nonprofit organizations that you want to help. They are somewhat complex with their own accounting rules, actuarial assumptions, and income limitations. If your financial advisor is not accustomed to working in this area of financial and gift planning, suggest that you bring in an expert to help design a plan for the optimal benefit for all involved.

Estate Giving

You may feel that it is more appealing to wait and to give large sums of money as part of your estate. During your lifetime, you could give smaller amounts and be involved in the organization. Some families hold off with large lifetime donations because they are concerned with needing the money to live on. There are many kinds of testamentary trusts (trusts set up at death) that can be created to address various family requirements, several of which were described previously. Some give income to the children for a period of years and then the money goes to a nonprofit organization at the end of the term (CRT). Others allow the nonprofit organization to get the income for a period of years, and then the money goes to the children (CLT). Both can be set up during your lifetime or as part of your estate settlement. With careful estate planning, you can address your children's income needs, your charitable intentions, pass on a legacy of giving, and receive some important estate tax advantages.

Find Your Own Direction

I want to urge you to start now. Don't postpone your charitable giving until you have more money or more time. Like good nutrition, the positive effects of giving accumulate over time, producing a deeper and more profound sense of satisfaction and well-being. I left this topic for the last because for it to be all it should be in your life, you must be ready to open your mind, your heart, and your checkbook. It is difficult to be ready if you are not sure how much income you have after the Sudden Money, where to invest, what your new tax bracket is, and so on. It is also difficult to begin your personal, intentional journey down your Giving Path if you have not thought about what your beginning should look like.

Find Your Beginning Point

You don't need to begin with large donations, you can start just by becoming involved with the local events or projects. Perhaps make small donations first, particularly if your cause is a smaller, local nonprofit organization. See how they handle the small money before you give them the large amounts. Ask for accountability: Have them explain to you what they spent your money on. If they can't or you are not pleased with how they spent it, move on to another nonprofit organization.

Think about this: Rather than donating to a public nonprofit organization, how about starting your own private foundation? Though the laws make them more cumbersome and not as tax efficient as public nonprofit organizations, your own private foundation may bring you the greatest sense of purpose and significance. As an alternative to your own foundation, you could set up a named account with your local community foundation or work with one of the umbrella public charities that allows you to set up a named account under their name.

Final Thought

Your Sudden Money will present you with an amazing range of experiences and opportunities. Giving and sharing are so personal; no one can tell you what to give, how to give, or even if giving is the right thing for you to do. I have tried not to use the word *philanthropy*, because I think many people don't personally relate to the word. They think philanthropists are larger than life. A philanthropist, however, is a lover of life. Their giving comes from the heart, and their reward is a progressively deeper sense of love for life.

Give yourself the gift of giving and enjoy what comes back to you. If you do, I suspect that, as time goes by, you will be more and more grateful for your Sudden Money. Sudden Money can help you discover your own inner sense of humanity and can allow you the opportunity to be part of the world in ways you might not ever have imagined.

THE SUDDEN MONEY EVENTS

Inheritance

Regardless of your level of money maturity or investment sophistication, when you receive a substantial inheritance, you might be thrust into a realm where your financial decisions affect not only the rest of your life, but the lives of future generations, as well. You can use the Sudden Money Process to increase your financial literacy and to help you create a plan for your money that also includes preparing future generations for their inheritances.

I counsel families on inherited wealth issues, and I have found that the biggest obstacle facing the recipient is lack of preparedness. In this chapter, I'll show you how you can minimize the negative effects of your own Sudden Money, and create an atmosphere in which your heirs will make their financial transitions in the most meaningful, peaceful manner.

The Spectrum of Inheritance

Your inheritance may be money that was accumulated throughout your parents' lifetime of hard work and sacrifice, or it may be money that has been in your family for generations. However the money you have received was accumulated, it is your turn to decide how to invest, spend, and share it. You may have just enough to retire on, or you may now be the steward of a family fortune. Either way, it is important that you don't let the arrival of the money and all the new decisions overwhelm you. Your life may be different now that you have your inheritance, even if you are used to having money. No matter what your position before, your inheritance presents you with more options, more freedom, and more responsibilities.

Long-Term Potential of a Modest Inheritance

If the amount you have received is a modest amount, it may not be your immediate ticket to financial independence—at least not right away. However, don't underestimate the long-term potential of this money. If the money is invested in stocks and you get the average long-term annual return of 11%, your inheritance will double every 6.5 years. An inheritance of $125,000 cannot provide much of an annual income. But if it is invested for 15 years and grows at the average annual rate of 11%, you will have almost $600,000.

Assuming you take an income of 6% per year, you'll have a $36,000-per-year income, which is almost five times the $7,500 income you'd get from $125,000. Waiting another five years would put you just over $1 million with an income of $60,000.

Give yourself as much time as you can to let your money grow. The longer it is invested, the more momentum it will pick up. Using the same example of 11%, the money increased by over $500,000 the last seven years. From year 13 to year 20, this hypothetical inheritance grew from $485,000 to $1,006,000—*eight times the original amount of $125,000*. If the money were left to grow at 11% for another seven years, it would increase by just over $1 million. The $125,000 would then total $2,088,000.

Struggles and Potential of a Large Inheritance

If you have received a large inheritance, chances are you are used to having money to spend, but you may not be accustomed to having sole responsibility for such a large amount of money. It is common for families to not talk about money or investing, particularly with their daughters. You are not alone if you feel unprepared to manage this money.

The Chute of Emotions

Take time to do the planning outlined in Phase One, and give yourself plenty of time in the Decision Free Zone. Though your inheritance may be in various forms of money, it is more than just money. Emotions, both positive and negative, may seem to surround your new money. You may find that sibling rivalries reignite, or that old wounds from long ago start to hurt once again. Feelings that you were sure you had outgrown may seem as fresh and real as they had once been long ago.

This emotional time usually doesn't last long, but while you are experiencing it, it can be the source of significant damage. Again, I strongly suggest you work through these issues before you begin to invest the money and make changes in your lifestyle. There are therapists trained in the psychology of money, and there are some that specialize in inherited wealth. Without help, the results can be unfortunate or even tragic.

Using Money to Express Emotion

Some families never recover from the bad feelings created while the estate was being settled. If there was infighting or conflicting opinions over what the deceased wanted or meant, you might come away from the process with emotional baggage capable of swaying your otherwise good judgment. Since most people are not aware of the moment their judgment is beginning to falter, my recommendation is this: *Don't use your money to get even or to make a point.* If you use your money for the good of your immediate family and yourself, and refrain from making financial decisions when you are emotionally upset, you will avoid many of the big mistakes.

Honoring Those Who Came before You

Receiving an inheritance is a very personal moment and may be accompanied by gentle whispers from your lineage. It may seem like your ancestors, including the ones who have recently passed away, are surrounding you, animated and in Technicolor, making demands. Whether you honor or ignore the feelings you get as you receive and subsequently use this money is a serious decision deserving much contemplation.

Seeking Approval

Psychologists tell us that seeking approval or disapproval from our parents is a very strong drive, even after our parents are gone. This sentiment often manifests itself in the investment behavior of the heir. Many people get stuck trying to invest the money like their parents had, or trying to live a lifestyle their parents would approve of.

Just because your father always bought bonds does not mean you cannot, or should not, invest in stocks. Your father might have lived on his pension and social security and not needed his bonds to live on. If that was the case, he had less of a need for the kind of inflation protection that the stock market has historically provided. *He* could afford to avoid the risks associated with the stock market. *You,* on the other hand, may want to use this money for growth and income that needs to keep up with inflation. Your investment goals may be quite different from your father's. If they are, your investment plan should also be different.

Guilt

Inherited wealth is viewed by the general population as a blessing and a privilege: something to be envied. However, when the amount of inherited wealth is large enough to allow the inheritor to not have to earn their own living, life can become unbalanced. Many who have grown up with inherited wealth report guilt, shame, and a lack of meaning in their lives. These emotions manifest in dysfunction within the family and in the relationships the heirs form outside the family. The first reaction may be to give it all away.

Those who have successfully dealt with their feelings of guilt and inadequacy say that it is important to find true meaning for your life and your money. You can work toward this goal by:

- Finding an inspiring career to pursue, particularly if you don't have to work

- Working on a philanthropic cause that you are passionate about

- Taking on a physical challenge such as a triathlon or mountain climbing

- Working with a therapist on financial and family-related issues

- Learning more about and getting involved with the management of your money

Conflicts between Spouses

Who gets control over your inheritance? Will it be joint money or segregated and kept in your name alone? There may be a desire to keep it separate, but to use it for your common needs and enjoyment. What is important is that you and your spouse discuss your feelings and intentions. Your spouse may have his or her own expectations regarding the inheritance, and those expectations might conflict with yours. This is an area that can cause marital trouble that may last a very long time if it is not dealt with properly.

What to Do

Money is a stressful topic in most marriages, and the arrival of an inheritance can exacerbate any existing money problems. There are no rules on how couples should deal with an inheritance. In most states, it is considered an individual asset—not a marital asset—as long as the money has not been put in joint name. This is an area that needs to be discussed and negotiated to avoid, or at least to minimize, problems.

One potentially problematic issue that frequently arises is when a family desires to keep their money within the bloodline, and those outside of it feel jilted. For instance, many wealthy parents express concerns about what will happen to the money if their children get divorced (i.e., they don't want their money going to the ex-spouse). Another concern is what will happen if their child dies before their spouse (i.e., they don't want the son or daughter-in-law to gain control of the family money). To prevent arguments, anyone who will be affected by financial decisions should be apprised of their inclusion or exclusion.

A possible solution to the potentially uncomfortable situation of exclusion of certain parties is to put the money into a trust that you have control over during your lifetime. At your death, your spouse has access to the income and some principal to maintain his or her lifestyle. However, your spouse will not have control over who inherits the money when he or she dies. Instead, *you* can name who gets the money when your spouse dies. This approach protects your spouse and your children. Trusts can be very flexible or quite strict; if you work with an experienced estate planning attorney, you will be able to create a trust that meets both lifetime needs and estate planning desires.

Immediate Decisions

Liquidating an estate takes time and the expertise of attorneys, accountants, and financial planners. You will have papers to sign, accounts to transfer, and time-sensitive decisions to make.

Paying Taxes and Collecting Your Inherited Assets

All estates must file final income tax returns and final estate tax returns. The executor is responsible for overseeing this process. Once the accountants and attorneys have filed the necessary returns, the personal representative pays the taxes. The heirs receive what is left after all taxes, debts, and fees are paid.

Receiving the assets does not usually mean you will receive a check for your share of the estate. You may be entitled to a portion of various brokerage accounts, real estate, businesses, bank accounts, retirement accounts, and company benefits such as stock options. Along with these financial assets you may have inherited collectibles, antiques, stamp collections, jewelry, and/or automobiles. Once you have the assets put in your name, you can begin to use and manage them.

It is a good idea to actually make a list of all of the assets. This itemized list will help you to not forget any of the assets you now have rights to. Each asset will have to be treated separately. Some may be easy to deal with; others may be complicated and take time to have titles switched or to liquidate. Many people put all their time and attention into dealing with the few biggest or most complicated assets and forget about others that seem less significant. Your list should help prevent you from losing track and forgetting about seemingly less important assets.

Real Estate and Businesses

As I have said, some assets are more difficult to deal with than others. Real estate and privately owned businesses are best liquidated with the assistance of an attorney who specializes in that area. Along with the attorney, you will need to work with a real estate broker and a business broker. If you feel that either of these kinds of assets are worth a lot of money, it will be worthwhile to hire a consultant to evaluate the asset and devise a plan to obtain the highest price and a deal structure to meet your needs.

Bank and Brokerage Accounts

Bank and brokerage accounts are transferred into your name once you present a certified death certificate, a will, or a trust document naming you as beneficiary. When there is more than one beneficiary of a brokerage account, you can either decide among yourselves who should take which asset, or you can divide each asset into the appropriate percentages.

Antiques and Collectibles

If you have received family antiques, art collections, jewelry, or other valuable collectibles, be sure you properly insure them. This might include the authentication and appraisal of things you take for granted, like the Chippendale chairs you sat on every holiday family dinner, the art hanging on the walls of your parents' home, or the jewelry your mother has been wearing since your childhood. It is easy for this familiarity to make you forget the value of these items. Particularly valuable items may need separate policies or at least a separate rider added to your policy.

While you are meeting with your insurance agent, consider increasing your personal liability umbrella coverage. If your inheritance has substantially increased your net worth, you may have to increase your liability coverage. Unfortunately, the wealthier you are, the more of a target you are for nuisance suits.

Retirement Accounts

IRAS Part of your inheritance is likely to be in an individual retirement account (IRA). The general idea with inherited IRAs is to keep required distributions to a minimum. Distributions are taxed as income for the year they are taken out. Minimizing the amount you take out not only reduces your income taxes, it also allows the money in the IRA account to grow tax-deferred. The amount you will be required to take will depend upon the age of the deceased IRA holder and the calculation method used if they had already begun required minimum distributions (RMDs). You should consult a tax attorney with experience in IRA distribution rules, as many mistakes occur in this area.

If the deceased was older than 70½.   The rules for required withdrawals can be complicated, and they depend upon the age of the deceased owner at their death. If the owner was over 70½, he or she had reached the age when RMDs began. When RMDs are not taken out, there is a steep IRS penalty of 50% of the required amount. Therefore, if he or she had been required to take a $10,000-per-year distribution and neglected to, the penalty would be $5,000 plus the regular income tax that would be owed. Be sure you take out the amount they would have been required to take the year death occurred.

After the first year, new rules apply. The amount *you* will be required to take will depend upon how the owner chose to calculate his or her required amount. The IRA custodian and the deceased owner's financial advisor can help you find out if he or she had elected the recalculation or nonrecalculation method. Your RMD will depend on what elections the IRA holder had made. In most cases, the financial advisor will tell you each year what amount you need to withdraw. To avoid the 50% penalty, withdrawals must be made by December 31. Don't wait until the last day, because some IRA custodians take several days to actually process the request.

If the deceased was younger than 70½. If the IRA holder died before reaching the required beginning date, you must elect a distribution method by no later than December 31 of the year following the year of the IRA holder's death. Meeting this deadline prevents the default provisions under the IRA plan agreement from kicking in. IRA plans have default provisions that will assign distribution options to a beneficiary if the individual does not make a timely election regarding his or her distribution option. You will have two options.

Option 1—The Five-Year Rule. Under this option, you may take distributions at any given time and in any given amount, provided you deplete the entire IRA account by December 31 of the year containing the fifth anniversary of the IRA holder's death.

Option 2—The Life Expectancy Rule. Your other option is to take the distributions over your single life expectancy. This allows you to let the bulk of the money continue to grow tax-deferred due to the lower required distribution amount each year. Distributions under this option must begin by December 31 of the year following the IRA holder's death. The early withdrawal penalty of 10% does not apply to inherited IRAs.

The name on the IRA. It is important to keep the IRA in the name of the deceased owner with the date of death, your name, and your social security number added to the title. If the new account is not titled correctly, you may be required to take the entire amount as a fully taxed distribution and lose the tax advantages of the delayed distributions.

If you have partial interest in an IRA account, you have the right to transfer your share to your own IRA account. By transferring your portion, you can invest the money according to your overall investment plan. The IRA will be held by a brokerage firm, bank, mutual fund, or other custodial firm. You will need to present a death certificate and the estate planning documents giving you rights to your portion of the IRA, before they will make the transfers.

COMPANY RETIREMENT ACCOUNTS If your assets include a company pension plan, a 401(k) plan, or other qualified pension plan, you must present the death certificate to gain your right to access the money. The employee benefits department will have forms to fill out, and the money may be available only on certain dates throughout the year. You will not be able to roll these accounts to an IRA as your parents could have done. You must take the money the year it becomes available to you and pay the income taxes on the full amount received.

EMPLOYEE STOCK OPTIONS Today, it is not uncommon to find large amounts of money tied up in company stock options and employer stock ownership plans. There are two categories of stock options:

1. Incentive stock options (ISOs)

2. Nonqualified stock options (NQSOs)

Both ISOs and NQSOs can be sold as part of the estate liquidation, even though there might have been time restrictions that the deceased employee was required to observe.

The tax treatment of an ISO depends on whether the options had been exercised before death, which would make the estate the holder of the option stock. If this is the case, the stock can be sold and will receive a step-up in basis as of the date of death. The only tax owed would be the difference between the price on the date of death and the price you sell it for.

If the options had not been exercised before death, you can exercise them and sell the stock, but there is no step-up in basis. You will owe capital gains tax on the difference between the option price and the price you sell the stock for.

You do not have to sell the optioned stock before any deadline. If you think the stock is a good long-term hold and if it meets your overall investment objectives, hold on to it and defer the tax until you are ready to sell.

Employee stock ownership plans (ESOPs) are qualified retirement plans. You will pay ordinary income tax on the distributions taken out of these plans. The distributions are made either in cash or in employer securities, depending upon what the plan requires. Distribution must commence no later than one year after the date of death. Some plans allow for the distributions to be taken over a five-year period. For others, the entire lump sum is distributed within 12 months of death.

Other Decisions

Capital Gains Tax Break

When you sell a stock for a profit, you may owe taxes. The amount originally paid for the investment is called its *basis*. The difference between the basis and what it is sold for is called *capital gain* (or *capital loss* if money is lost). Therefore, you will owe a capital gains tax when you sell a stock for a profit. However, when you inherit a stock, you receive a *step-up in basis* (your basis becomes the price of the stock on the date of the person's death or six months later, not on the date they purchased the stock).

Your Own Estate

Now that you have a sense of what the estate settlement process is like, consider your own estate. Will your estate be easily settled with as little tax as possible, or will there be confusion, expenses, delays, and serious estate shrinkage because of heavy taxes owed? If you feel comfortable with the attorney who settled your parents' estate, start to discuss strategies for your own heirs.

You may have the advantage of addressing these tough issues at an earlier age than your parents had. Because of this, you may have options to eliminate some of the problems you had settling their estate.

Also consider how your heirs will feel about and manage the money that you may pass on to them. Pay attention to your feelings, as you may gain insight on how to help your heirs be good custodians when their time comes. If it is time for you to learn more about investing and wealth management, bring them into the learning process. As they develop financial maturity, they will have a great sense of self-esteem and control in their own lives.

The Family Legacy

Consider annual family retreats to discuss the affairs of the family. When money is kept as a taboo topic, it can become toxic. Though it may not be easy at first, bring the financial position of the family out in the open, and encourage your children and grandchildren to ask questions.

I suggest you openly place value on the nonfinancial assets of the family as well. Consider the fact that you have human and intellectual capital as well as financial capital. Child-rearing skills, community service, artistic abilities, educational endeavors, and your family history are all important parts that make up the whole you call your family.

I know that what I am suggesting may not be easy at first. I usually begin by creating a flexible structure with a very general agenda and interesting discussion topics. As a facilitator, I allow the family to find their comfort level, and I continue to make suggestions and to share how other families have found satisfaction through their retreats. If you don't have a facilitator and if you are not sure you want to talk about your money with your kids, start by telling them the family history. Your legacy is made up of more than money; let your children know who came before them and what contributions these ancestors made to their lives today. The money discussion is eventually essential, but you don't have to start there.

Stock Options

tock options are not guarantees; they are potential. It is precisely that lack of certainty that makes the initial stage of this type of Sudden Money different. When you get your stock options, you cannot make lifestyle commitments, quit your job, or make generous gifts, because you really don't know how much new money you have. In order to calculate how much you have, you must exercise the options, sell the option stock, pay taxes, and pay for the cost of exercising and selling.

Many of the decisions involved in this type of Sudden Money are unique to stock options, and many option holders, as well as many financial advisors, are unfamiliar with them. This makes educating yourself and finding the right financial advisor a crucial part of your Sudden Money Process.

Know the Terminology

A *stock option* is the right *granted* by a company to purchase its stock at a predetermined price (called the *exercise price*, or the *strike price*). Typically, there is a delay from the date the option is *granted* to the date it is *exercisable*. This period of time is called the *vesting* period. So if you are *vested*, you are able to purchase at the price at which the option was *granted*.

Types of Stock Options

There are essentially two types of stock options:

1. *Nonqualified stock options (NQSOs).* Issued to employees, directors, and outside contractors. They allow employees ownership and participation in the company's profits. Nonqualified stock options are a flexible and less expensive way for employers to compensate their employees. (The company gets a tax deduction when the options are exercised.)

2. *Incentive stock options (ISOs).* Granted only to employees. They give employees an ownership interest in the company and the opportunity to convert compensation into capital gains income. This is particularly valuable for high–tax bracket employees, lowering the tax on this compensation from 39.6% to 20%.

When Is the Right Time

As an option holder, you are likely to go through a series of what-if scenarios in search of clarification of two burning issues: when to exercise and when to sell. You then have to organize the results of all of your projections in order to *make the best-guess decisions.*

How to Exercise

When you exercise an option, you must have a way to pay for the transaction. You can pay cash, borrow against other securities, or make a cashless transaction. With each method, you have variables to factor in.

Paying Cash

When you pay cash, which is the simplest method, you lose the liquidity of that money. Don't pay cash if it will leave you without emergency funds. You may later regret having to sell shares of the optioned stock to cover one of life's unexpected expenses. This is particularly true if you must sell within 12 months and pay short-term capital gains or if the price of the stock has tanked.

Borrowing

You can borrow against other securities you own or even against existing optioned stock exercised at an early date. One way to borrow against your securities is to take out a margin loan through your broker. The rates charged for margin loans are comparatively low and the interest may be tax-deductible. You might prefer this approach over selling an investment you had hoped to keep for a long time, especially if you will owe capital gains tax when you sell it.

Typically, you would pay off the margin loan when the optioned stock qualifies for long-term capital gains treatment (12 months after the exercise date). In the meantime, you would still own the asset you put as collateral, and you would have avoided the capital gains tax you would have to pay if you had sold it. Keep in mind that the margin loan may be called if the investment you pledge as collateral drops in value. Before taking a margin loan, find out the price at which you would have a margin call.

Cashless

You may be able to simultaneously exercise and sell all or a portion of the stock. The main drawback of this method is that the stock sold will be subject to higher short-term capital gains rates. However, for many option owners this may be the only choice, because they do not have cash or other investments to sell or margin. Options commonly represent the vast majority of net worth outside of a home and retirement accounts. It is usually unwise to borrow against your home for investment purposes, and retirement plans cannot be used for collateral.

Stock Swaps

If you already own company stock, you might be allowed to swap that stock to pay for the exercise of options, both NQSOs and ISOs. When the previously exercised stock is ISO stock, be sure that it has met the requirement of being two years from grant and one year from exercise, or it will be considered a disqualifying distribution and will lose its tax-deferred status. In the case of both ISO and NQSO stock, the transfer qualifies for nonrecognition treatment, meaning there is no capital gains recognition and no capital gains tax.

Exercising Your Options

Without the benefit of option planning, the question of when to exercise your options will be answered for you. Each option granted will have a vesting period before you can exercise and an expiration date. The expiration date is usually from 5 to 10 years from the grant date.

- ISOs must be exercised within 90 days after you leave the company or they will lapse (some will revert to NQSO based on contract provisions).

- NQSOs may have a similar time frame, but frequently have extended time frames (usually five years from the last date of employment). If you are fired, your options may immediately expire.

Exercising ISOs

Because an ISO may be exercised without up-front income tax consequences, it is easier to decide when to exercise. However, if you have a large number of options, the "bargain element" (i.e., the difference between the exercise price and stock price at the time of exercise) may cause you to fall under the alternative minimum tax. This would happen often if the bargain element is substantially higher than your regular taxable income for the year you exercise. If possible, exercise in two different years, or wait until your income from other sources will be higher (or your deductions lower).

Besides the tax difference between ISOs and NQSOs, the strategies for exercising are similar for both kinds of options. The what-if projections will be based upon how you think the optioned stock will perform in the future. It makes sense to use moderate to low assumptions, but if you really think the stock is a big winner, run some projections at the high end.

When Your Investment Goal Is Income

If you need current income, you will have to start exercising and selling the optioned stock immediately. You will need to determine if you are better off exercising and selling all the options at once or doing a portion each year until expiration. If the optioned stock is doing well and you think it will continue to do so, then take the full amount of time that you have and that your income needs allow. If the stock is not doing well or if you expect the company to be entering a tough period with lower earnings, exercise and sell sooner, and reinvest in assets that you feel have better potential.

When Your Investment Goal Is Growth

If your investment goal is growth and you think the optioned stock will perform well, it may seem obvious that you exercise early, paying tax on the lower present amount. However, this is not the case when you factor in the delay of taxation and the increasing leverage you have as the stock price rises. If you think that the optioned stock will continue to do well in comparison with the exercise price and with alternative investments, it is not wise to exercise early.

If you plan to delay exercising until the expiration date, be mindful of your employment status, career goals, and the evolving condition of the company. The longer you stay with the company, the more option grants you are likely to receive. I recommend you add all new grants to your list and do an options audit each year to see how you are doing.

Use Net Numbers

Remember to use the net, after-tax values when you make long-term income projections with your options. Having 50,000 options at $20 does not mean you have $1 million. If the current price is $30, you have a before-tax value of $500,000. After tax, you will have $300,000 (or less if you are subject to state income tax). Making future income projections based on $1 million is very misleading, by more than two-thirds. If you assume you will receive a 6% income from your investment portfolio, it is the difference between $60,000 and $18,000. I recommend that you do the after-tax projections for your options strategies *before you do the Bliss List and the Reality Check exercises.*

Know Your Tax Consequences

Nonqualified stock options and ISOs have different timelines and tax consequences, and both are crucial factors in your decisions of when to exercise and when to sell.

NQSOs

There is no tax consequence when NQSOs are *granted.* When these options are *exercised,* the difference between the exercised price and current stock price is considered earned income. This amount is subject to income tax and possibly FICA tax and Medicare.

When the optioned stock from an NQSO is *sold,* however, it is taxed as capital gains, either long-term or short-term. To qualify for the lower, long-term rates, the stock must be held at least 12 months after exercise. The maximum long-term capital gains rate at this writing is 20%. Therefore, if the stock is not held for 12 months, perhaps sold immediately to pay for exercising, the proceeds are subject to short-term capital gains rates (maximum short-term rates are currently 39.6%).

ISOs

As with NQSOs, there is no tax consequence when ISOs are *granted*. When ISOs are *exercised*, there is no income or FICA tax, but there may be an alternative minimum tax (AMT). Before you exercise ISOs, it is possible to determine if the difference between the exercise price and the current stock price will need to be included as a preference item on your upcoming tax return. Tax-planning strategies to avoid AMT are reverse strategies. They include accelerating income for the year you exercise and postponing deductions.

The sale of the ISO stock will qualify for favorable capital gains taxation if certain requirements have been met. For example, the stock must not be sold for two years from the date of grant and one year from the date of exercise. These are important dates to include on your options list. Another way to lose favorable tax advantage of an ISO occurs the year the recipient vests. When the exercise value of options in the year vested exceeds $100,000, the options over $100,000 become less desirable NQSOs. If these requirements are not met, the options are reclassified as nonqualified stock options and taxed accordingly.

Incentive stock options cannot be transferred; they must remain in the ownership of the employee. If they are transferred, except at death, they will be disqualified and will become NQSOs. ISOs cannot be split with or transferred to a spouse as part of a divorce settlement. Typically they are kept by the employee spouse, while the nonemployee spouse takes other assets.

The Chute of Emotions
and the Thoughts You'll Wrestle With

While you go through the process of deciding when and how to exercise, you may find yourself wrestling with fear, impatience, entitlement issues, disappointment, denial, and unrealistic expectations. Any one of these emotions can trip you up enough to cause you to lose the real potential of your stock options.

High/Unrealistic Expectations

Sergio sold his information technology company after seven years of very long workweeks. The take-home income that he and his much younger wife lived on had averaged $175,000 per year. After the sale of his company, he was ready to retire and help raise the family he and his wife were trying to start. Besides several hundred thousand dollars in his pension, 401(k), and IRAs, all of their assets were in the business.

Sergio told his financial planner that he received $20 million for the company. In reality, he had 1 million stock options at $9 each. The stock had a price range from a low of $17 to a high of $31. For his options to be worth $20 million, the stock price had to be $29, and that seemed possible.

However, receiving $20 million in options is not the same as receiving $20 million in cash. Sergio's options would be taxed twice before this money would be usable for income and diversification.

Denial

I have observed a common tendency to not take stock option wealth seriously. The prevailing feeling is that it could all go away tomorrow, so you shouldn't count on it. This is a healthy attitude up to a point, as it helps prevent overspending or creating a lifestyle that cannot be maintained. However, ignoring the options will cause you to miss planning opportunities and omit critical estate planning.

It is true that options do not have any market value until they are vested (the point at which you can exercise). Once they are exercisable, it is common to see them only as peripheral wealth, to be dealt with just before they expire. However, their potential value can add up to a very large percentage of your net worth. You may have real diversification issues and not want to be buying company stock inside your retirement plan or as an outside investment. You may have early retirement possibilities, or career change opportunities available.

It is not uncommon for options to be left out of the estate planning process, again because they don't seem real. If you die with vested options, the IRS will see them as real assets—real *taxable* assets. Acknowledging their present value may help you take advantage of strategies to minimize estate and income taxes, create liquidity, and ease the settling of your estate.

Impatience

The flip side of denial is the impatience that some options holders experience. It is tempting to cash in and exit a career that is no longer satisfying. For some, it is equally tempting to make a super-expensive purchase. Like Sergio in the story earlier, you might be counting on more money than you actually have. If you are impatient, you probably won't wait long enough to get a lower long-term capital gains rate.

Consequences of Cashing Out

If cashing out has strong appeal, move carefully. Keep in mind that in order to turn your options into an income source, they may have to be sold (and options do not pay dividends). Selling also means that taxes will have to be paid. As you do your projections, you will notice how much more money you have if your sale of stock is subject to long-term capital gains rather than short-term capital gains. This means you wait 12 months after they have been exercised.

If you are cashing out, make an alternative income plan for the first 12 months. Better yet, if you plan your departure in advance, you can exercise a year before you leave, and then sell stock at the long-term capital gains rate. The price of impatience may be lower income in years to come.

Discomfort

Wealth that does not fit well can feel uncomfortable for some time. I have met with many families who still see themselves as middle income, middle America people. They have lived in average homes and spent average amounts of money on vacations, cars, and general lifestyles. However, they have tens of millions of dollars in stock options, or optioned stock that never really seems like it is theirs.

Stock option wealth can come overnight without you doing anything to create the windfall. If your company goes public or is acquired, you may have a magnification of wealth beyond your ability to understand. It may take some time to settle into it, and you may have some surprising self-esteem issues to deal with. You may also feel guilty that your company did so well while your friends' did not. Sudden Money from stock options can seem random to some recipients. All of your friends worked as hard as you did, but your company stock made you rich, and theirs did not. These feelings are natural, and you might want to meet with a therapist to discuss them. With a little help, they are not too difficult to adjust to.

Managing Your Options—Keeping Track

The key issue when managing your options is to keep track of the types of options you have, the date they were granted, how many options were granted, the exercise price, the vesting date, and the expiration date. You are likely to have several batches of options issued over your years of employment. Before you can do any strategizing on when and how to exercise and sell, you need to know what you have.

I recommend you keep a list of all your options by date of grant. I prefer to use a spreadsheet to keep track and to do what-if scenarios to assist in deciding when to exercise and when to sell. If you use this kind of planning tool, be sure it is flexible enough to be customized to your specific situation.

Selling Your Optioned Stock

Once the options are exercised, you are free to sell the optioned stock. The issues surrounding the sale of the optioned stock are taxes, your investment goals, your risk tolerance, and your need for diversification.

In most cases, it is best to wait at least 12 months before you sell the optioned stock in order to qualify for lower long-term capital gains rates. However, if you need to sell some stock to pay for the cost of exercising, you won't have the luxury of waiting 12 months. If you need to sell stock to pay for taxes, it may make sense to consider using a margin loan (described earlier). This loan will give you the cash for the taxes without having to sell the stock. Once the 12 months have passed, you can sell the stock and pay off the loan.

Unless your stock pays a hefty dividend, you will have to seek other investment vehicles that produce predictable income, thus causing you to sell some of the optioned stock. However, it is possible to hold on to the stock and to sell some shares each time you need income. This is best done on a systematic basis. You could, for instance, sell 0.5% of the value each month, and you'd receive a 6% annual income. If you time this cash flow strategy properly, waiting 12 months from the date of exercise before you begin, you will pay the long-term capital gains tax rather than the higher ordinary income tax rate.

Don't Ignore Diversification

I recommend that you diversify both your income sources and your growth investments. Even if you foresee great appreciation potential for the optioned stock, use prudent personal money management guidelines and sell some of it. As an advisor, I like to keep no more than 10% of a portfolio in a single asset. However, I have found that many option holders are devoted to their optioned stock. At times, they are equally devoted to delaying the capital gains tax they would owe if they sold. Therefore, the idea of diversification, though it may sound logical, is at times a very hard sell.

Be fair to yourself. Use very low assumptions in your what-if projections, and then use the assumption that the stock price drops and does not come back up. Though you may feel these are unlikely scenarios, you need to see the possibility and decide how it makes you feel.

If your option stock represents a large percentage of your net worth, sell at least one-half, assuming you foresee good future gains for the stock, and reposition the money in various appropriate investments. You will have to pay tax upon selling, but your financial future will be more secure.

Solving the diversification problem produces two big blocks:

1. The taxes that will be owed

2. The belief that the company stock is the best single asset to own

I respond with two absolutes:

1. There is no such thing as the single best investment for all times, as every investment has its cycles.

2. There is no place for emotions within investment portfolio management.

Work with your financial advisor to identify other investments with excellent track records, good future prospects, and the ability to meet your investment goals. Once you find good alternative investments, make a commitment to move a percentage of your stock into them. Either do this as one big move, or take a few years to gradually rebalance your portfolio.

If you can't wait to diversify because you no longer believe the stock will appreciate, run your what-if scenarios, waiting 12 months to qualify for capital gains and immediately paying higher taxes. Build into these scenarios the stock prices you believe are possible, including a drop in price. Find out the tax cost of not waiting, and weigh that against the possible drop in price.

Estate Planning

Since stock options may be a significant percentage of your net worth, you need to pay attention to the estate planning issues.

- Incentive stock options cannot be owned or exercised by anyone but the option holder. At death, the ISO can be exercised and the stock sold by the executor. The required holding periods and employment tests do not apply. However the ISO itself does not receive a step-up in basis at death. The difference between the exercise price and the value of the optioned stock on the date of death is considered income with respect to the decedent, and it is taxable.

- Stock owned via the exercise of ISOs and NQSOs is given the advantage of a step-up in basis at death, even if the time requirements have not been met and there is no capital gains tax.

- You should be sure to use the net value of the options you hold when you do an estate planning audit as part of your Sudden Money financial plan. Also, consider your heirs' need for liquidity to pay for the costs of exercising and estate taxes when settling your estate. The presence of the options in your name, even if they have not been exercised yet, may catapult you into a surprisingly high estate tax position. Review the estate planning chapter in this book, and meet with your financial planner and estate planning attorney. Prepare yourself to make some decisions you never thought you'd have to make. Even though your options may represent only potential until they are exercised, they will become part of your estate and will be subject to estate taxes.

Charitable Giving

When you think about sharing your good fortune, pay attention to the tax issues, as minimizing taxes will give you more money to share. It is not possible to avoid the income taxes due when NQSOs are exercised. You might have thought you could donate stock options to a charitable remainder trust to avoid the income and the capital gains taxes, but neither will be avoided. It is a compelling idea because these trusts would pay you an income for life and the income would be higher if the donated amount was the before-tax amount. But as always, the IRS still wants its taxes. If your intention is to donate to charities, it is better to donate the optioned stock with long-term gains (held 12 months or longer) rather than the unexercised options.

Divorce

ivorce propels you through one of life's toughest transitions. In order for this transition to be successful, it usually takes time, good planning, and a willingness to face the myriad changes around every corner.

You might find that your personal, social, and financial situations are drastically different from when you were married. It is easy to become fixated on what you have lost instead of what you have and how you are going to make the best use of it. This is especially true when it comes to money. But rather than focus on what you did or didn't get, concentrate on using what you have to help you become financially secure and emotionally well. Use your Sudden Money to help you build a foundation for your new life.

Not-So-Sudden Money

Divorce is a legal process that is often charged by emotion and riddled with uncertainty, denial, and confusion. In a perfect world, you would go through the legal process and be able to deal with your financial decisions with a calm, clear mind. Your passage from a married person to a happy, well-adjusted single person would go swimmingly, and you would know exactly where you stood financially. After all, you understood your tax consequences, your insurance situation, and your social security benefits, and you invested your money wisely with a wonderful advisor with whom you have developed a great relationship.

In our imperfect world, however, the average story reads a bit differently. First of all, the legal proceedings are mostly about money: Who gets it? Who pays it? How much is involved? And that entire conversation is usually clouded by the intense chute of emotions that you experience as a consequence of the termination of your marriage. The result is that you are forced to make financial decisions at a time when you are vulnerable. When your settlement is reached, you may not be clear about what you have, what your income will be, and what details still need to be taken care of. As for a financial advisor, you probably don't have one because you were so overwhelmed by the flood of emotions stirred up by the divorce process that you haven't had time to think about anything else. And you don't want to use the same advisor as your ex-spouse.

The Chute of Emotions

Even though this form of Sudden Money does not just materialize overnight, what makes it so challenging is that it often arrives with an enormous amount of emotional baggage. The most common emotions are abandonment, fear, and anger. Once again, your best defense against becoming overwhelmed by the emotions and, consequently, making bad financial decisions, is *time*. You must allow yourself adequate time in your Decision Free Zone (DFZ) to understand your new goals and to educate yourself about your financial options.

Abandonment

The months and possibly years prior to divorce settlements are usually dominated by the legal and accounting work necessary to reach the settlement. Once it is reached, the lawyers and accountants go on to the next case, leaving you with serious financial decisions to make while you're still reeling with emotions. Many people say they feel abandoned all over again when their settlement is reached and their divorce attorneys and accountants "leave" them. The key here is to look at the dissolution of those relationships more positively.

At this point, you have to put together a new team, and you are the captain. Take time to research the kinds of professionals who are most appropriate for your situation. Along with needing a financial advisor, an accountant, and possibly an attorney, you also need the support and companionship of your friends and family. Your personal support team may have changed as a result of your divorce. Now might be a time to seek out new friendships. Be careful to avoid negative people, however, especially those who are still bitter about their own divorces.

Fear

The most common fears in the early stages following a divorce are:

- Being alone financially
- Having insufficient money to live on
- Losing your settlement money through risky investments
- Wondering if, even with sound investments, the money will run out someday

As you go through the financial planning process of the DFZ, the answers to most income questions will become clear to you. Your Reality Check will tell you how much income you will really have, where you can afford to live, where your income will come from, and how dependable it is. You will also learn about your new tax position, your credit rating, and your debts, and you will develop a plan for your retirement.

If you follow the DFZ guidelines, you won't make long-term investment decisions until you have developed a plan that you have confidence in and that you understand. When you implement your plan in Phase Two, you know you will have enough income to comfortably support yourself now and in the future. All of the common fears, then, will be alleviated if you follow the steps of the Sudden Money Process.

Grief

Grief is often associated with death, but it is a common part of the healing process for divorced people as well. In most cases—even if it was your idea to get divorced—there is a sense of losing a part of you. If it wasn't your idea, you might feel the loss of the marriage that you thought could be saved. There are many excellent books specifically written about the grieving process, and there are others on surviving a divorce. I recommend that you familiarize yourself with the research on the grieving process and that you wait until you have worked through most of the process before you make investment or lifestyle decisions. It could take over a year.

Low Self-Esteem

Many people see their divorce as a personal failure; others focus on their feelings of rejection. The cause of both reactions is usually low self-esteem. The impact of low self-esteem can show up in many areas of our lives: in our careers, in our relationships, and in our shopping patterns.

Spending and gambling are two destructive behaviors that spring from low self-esteem. Many people would rather go shopping or gambling as a way of temporarily feeling important and good about themselves. For them, the act of buying or gambling is like a drug, a temporary fix that must be repeated over and over again in order to maintain the "high." Unfortunately, the ultimate destructive consequence of these behaviors, which do not easily cease, is financial ruin.

Essential Decisions/Actions

There are many details, legal and practical, involved in building your new life. Even though you may feel emotionally incapable, some things must be done. Many of the essential actions and decisions are listed below. If something not on this list comes up, find out if it truly must be done now or can it be put off.

Retitle Assets, Draft New Legal Documents, Change Beneficiaries

No matter what is spelled out in your legal, filed divorce settlement, you still have to change names and beneficiaries on your will, trusts, insurance policies, annuities, retirement plans, and credit cards. If you don't make these changes, you could lose control of the assets, your money could go to the wrong person when you die, and you could end up paying off your former spouse's credit card charges. Just because you agreed to the changes as part of your divorce does not mean the changes have legally taken place. It is *your* responsibility to see that the process is completed.

BANK AND BROKERAGE ACCOUNTS If your bank and brokerage accounts were held either jointly or in your former spouse's name, they must be changed as soon as possible. Each institution will have its own forms for you to sign, and in many cases, you need to submit a copy of the portion of the divorce decree that assigns the accounts to you. You might even need a letter of instruction signed by your former spouse.

It is your responsibility to check and double-check that the name change has been done properly. Many companies are sloppy with their paperwork, and if you don't catch a mistake, it might never get corrected. The consequence of your account not being properly titled is that you will have trouble exercising control over your money. For example, you might not be able to make a trade or to withdraw funds when you need to. The company's point of view is that whoever is named owner of the account is the person who owns and controls the money; they don't care about what your divorce documents say.

WILLS AND TRUSTS Your will and any trusts you have established must also be changed if your former spouse was named as beneficiary or guardian. Be sure to make new appointments within your personal legal documents regarding your power of attorney, living will, guardianship, and any new beneficiaries.

LIFE INSURANCE Life insurance policies have three key positions:

1. The owner
2. The insured
3. The beneficiary

If you have a policy on your own life, meaning the policy states that you are the insured, make sure the beneficiary named is correct. If the beneficiary was your former spouse and now it should be your children, you must make the change with the insurance company directly. Most companies have their own forms they want you to use, so either call the company directly and request instructions, or call the person who sold you the policy.

The policy owner controls the policy, and all the correspondence from the company is sent to that person. If you have been given rights to have insurance on your ex-spouse, maybe to cover alimony payments if he or she should die, you should be the policy owner. If your former spouse is the owner, he or she can take cash out of the policy, perhaps forget to pay the premium (in which case the policy will be cancelled), or choose to cancel the policy. And all of this can happen without you being notified. My advice is that if the insurance is important to you, you should pay the premiums, carefully read all correspondence, and ask questions if there is anything you do not fully understand.

ANNUITIES Annuity contracts have an owner, an annuitant (upon whose death the annuity contract ends), and a beneficiary. They are similar to life insurance policies in that the owner controls the contract. In addition, all changes of beneficiaries must be done directly with the company. If the ownership is going to change, you need to sign the company's form to make that change. If the annuity contract was set up with joint annuitants, it is a good idea to have only you listed as the annuitant. Again, use the company's form to make this change.

HOMEOWNER'S INSURANCE Homeowner's insurance and auto insurance policies must also be changed after a divorce. They, too, need specific forms and the permission of your former spouse. In one case I know of, a man took two years to sign the release form allowing the insurance company to drop his auto insurance. (When he was married, he and his wife's auto insurance and their homeowner's insurance were under one contract.) The company insisted on having his permission before taking him off. Meanwhile, the man's former wife needed to keep the coverage because it was the only company in her area willing to insure waterfront property. She ended up paying for his auto insurance for two years.

RETIREMENT PLANS, IRAS, AND 401(K) PLANS The information regarding a person's retirement benefits is private and not released to anyone but the named employee. If your divorce settlement includes the rights to a portion of your former spouse's retirement, pension, individual retirement account (IRA), or 401(k), you must secure these rights by filing a Qualified Domestic Relations Order (QDRO) with the courts and with the plan administrator. Once that document is filed and accepted by the plan administrator, you become the alternate payee and you should receive information on the plan without much difficulty.

It is important that you file this paperwork as soon as possible, because you could lose your position to a creditor, to the IRS, or to another former spouse if one of those parties has acted before you. The rule is that once you have staked your claim to your agreed-upon portion of the plan, no other alternate payee can replace you—*as long as you filed first.*

Sara and Ron agreed to separate and intended to get divorced. They agreed Sara would get the house and one-half of Ron's retirement benefits. However, when they discovered that Sara and the children would lose the insurance benefits from Ron's company, they decided to live as though they were divorced without actually filing for divorce at the time.

Later, when Ron wanted to marry his long-time girlfriend, he and Sara filed for divorce. Soon after his second marriage began, Ron was divorced again. Sara had no idea that Ron's second wife had also been given one-half of Ron's retirement benefits.

Sara had represented herself in the divorce, and the plan administrator had rejected the QDRO she presented because of technicalities. Sara intended to hire a lawyer to refile the QDRO, but she let it go for a year. During that time, the second wife's attorney properly filed the second QDRO and she became the alternate payee, not Sara, even though Sara had been married to Ron for 20 years.

In some cases, such as an IRA or a 401(k) plan, you may roll the money into your own IRA account or take it out and spend it. Ordinarily there is a 10% early withdrawal penalty, but it will not apply *if this money is part of a divorce settlement.* You will, however, owe income taxes on the full amount you take out. Whether you should take the money out or leave it in the new IRA to grow for the future is something to address within the context of your cash management and retirement planning (discussed later in the chapter). Once the money is rolled over, you will have the responsibility to manage it based on the investment goals you set for yourself as you work through Phase One.

ACCESS TO COMPANY PENSION PLAN MONEY Many company pension plans will not allow you access to the assets within a pension plan until your former spouse reaches a specific age. Each plan has different rules regarding the ages and conditions under which the money can be withdrawn. You will be subject to all the rules of the plan, and it is up to you and your advisors to understand those rules and to plan accordingly.

Until you take the money out, the company will be managing the money, and you will not have any say in the investments it chooses. If you have rights to a retirement account that is self-directed but not available for a rollover, find out if you can separate your portion from your former spouse's. This will give you control over the investments within the account, allowing you to manage this money according to your personal goals and risk tolerance.

CREDIT CARDS Regardless of your marital status, you should establish your own credit rating and your own credit cards. If your former spouse is on any of the cards, you could be responsible for their charges. Call your credit card companies and have new cards issued with you as the only authorized user. Be sure to cancel all the cards that list your former spouse as an authorized person. Do this by phone to be expedient, but also be sure to confirm the cancellation in writing.

If you and your former spouse had joint debts, it is possible for you to get stuck with more than you bargained for. Credit card companies, department stores, and collection agencies will hold both of you responsible for debts incurred. This means that if they cannot collect from one of you, they will go after the other. Your divorce settlement means nothing to them—they want their money.

Now that you are on your own financially, you may find it challenging to resist the lure of easy money that credit cards represent. As many of you have already discovered, there is nothing easy about big credit card debt. It has been the ruin of many otherwise financially secure individuals, and it takes many people a lot of time to get used to living within the constraints of a much lower income. Credit cards can make it easy to keep up the old lifestyle, but the cost is usually way out of line with what the new budget calls for.

UTILITY COMPANIES Utility companies (e.g., electric, phone, and cable) originally gave you service based upon someone's credit history with the company. If the credit history was your former spouse's, you may have to put down deposits when you have the utilities turned on in a new home or when you have your former spouse's name taken off the account. It is wise to take care of this matter immediately by paying any deposits required and by making certain that your name is the only one on the account. You might be tempted to leave everything as it is, but that leaves room for the possibility that the bills will be forwarded to your former spouse and will go unpaid, and/or that you won't be able to make changes in service without your former spouse's permission.

Your New Identity

In addition to losing your spouse, when you get divorced, you often lose your social identity. Ask anyone who has been recently divorced or widowed, and they'll tell you that the single's world is very different from the couple's world. If your postdivorce income will be substantially lower, you may have to make some dramatic adjustments, such as moving to another neighborhood, canceling your club memberships, and selling your boat or vacation home. Making these adjustments to accommodate your new financial reality may cut you off from the social network of which you were part when you were married.

It is common to try to hold on to the lifestyle and friends you had before your divorce. Many people will try to convince themselves that spending the extra money to maintain their old lifestyle is emotionally worthwhile. The financial strain that becomes evident over time, however, will not be so easy to rationalize. If you are paying attention to your finances and you are regularly overspending, it will become clear that, in addition to depleting your money *today*, you are creating a very difficult financial *future* for yourself. It is best to do a Reality Check with your advisor as soon as possible, then live within your income limitations.

The Spending Spree

Whether you are glad to be rid of your former spouse or are still feeling very wounded, you may feel the need to go out and live it up a bit. Sometimes a new outfit or a piece of new furniture is a way of signaling a new beginning. It is common for people to go on a spending spree in order to make themselves feel better, as a form of revenge, as feel-good therapy, or to celebrate their new freedom. If this is where you're at, I suggest you set some limits.

Before you take off on a grand vacation, buy new furniture, a new car or some jewelry, or get cosmetic surgery, get a clear idea of what these expenses will do to your overall financial picture. If a spending spree is in order, do it within your preset limits, which will help you minimize buyer's or celebrator's regret. Before you set your spending limits, ask yourself the fundamental question: Is a spending spree really in order?

Income

The composition of assets (and debts) tends to be in a constant state of flux while the negotiation or litigation progresses. Even after a settlement or a court award is made, several events may occur that can delay the actual receipt of funds. In the worst-case scenario, the assets may never arrive.

The most important step toward achieving a sense of financial security is finding out as much as possible about how much income you are supposed to have and where it should be coming from. If you have fixed income (e.g., alimony, pension income, or social security), you need to know when the checks will arrive each month. Know also *where* they will arrive: Will they be deposited directly into your bank account or your brokerage account, or will they be sent to your home address?

Social Security

If you were married for 10 years or more, you are entitled to receive social security based on your former spouse's earnings. Your claim does not affect the amount your former spouse will receive, nor does it change the benefits to their current spouse should they remarry. To be eligible, the following criteria must be met:

- That you must be divorced for two years before you collect
- That one-half of your former spouse's age-65 benefit must be larger than the benefit that you would receive based upon your work history
- That you are not married to someone else at the time you start to get your social security checks
- That you and your former spouse must both be at least age 62

If you remarry after you start collecting on your former spouse's social security, you lose these benefits, but you can still apply for benefits based upon your own work history or receive spousal benefits.

Alimony and Temporary Maintenance

If you have been awarded maintenance or alimony, chances are you need this money to live on. You may have been given temporary maintenance to give you time to go back to school or to otherwise prepare to support yourself. In this case you will have to be aware of the need for a replacement plan for when the money stops coming.

It may also mean that you make certain investment choices, such as keeping the money liquid and invested in low-risk investments until you have gotten your career in place and are receiving a predictable paycheck. Once you know you won't need the settlement money to live on, you can choose long-term investments capable of providing you with a comfortable retirement. If you are starting your career later in life, the settlement money may make the difference between being able to retire or having to always work.

ALIMONY AND INFLATION Alimony is not usually increased for inflation. As you do your Reality Check, determine if you need to save a portion of each payment to build up additional money to supplement your alimony in the future. This may seem impossible if your budget is already tight, but just imagine living on one-half of that amount 15 years from now. That's what inflation will due to your income over time.

RELIABILITY OF PAYMENTS If your alimony is permanent and if you intend to rely on it for your income, you have to be concerned with how reliable it will be. A variety of things can threaten this income, and several of the potential variables are impossible to control. One variable you can protect yourself against is loss due to the death of the payor. You can buy life insurance on the payor, with their consent (and for an annual premium payment), so you are effectively guaranteeing your own future income.

Whether the insurance replacement plan will work depends upon whether your former spouse is healthy enough to qualify and whether you can afford the cost of the coverage. It is usually stated in your divorce agreement that you have the right to buy insurance on your former spouse, and he or she must cooperate by submitting to a physical, providing medical records, and signing the application.

ALIMONY INSURANCE If you choose to buy what we call "alimony insurance," shop carefully. It is not only expensive, but the cost can change over the years. If you need this kind of insurance, you will presumably need it for a long period of time. It will be much more difficult to change to a new policy years down the road when your former spouse has aged, may not be insurable, or is uncooperative.

In other words, educate yourself on the various kinds of insurance available to you and try to make a permanent decision. And don't forget to add the cost of this insurance to your annual budget.

THE ANNUITY PLAN Another way to make the payments reliable for the rest of your life is to have the payor buy an immediate annuity, which pays you a fixed amount of money each month. An immediate annuity is a contract with an insurance company. You give them a lump sum of money, and they agree to make specific payments to you for a period of time. The payments can continue for your lifetime, and you can arrange for the payments to be made to the payor if you die before he or she does.

The annuity plan simplifies and guarantees the payment, the payor does not have to write an alimony check every month for the rest of his or her life, and you don't have to worry about the payments stopping for any reason. The drawback is that the payor must come up with a large amount of money to produce the lifetime of payments. You also must be certain the insurance company is a solid company unlikely to go into default. An alternative to that one annuity is to diversify by buying several smaller immediate annuity contracts from different insurance companies.

CHILD SUPPORT INSURANCE Along with considering buying insurance to protect your alimony, you should buy enough to protect any child support payments as well. The alimony insurance and/or the annuity plan will work for these payments just as it did for the alimony, but since child support is temporary, the death benefit needed is not as high. An inexpensive term policy would be best in this case because you will need it for a shorter period of time.

Child support payments might cover most of the expenses related to raising children, but they probably won't cover everything. Your daily care and the income you bring in would be missed if you were to die while the children were still young. The best way to prevent this potential problem is to buy a *term policy on your own life* for the children. This entails having your lawyer set up a trust to receive the money and naming a guardian for while the children are still in school.

REPLACEMENT PLAN FOR CHILD SUPPORT MONEY It is not unusual for the child support payments to be enough to allow the custodial parent to remain out of work while the children are in school. If this is the case, be sure you set up a replacement plan for when the payments stop, because it is not uncommon for the children to still be living at home at this point. You will need to either manage your investments for the future income, or plan to *earn* the replacement money. You can ask the stay-home children for rent, but they have their own lives to lead and will eventually be ready to move out. Your replacement plan should not be based on the collection of rent from your children.

Taxes

NEW TAX BRACKET, NEW FILING STATUS As a result of your divorce, you will be in a new tax position. As a result of filing your taxes as a single taxpayer, you might end up in a new tax bracket. You should file your income to the IRS as a single taxpayer—not *married filing jointly*—if your divorce is finalized by the end of the year.

ALIMONY AND TAXES If you are awarded alimony, you will owe taxes on the full amount you receive. Remember that alimony is taxable, but child support isn't.

A point that surprises many is that alimony is considered *earned income* and that it qualifies you to make an IRA contribution. It makes sense to put some money away for the future and to get the tax benefits unique to IRAs at the same time. Discuss with your financial advisor what kind of IRA you should have and what amount you should put in each year.

QUARTERLY TAX PAYMENTS Taxes will not be withheld from your alimony or maintenance. In most cases, taxes are not withheld from investment income either. This means that *you will be responsible for making quarterly tax payments*, which is something that may be new to you. When you work for a company, the company withholds taxes from your pay each pay period. They send the money to the IRS on your behalf. Then, in January or February, you get a W-2 form showing how much was paid toward your tax bill. *If you are receiving income from sources other than a paycheck, you must make quarterly payments.*

Your accountant will help you to estimate the amount you will owe and how much should be paid each quarter. There are specific forms to use when you file your quarterly taxes. Once you do it a couple of times, you will see that it is not all that complicated.

In most cases, the transfers of assets between you and your spouse are not subject to income taxes or capital gains tax. Once the transfer has taken place, you will owe tax on your investment income, with the exception of interest from tax-free municipal bonds. Whether you choose to receive or to reinvest your interest and dividend income, you will owe taxes. Each January or February, you will receive IRS 1099 forms reporting how much income and dividends you received the previous year.

The sale of investments may trigger a capital gains tax if the amount you receive is higher than the amount of the investment cost. If you have investments that you have received as part of the settlement, find out what the capital gains consequences will be before you sell. If you have not settled yet, require the original cost information as part of your settlement process.

SALE OF THE FAMILY HOME If you have received the house as part of your divorce settlement, you may need to sell it in order to cut your living expenses. If the house has been your primary residence for two of the last five years, you will get beneficial tax treatment for the first $500,000 of profits from the sale. For example, if you bought the house for $300,000 and sold it for $500,000, the $200,000 profit would be excluded from tax.

If you have lived in the house for less than two years, you get a portion of the $500,000 exclusion. If you have lived there for one year, you would get one-half of the exclusion (i.e., if you sold the house after one year, you would have up to a $250,000 exclusion).

Conclusion

Each action you take—or elect to postpone—will shape what you can do later. Each step you take toward acknowledging and reconciling your emotions, whatever they may be, will shape how you feel about yourself, your money, and your marriage. When the suddenness is gone and you have given yourself time to work through many of your emotional issues, you will be able to comfortably settle into your new identity. Use the Sudden Money Process to help create the optimal new you.

When Two Become One

When many new widows begin to process what has happened to their lives, they are faced with two major issues: the grief over their loss, and the new financial situation that has been thrust upon them. Both of these areas are so powerful and even overwhelming that many widows choose to act as if one or both of them do not exist.

In my experience, the sooner you deal with your emotions, the sooner you will be able to begin to heal. This is not one of those miserable situations that you can work *around*—this is one you have to work *through*. The Sudden Money Process gives you a useful structure to get you through this challenging time.

Naturally, this category usually involves a lengthy Decision Free Zone because grieving the loss of a spouse is one of the most traumatic events of your life. However, this is also a situation that may require important, immediate decisions that affect your future financial security. I'll tell you what to expect and what decisions

---

This chapter has been written to address widows because conventional thinking tells us that women have more difficulty dealing with the financial aftermath of the death of their spouse. However, in my experience, the issues and feelings involved pertain equally to men. For convenience of language, I am addressing this chapter to women.

you need to address, and I'll guide you through the practical side of what happens when two become one.

The Importance of the Decision Free Zone

When widows describe their emotional state immediately following the death of their spouses, they tend to use words like *shock, numb, empty,* and *dead inside.* They say that nothing matters to them. Naturally, making any inessential decisions when you are feeling so horrible is probably not a good idea.

My Recommendations

I recommend that every widow, regardless of emotional state, wait at least one year before making any unnecessary major decisions, particularly regarding finances. The only things you need to do are:

- Experience your emotions, perhaps with the aid of a therapist and/or support group.

- Settle the estate, secure your income, and collect your assets. This will include hiring an attorney, an accountant, and a financial planner.

The second set of items is why I often refer to this category as *sudden responsibility.* Although you are grieving your loss, putting these things off can ruin you financially. You must be personally involved in these decisions to ensure the outcome that is best for you.

By working on these items, you will not only be doing the things that must be done, but you will be progressively regaining your sense of self. You will be gaining control of your life during a time when it may feel as if nothing is in your control. There may be days when you feel like the slightest responsibility is impossible to face. Nevertheless, each day you should try to deal with at least one thing, even if it is very small. Eventually, you will have your financial life in order and your future will seem less frightening.

A Caveat on Selling Your House

While you are grieving, your ability to make rational decisions may be limited. Nevertheless, whether to sell the house and move away is often the first decision that new widows try to tackle. That could be a bad idea for you emotionally and financially, but since you would be thinking about neither with a clear head, you might not notice or care at the time.

The same recommendation of waiting to make decisions applies to the sale of anything, large or small, that reminds you of your spouse.

It was assumed that Donna would sell the stables that Stan loved so much when he was alive. Local real estate agents brought her several offers, and she was advised to consider them. Luckily, Donna did not accept the offers, even though she was strongly advised to sell the property and take the money. Once she was able to deal with her financial affairs, she realized that not selling was one of her best decisions. By not allowing herself to be pushed into what seemed like an obvious decision, she found out later that she was able to rent the stables. As a result, they became an important source of income.

However urgent the impulse or need to sell appears, you should hold off until you have had time to discover what you want the next part of your life to look like. Explore alternatives and take at least six months to begin to process what has happened and to decide where you belong.

Shopping: The False Solution

While you are feeling numb and exhausted, be careful not to overspend. Some people find themselves shopping as a way to kill time or to try to feel better. It is easy to overspend when you don't know what your limits are and you are searching for anything to make you feel better. Shopping may make you feel better for a few hours, but it is no solution to the grief you are dealing with. In fact, it may cause its own kind of stress, created by the fear that you are doing something irresponsible and wrong by spending too much. Even if you are not ready to invest, meet with an advisor to determine what amount you can spend without jeopardizing your future security.

The Chute of Emotions

Losing a spouse is one of the most stressful experiences in life. The following are the most common emotions experienced by widows and widowers.

Grief

The most common emotion that results from the death of a loved one is grief. Experts in the fields of anthropology, sociology, and psychology have studied grief for years, and while they differ on their approaches to it, they generally agree on what it is.

Grieving is a process that can last for years. It involves several stages, including shock, anger, denial, and depression, and it usually culminates with some version of peaceful acceptance and moving forward. There is not a predictable timetable for this process, not everyone experiences every stage, and some people repeat a state or two.

A vital part of the grieving process is allowing yourself the time and space to grieve. This means seeking support and permitting others to help you through your process. There are therapists, support groups, and chat groups on the Internet created to address the emotional needs of people just like you.

If your loved one was terminally ill, the process may have begun when the illness was diagnosed. Though you may have felt you had come to terms with your loss before the death occurred, don't be surprised to find that you have a new level of grief to confront now. As much pain as you may be feeling and as unique as it is, there are others who have experienced similar pain. Contact them and let them help you.

Fear

Many kinds of fear may arise as a result of the death of a spouse. There is the fear of being alone, the fear of losing your financial security, the fear of making poor investment decisions, and the fear of not having enough money to produce the income you will need. Worst of all, many widows fear they will never feel like a complete person again.

The fears about money need to be dealt with rationally and openly, with the help of your therapist and your financial planner. Many of these fears stem from a lack of understanding and confidence, particularly when investment and budgeting decisions are a new experience for you. New things can be scary; when you are facing them alone, they can seem terrifying.

Your advisor can work with you to increase your knowledge and confidence before you invest in unfamiliar investments. Like all investors, you will make mistakes. If you are following an investment plan designed to meet your specific needs and risk level, however, your mistakes won't be so awful in the end.

.As you learn more about investing, interest rates, and taxes, you will begin to feel more confident. Find a financial planner who is willing to teach you about each decision you are confronted with. Rather than telling you to buy this or that investment or to take one kind of a mortgage over another, you want someone who will help you to think through the pros and cons, and help you to understand your range of possibilities with each decision.

Loneliness and the Influence of Others

Loneliness is a common feeling among widows. The isolation that often results can be exacerbated by all of the pressure coming from family and friends. Turning down the helpful offers of people who love you might seem like rejection to them, and this is not a time for alienating anyone. You can avoid isolating yourself and alienating others by listening to their suggestions and thanking them for their support and kindness. Explain that once you have hired your team of advisors, you will be in a better position to act on outside advice.

Once your friends and family realize that you have a financial planner, an attorney, and an accountant, they will have less of a need to oversee your decisions. If it seems necessary or feels right, you can share with them the professional advice that you are receiving and acting on. Remember that most well-intentioned people just want to be sure that you are not going to be taken advantage of. They want to believe that you are making logical decisions, that you have a plan, and that you are getting expert help.

Taking Responsibility for Your Finances for the First Time

When asked, most women admit that they would not be ready to take over the family finances if their husbands died before they did. In fact, not only are they unprepared, but they say they would feel lost and overwhelmed.

If the person you have lost was the one you relied upon to make financial and investment decisions, you have been compelled to assume *sudden responsibility*. You must now begin to learn things you never needed to know before, when you had an in-house expert.

If you always had someone to tell you whether it was better to buy or lease a car, how much mortgage you could afford, and what investments were best, you may feel like you are in a precarious position, with many potential mistakes to be made. For the record, you will make mistakes. Everyone does. You might choose a losing investment now and then, although if you avoid the common investment mistakes listed in the Appendix, it shouldn't happen very often. When it does happen, you'll just sell it and go on, and you'll learn not to keep looking back with regret. You might even choose a mortgage and then find out another bank had a lower rate. But if you received a good rate that met your requirements, you shouldn't worry about what other offers are available.

Immediate Decisions/Actions

You should seek to learn three main things during your DFZ:

1. What your family's financial assets are and what debts, if any, need to be paid on a regular basis or in a lump sum, and when.

2. How much you will have to live on in the immediate future and in the long run.

3. How much you are spending now and what changes, if any, will be necessary in the way you live in order to match your future expenses to your future income.

Reviewing the Family Assets

Document what stocks, bonds, bank accounts, real estate, partnerships, retirement plans (such as IRAs, Keoghs, and pension plans), and insurance both of you own, either separately or jointly. Here's a list of what to look for when compiling your list.

- Bank statements, checkbooks, canceled checks, savings accounts, and money market records. For example, payments to an insurance company, brokerage firm, or another bank may lead to other assets that you may not have known about. Payments to a lawyer or an accountant will identify advisors who will be able to tell you about your husband's will or his finances. Payments to a bank may reveal a safe deposit box.

- Homeowner's insurance policies may include a list of family valuables that are under insurance coverage.

- If your husband was an officer, director, or owner of 5% or more of a publicly held company, there are forms (SEC 13D, Nos. 3 and 4) that indicate his securities holdings. You can get copies of these reports by writing to the Securities and Exchange Commission (SEC), Washington, D.C. 20549. Attn: Public Reference.

- Track down any executive or employee pension benefits for which you may be eligible. Ask the personnel department of your husband's company if there was life insurance coverage, a pension, profit-sharing, deferred-compensation, or any other executive savings plans, and if so, what this means to you. Also, find out if payment is due on his salary or commissions, unused vacation or sick pay, and if the company pays a death benefit.

- Check also for IRA and rollover IRA accounts at *former* employers. You may be eligible either now or at some later date for pension or life insurance benefits that your husband earned at previous companies. If he worked for the federal government or if he served in the Armed Services, contact the Office of Personnel Management in Washington, D.C., or the nearest Veterans Administration office to see if you are eligible for benefits from them. Again, you will need death certificates.

  There are many alternative ways to take pension benefits: in a lump sum, for example, or as an annuity over longer or shorter time periods. Each has its own income tax consequences. Before deciding to take your benefits, make sure you know your investment options. Take the time to consult your accountant and investment advisor.

- If your husband had his own business, you, your accountant, and your planner should review its *financial statements* in addition to checking tax returns. There should be a profit and loss (i.e., income and expense) statement for each quarter, or at least annually, and a balance sheet to reflect assets, liabilities, and capital (i.e., retained net earnings). These reports are not hard to understand, and it's easy to get help with them if you need it.

- If your husband was covered by *social security,* you are probably entitled to a one-time lump sum settlement death benefit of $255 to help with funeral expenses plus monthly support of any of his children up to age 18. If you are over 60, you can start to collect retirement benefits on a reduced basis or wait until 65 and collect full benefits. If you work and your earnings are above a minimum level, retirement benefits will be reduced until you stop working or until you reach age 70. If you are eligible for retirement or child support, apply to your nearest Social Security office immediately after your husband's death. Don't expect the Social Security Service to make up monthly payments for a period you didn't file. You will simply lose the rights to that money.

Tax Returns Are Valuable Sources

It is not uncommon for assets to go unclaimed or lost because they were not claimed before a deadline. This can easily happen when you are in the throes of grief and trying to work your way through settling your spouse's estate. Periodically, state governments will publish lists of unclaimed assets: retirement plans left with companies, bank accounts, tax refunds, and real estate interest. The best way to search for this information is your tax returns. If you don't know where the copies are in the house, ask your accountant or get an IRS form 4506: *Request for Copy of Tax Return,* from your nearest regional IRS office. Each return will cost you $5.00.

Retitling Assets

Although ownership of property held jointly with right of survivorship by law passes directly to the survivor, that passage is not necessarily automatic. If your joint accounts are temporarily frozen, you should ask your bank about the procedures for *un*freezing them.

You should have the title or registration changed for your house and any other real estate. All brokerage accounts registered in both names or in your husband's name should be corrected as well. The same goes for your real estate title insurance, homeowner's insurance, and auto insurance.

Change the ownership on any other jointly held assets, including the family car and credit cards, to your own name. A death certificate will be required for each institution that you have to deal with. The credit card company may ask you to file a new application and may reduce your line of credit. Destroy any credit cards that were issued in your spouse's name.

Notify Social Security

Your next step is to notify the nearest Social Security office of your husband's death. Bring with you a certified copy of the death certificate, your marriage certificate, a birth certificate, and the Social Security numbers of your husband and everyone in the family who is eligible for support. Include your husband's name, address, and approximate income in the year of his death. You can get a statement of the earnings credited to your husband's account by calling your local Social Security office and asking for an SSA-7704 Form, which is a request for this information. Even if you start on this immediately, it may still take several months for any Social Security payments to arrive.

Notify Each Insurance Company

Life insurance may be one of your first and main sources of money after your spouse's death. Insurance companies generally pay benefits promptly. If you or your children are the named beneficiaries in any of your spouse's life insurance policies, you should immediately notify each insurance company. Contact them directly or with the help of your insurance agent or financial advisor. You will receive a claim form which will tell you what information is needed to support your claim. You will need an original of the death certificate, and you may need other items, depending on the insurance company.

- If there is an insurance death benefit to which you are entitled, you will have to decide how you want to be paid by the insurance company. Most policies offer four options:

  1. You may take the full amount as a lump sum immediately. Most companies will send you a lump sum unless you specify another option.

  2. You may leave the money with the company and receive only the interest on it. Many companies will allow you to retain the right to receive as much of the principal as you want when you want it. That is an important right, and you should not settle for less because it assures you of liquidity in what would otherwise amount to a frozen investment.

  3. You can receive an annuity that will provide a fixed income throughout the rest of your life. Be forewarned that as the years go by, inflation may reduce the value and purchasing power of that income. Also, the benefit ends with your death.

  4. You can receive fixed amounts over a specified period of time, depending upon your needs, until the proceeds are exhausted. Inflation may reduce the value and purchasing power of that income and this benefit ends with your death.

- If you don't need the money immediately, you can notify the insurance company that you want to leave the money earning interest for the time being and will make a final decision later. Before you make that decision, be sure that the rate of interest you will receive is at least as good as you would get in any other money market fund.

Review Liabilities

Review and document the family's liabilities and what each of you owes to others (e.g., mortgages, car loans, or other debts of any kind). Give this list to your financial planner, who will prioritize it with you and create a plan for addressing each item.

Probate

Probate is the process required by law for court supervision of transfer of assets from the decedent (the person who died) to the inheritors under the will, after all creditors are paid off. It is carried out under the local court system and varies from state to state. No matter how simple the will and estate, no matter how well prepared the widow or how expert her attorneys, probate will probably take more time and cost more than you expect. If property is located in several states, it may be necessary to file for probate in each of them, which will add to delays and expenses. Most estates must go through probate, but if you plan in advance, with the use of life insurance and trusts, you can avoid it.

The probate process is as follows:

- The court appoints a personal representative (usually the person named in the will). If there is no will, an extreme circumstance, the court usually appoints the nearest living relative. The personal representative is responsible for taking control of the assets of the estate. This includes keeping financial accounts, paying debts and taxes, distributing assets to the inheritors as called for in the will, or if there is no will as specified under state law, and filing all necessary reports.

- To do this, the personal representative needs to obtain a taxpayer identification number for the estate; open estate checking, savings, and brokerage accounts as needed; transfer titles to all estate assets, and obtain a valuation for all assets. The personal representative is also responsible for paying the decedent's final medical bills and for filing claims and collecting on any medical insurance policies and/or Medicare. An outside personal representative almost certainly will be entitled to a substantial fee.

■ If you are the personal representative, you will need to hire an accountant to prepare the estate tax return and an attorney to help with legal procedures. The tax to be filed includes returns for federal and state income taxes for both the decedent and the estate, the federal estate tax, and the state inheritance tax.

■ All claims against the estate, both by creditors and by any disgruntled or disappointed potential heirs, must be settled during probate. For this reason, the personal representative is generally required to publish notices in the newspaper for all creditors to make their claims. Legal notice must be given also to all those named in the will as well as all others who might have a claim against the estate.

■ Within a specified period, the personal representative must file with the court, an inventory and appraisal of the value at death of all the assets of the deceased as well as periodic reports of what has been done with them (i.e., whether they have sold or otherwise liquidated, or distributed). In addition, the personal representative must eventually distribute all of the assets to the beneficiaries as directed by the will. Probate may take six to nine months for an uncomplicated small estate. If the estate is large, which is defined as more than $675,000, probate may go on for several years.

What Do I Do during That Time?

While many of the assets of an estate will remain tied up until the estate is settled, the personal representative may permit you to draw out limited amounts immediately for urgent needs. Some jurisdictions limit the amount that can be drawn, and larger amounts require court approval. Some states allow for a family allowance of several thousand dollars that can be paid immediately and that has priority over payment to creditors other than the funeral home.

If your completed Reality Check demonstrates that you won't need all of the assets of the estate for your own livelihood, you may want to consider what is called a *disclaimer of part or all of your husband's estate*. This allows the disclaimed portion of the estate to go directly to someone else, presumably your children or a trust, rather than to your own estate. This step can bring significant tax savings, especially if your husband did not plan your estate carefully. However, this is also a special situation requiring technical study and professional advice.

If No Assets Are Subject to Probate

If your assets consist of insurance to a named beneficiary, assets held jointly, or assets held in a living trust, estate and income tax returns must be filed within a few months.

Death Certificates

One of the deceptively simple questions you will be asked by the funeral director is how many copies of the death certificate you want. Most widows underestimate this number because they do not realize how many parties are going to need a copy. Though you can purchase additional copies, it will add extra time to the already lengthy process of settling all aspects of the estate. In case you weren't counting, I have already mentioned at least five parties who will need a death certificate. I suggest you get a dozen to cover unexpected items.

Medical Coverage

If you were covered under your spouse's group health plan, you need to find your own medical coverage. If your spouse worked for a private company with more than 20 employees, you and your minor children can continue to be covered under that plan for up to three years, but at your own expense. Widows of employees of the federal government and many state and local governments have similar protection. This group coverage is far better that you can arrange on your own. If you are over 65, you should be able to get a "medi-gap" policy to cover most of the medical and hospital expenses not paid by Medicare. A few strong companies pay all of such expenses.

Congress, of course, may change the whole landscape of medical insurance. In the meantime, if you purchase medical insurance of any kind, be sure to get at least two proposals. Life insurance on your own life, which might not have been necessary before your spouse's death, may now be vital for protection of your estate against taxation.

- Your own will should be reviewed with your attorney to make sure it reflects your new status as a single person and all of your own personal wishes for your estate. This review should also check the agreement of your will with existing plans for your estate.

- You should then consider other necessary legal documents needed to provide care for yourself and your family in case of a catastrophe. A power of attorney or a living trust will permit someone to act for you if you are ill or incapacitated and cannot act for yourself. A living will can indicate your wishes if you should become terminally ill.

Review Your Husband's Investments

Many a wealthy widow has found her assets nearly wiped out at the collapse of her husband's favorite type of investment. Even if your husband was a successful and sound investor and left all of your combined funds fully invested, you will want to review these investments in the light of current economic conditions, changing tax laws, and your own particular circumstances.

Your husband may have preferred trading in special stocks, even speculating in the stock market, which obviously involves considerable time and risk. Unless you have a great deal of experience you may lack the temperament and skills for this kind of investing. If you can't carry on your husband's investment philosophy, don't turn around and invest with the first person who comes along with what sounds like a good idea.

Here are two potential investment problems for widows:

1. They stay too long in investments that were chosen by their husbands.

2. They fall into the clutches of a salesperson unfamiliar with their financial needs.

To avoid both, you need to learn something about the investment field for yourself and find someone trustworthy to advise you.

Your Children and Your Investments

Many widows who totally relied on their husbands when it came to money matters turn hastily to reliance on their adult children. This can be a bad idea no matter how good the family relationship is.

There is, potentially, a conflict of interest. You may need current income to live on, yet your children benefit if the estate grows larger during your lifetime. These different objectives require different kinds of investments.

On the other hand, if you are fortunate enough to have more than you will need for your lifetime, you will be able to give away more to your heirs (thereby avoiding heavy estate taxes) when you die. Your children might be reluctant to suggest this, or you might resist their suggestions. If you are on top of your financial situation yourself, or if you have an outside advisor whose advice you respect, you will be in a better position to make the right decision.

It is okay, if you wish, to listen to the advice of your children and others, but don't substitute that advice for a financial planner whom you trust. Read, study, take courses, and listen to tapes. Learn so that you understand what is going on and can judge the advice you receive. Remember, it's your money. With solid financial planning, you can take charge of your life by taking care of your financial future.

A Note on Taxes

Everyone is entitled to give away a tax-free amount of money called the *unified credit*. At this writing, that amount is $675,000. Married couples can give each other any amount of money during life or at death without taxation. This is called the *unlimited marital deduction.*

You are not likely to have any estate taxes due as you settle your spouse's estate due the unlimited marital deduction. However, you might have income taxes due. Your accountant will be an important member of your professional team. Income taxes may be owed on income that your spouse is due but has not received, on stock options that must be exercised, and on retirement assets or deferred compensation plans.

An estate tax return must be filed, usually within nine months, and the last joint income tax return will be due by April 15 of the year following the death. Your accountant will also help you determine if you should be making quarterly income tax payments. Even if making quarterly payments is not new to you, the amount may have changed and adjustments may need to be made.

Conclusion

Getting through the first year after the loss of your spouse is probably the hardest thing you will ever have to do. Emotionally, it is grueling; financially, it can be very overwhelming.

Take your time. Find out everything you need to make decisions for yourself. With the help of a good therapist or support group and a financial planner who understands what you are going through, you will do what is necessary and begin to heal.

Insurance Settlements

Money that comes from the settlement of a lawsuit is hardly a joyous windfall. Most of the time, this money is a recovery for damages, pain, suffering, and loss. It has probably taken many years of legal battling to secure your settlement. While getting the money might be nice, the real blessing is to have the matter over with so you can go on with your life.

Going on with your life, however, may not be so simple. You will need to make far-reaching investment decisions while simultaneously dealing with psychological and possibly physical pain. You may have a permanent disability, you may have become the caregiver for a family member who has been permanently injured, or you may be still suffering the effects of a tragic loss such as the death of a child or a spouse.

The emotional landscape is as important as the financial landscape. It is normal to see the financial component as more important and to give your attention and energy to the financial planning that is required. Because it is more factual, it may seem like safer ground, but your finances do not exist in isolation of your emotions.

The Emotional Landscape

It will be helpful if you keep in mind that emotional damage as well as physical damage may have occurred. You need to be aware of the effects of the pain, exhaustion, and uncertainty that you and your family may be experiencing.

The People Involved

Frequently, there are many individuals whose emotions need to be considered as a result of the event that made the insurance settlement necessary. While the victim or victims have obviously been affected, so have the caregiver and the rest of the family. If you are dealing with a long-term disability or illness, the person providing the ongoing daily care becomes a key person to consider and provide for. This person, called the *primary caregiver,* will be critical to the comfort and possibly the physical improvement of the injured party over the years. It is a tough job, and one that needs to be paid attention to and managed as part of the injured person's care.

If the primary caregiver is a family member, such as a spouse, a parent, or a sibling, it is easy to overlook their needs and take them for granted. They will need periodic breaks from caregiving, maybe certain days off each week or short vacations. Backup caregivers or teams should be identified and trained to step in and take over for the primary caregiver.

Along with the injured party and the primary caregiver, the other members of the family and the support team also need to be considered. They, too, will have emotional and other consequences as a result of the accident or the event that created the settlement. Their feelings may not have been addressed, because until now, everyone involved was in crisis mode while the legal battles continued. After the settlement, the brave fronts may disappear, and the quiet co-existence may begin to unravel. This may be the time to start or resume therapy.

Too Exhausted to Care

It is likely that you are exhausted and that you just want to rest and wake up to find out that what you have been through was just a bad dream. In Phase One, I discussed the need for a Bliss List to begin the goal-setting process. But I also advised you to do this exercise once the emotions of the Sudden Money event start to settle down. At this point in your life, a Bliss List may not seem very important, or it may even feel impossible. Many people in your position report that they are too exhausted to know or to care about what their passions and goals are; they just want to find a way to live with the circumstances they now have to confront.

Take your time and be gentle with yourself; there will be plenty of time to put your money to work later. If you are exhausted and overwhelmed, it is better to keep your money safe at the beginning and think about investing later.

Not Knowing What Your Goals Are

Once you are ready to meet with a financial advisor, they can help you to clarify your goals and needs. As you discuss your situation with a financial planner or with other advisors, they should be listening carefully and be able to pick out the things that are important to you.

Maggie was pregnant when her husband was killed in an industrial accident. Five years later, she received a very large settlement, but she didn't have a clue about what to do with it. She had continued to work since the accident because she needed to support herself and her daughter. Maggie intended to keep working even though the settlement money would allow her to never work again.

When Maggie met with her financial planner, she said she didn't need the money and wouldn't know what to do with it. After all, she was doing fine financially. But during their meeting, Maggie mentioned five separate things she would like to do someday:

- Provide for her daughter's financial security and education
- Go back to school herself and finish an advanced degree
- Give financial assistance to the people who helped her through her very rough times
- Find a way to help other women who have gone through similar tragedies
- Take a long and wonderful vacation with her daughter

Maggie's planner took copious notes during the meeting and read them back to Maggie. Maggie soon realized that she had dreams for her life that could be realized as a result of the settlement money. Although she didn't need the money to survive, she could use it to become fulfilled.

Maggie's planner worked with her to develop the particulars for each goal, including how much would be needed and how long it would be before she needed it. This goal-setting process helped Maggie focus on building a future for herself and her daughter, and on helping others outside her family. She found it to be a big step toward healing her broken heart.

The Chute of Emotions

Between the time the injury occurred and the settlement was reached, you may have experienced a number of different emotions. Some of them will continue as you progress in your healing process.

Numbness

It is not uncommon to feel numb and to feel guilty about being too numb to take action and make investment decisions. No one can tell you how long you will feel this way, and no one but you can heal the wounds that are the source of your numbness and fatigue. Furthermore, no one but you will have to live with the results of the financial decisions you make. Therefore, it is better to make only the most essential decisions and to let the investment decisions wait until the healing has begun.

Pain

Many people who receive insurance settlements are still in pain when they reach the end of the settlement battle. For some people, the pain is physical, caused by an accident or by improper medical treatment. For others, the pain is emotional. Frequently, it is both. The intense emotions that dominate the legal battles, combined with the reality of the loss or of years of caregiving, are too much for many families. Divorce is common, and estrangement of siblings or children is also unfortunately common. Therapy is the answer for many families. (Note that therapy for marital problems is different from therapy for kids who have been traumatized. Do your homework.)

It is good to start therapy immediately and to continue it as is needed. Once the settlement is reached, you'd think the strain would be over and the anguish would go away, but it can also be reignited or take a surprising turn. It makes sense to again use the services of a professional therapist to deal with what comes up during settlement time. Families that can take the strain frequently become closer. Tragedy can either pull a family apart or bring it closer together.

Envy of "Easy Money"

To outsiders, receiving a large financial settlement may seem like a wonderful thing, and some people may be envious of your new financial position. But they have no way of knowing what anguish it has cost you and what pain still lies ahead for you. Envy is much like invalidation. It seems to be saying: "But you got all this money; yeah, it was difficult, but now you are rich!" As you know, financial awards for misfortune are not the *rewards* they are thought to be.

To deal with the envious, I suggest you make a point of keeping your finances private. Try not to discuss how much things cost, how your investments are doing, how much you paid in taxes, or how much income you now have. There seems to be a natural tendency to be fascinated with other people's money, particularly if those other people are perceived to be rich. It is best to avoid these misinformed people, but family members are often the worst offenders and are difficult to avoid. The best way to deal with nosy people you can't otherwise avoid is to keep a low profile and not talk about your money.

Fear of the Unknown

Until the settlement happened, you probably had the fear that there *would not be* a settlement, and that somehow your case would be lost. Now that you have your judgment or your settlement, you may fear the unknowns that lie ahead, particularly anything having to do with your money. Though you now know how much you have recovered, you have no way of knowing the future costs of medical expenses, lost employment, and caregiving. Consequently, you may not know how long your money will last and if you will have enough to cover future expenses.

Questions to be pondered now are:

- Will you ever go back to work?
- Will your caregiver be physically and emotionally able to care for you long term?

- What would you do if something happened to the caregiver?

- Will the money be enough to support your needs for life, or will it run out someday?

- How do you want to use the money if medical expenses and caregiving are not required?

- How are you going to make the money last?

Many of these questions, whether they are related to fears, or not, are what will become your planning issues. They should be discussed with your planner, who should be able to demystify them by applying your numbers to them.

The Major Planning Issue

The toughest of the aforementioned issues are the unknown costs for medical, home care, nursing home care, medications, physical therapy, and the other items not covered by insurance. If these unknowns exist for you, the best way to plan for them is to keep your fixed and discretionary expenses as low as possible. By choosing to spend less money on your lifestyle, you allow more of your settlement money to grow and build for possible future needs. If the amount you have received is modest compared with the expenses you face now or may face in the future, limit the income you take from the investments.

There will undoubtedly be many costs that you cannot foresee, and there will be costs not covered by your insurance that you feel are necessary for your continued progress. The settlement may seem high to you at first, but it might not go as far as you would like it to go. The idea, once again, is to be very careful spending the money, because you have no idea what your needs will be years from now.

TAX-FREE VERSUS TAXABLE SETTLEMENT MONEY How you receive the money from the insurance company will determine whether your income is taxable or tax-free. This point is so important that it is worth reviewing, even though your attorneys undoubtedly drilled this into you. The *settlement money* received as a result of injury is *not taxable*. However, if you received a lump sum amount and invest that money, *the earnings* (i.e., interest, dividends, and capital gains) *are taxable*. The lump sum is not taxed, but the income it produces is taxed.

If you opted to take your settlement as an annuity, the income received is *not taxable*. The annuity income is still considered settlement money received because of an injury. It is possible that your settlement is a combination of an annuity and a lump sum. In this case, the annuity income will be excluded from taxes, and the investment income from your investments you bought with the lump sum will be taxed.

DISABILITY INCOME INSURANCE If you were covered by a disability income insurance policy at the time of the incident, you may still be receiving monthly benefits. Your settlement money, in the form of either a lump sum or an annuity, will not alter your eligibility for this income. If your policy was paid for by an employer, your income is taxable and will remain so after the settlement. If your policy was privately owned, the income is tax-free and continues to be tax-free.

It is likely that your disability income will stop at age 65. Be sure you develop a plan to replace this income. The plan should identify how much money you will need at age 65 to reproduce your disability income, and it should factor in annual increases to keep it rising with inflation. The plan should also identify what money will be allocated as replacement money. Your retirement plan money is a good choice, as is a portion of your lump sum. Your investment plan should address the specific needs of this sum of money and should not treat it as part of your portfolio, being managed to provide current income and growth.

If neither lump sum nor retirement plan money is available, then your only choice is to save a portion of your annuity income and monthly disability income. This may be a challenge if your income is low compared with your expenses. However difficult it is, it is necessary, not optional. If your disability income is important income and it will stop some day, you must have a plan to replace it.

SOCIAL SECURITY If you are permanently disabled and you will qualify for social security disability income, you should understand that it, too, ends when you reach 65. This income, however, is replaced by regular social security. Again, if this is important income, pay attention to the proposed changes in the social security system. It is possible that the amount, the age qualification, or how the money is managed, will change over time.

RETIREMENT MONEY If you are unable to work and continue to contribute to your retirement savings, carefully consider your long-term needs before you start to withdraw money from your retirement savings. If you are permanently disabled and under age 59½, you may be able to take money out of your 401(k), IRA, and other retirement plans without paying the 10% early withdrawal penalty. But you will still owe income tax on the full amount taken out. When you take the money out of these plans, you will also lose the tax-deferred growth.

If at all possible, keep the money set aside for retirement invested for your long-term needs. You are probably unsure of what your future expenses will be, and this money may be needed down the road. It behooves you to keep it growing tax-deferred for as long as you can.

A Final Word on Not-So-Easy Money

The receipt of an insurance settlement pushes you into circumstances that you would not ever have chosen. But now you must become a good steward of the money you have received and make money management a part of your life. If you have chosen an annuity payment that will last for life, you need to manage your expenses. If you have received a lump sum of money in addition to, or as an alternative to, a life annuity, you have investment and tax responsibilities to get used to. The two key points are to take your time and find the right advisor to work with. You have the time, and there are many financial planners around the country to help you.

Winning the Lottery

Many people purchase lottery tickets each week because they think: If I could win this X million dollars, all of my problems would be solved. But money cannot protect you from life's disappointments and frustrations: You will still feel pain when you lose a loved one; you probably will not be healthier than you were before; and you won't be any more (genuinely) loved and respected. What you will find as a result of your instant money is that a whole new world of opportunities and problems has been opened up to you. To make the most of the opportunities, you have to be able to avoid the problems. And to successfully avoid many of the problems, you have to know what they are. Here is that crucial information.

All Eyes Are on You

Winning the lottery is not usually a quiet, private event. Your win probably made the local news. Perhaps it also made the national news. When the national lottery, Powerball, gets high like it did one spring when the jackpot grew to $200 million, the entire country waits to see who will win. When an Illinois couple won that $200 million Powerball and celebrated by buying drinks for everyone at their local bar, people across America watched the footage of the celebration on their evening news. There was probably much lounge chair speculation about how the couple would handle their new fortune based on one short clip of them toasting their win. For a few days this couple had celebrity status, and their personal lives were judged by many who knew them and by millions who didn't.

Today this blue-collar family has moved to an upscale community. They live behind a security gate, have an unlisted phone number, and they are being sued by the friends who bought the winning ticket for them. They are sharing their lottery money with their kids, as long as the kids work. Friends say they are generous, quietly giving money to many people. For years to come, probably for the rest of their lives, the media will periodically run stories on this family.

The reality is that everyone will have an opinion about you and the way you choose to live. Living in a fishbowl may be glamorous at first, but it quickly becomes old and can be treacherous. It invites all kinds of unwanted people, opinions, and advice into your life. It is a good time to "circle the wagons" and form a tight inner circle of family and advisors. If you have a personal attorney, financial planner, and accountant, you will be able to minimize most of the initial stress by letting everyone know that your team of professionals has everything under control. All media requests and solicitations should go through your advisors, not directly to you. Unfortunately, most winners do not have established relationships with such a group of personal advisors. (See Chapter 5, "Search for the Right Financial Planner." You can find other advisors using that process as a guide.)

You Have Become Every Salesperson's Dream

If your win has received publicity, you may be hounded by people selling everything from luxury real estate to cars to investments. Most experienced and aggressive salespeople know how vulnerable you are immediately after winning. They will try to make it seem quite natural for you to buy flashy things or make exotic investments now that you are rich. They are hoping to get to you before you hire your team of advisors and before you discover that *it is far from the norm for people with real wealth to impulsively spend money on luxury items or to ever jump into exotic investments.*

The Chute of Emotions

Greed and Entitlement

Some of the people you should be wary of, unfortunately, are your friends and family, many of whom might treat you like the goose that laid the golden egg. You might be asked or expected to support parents or children, and you'll probably be approached for loans of all kinds. Remember that money is the topic of many family quarrels. Family disputes and the often permanent alienation that follows are phenomena common among lottery winners. However, there is a way to try to prevent such tragedies.

If someone bought the ticket for you and they feel entitled to share in the winnings, address their claim up front. Don't just let it go, chances are very good it won't just go away. Hire an attorney to represent you, and understand your rights and obligations. Stay in control and don't let the other person or the attorney talk you into something you really do not believe is right. It is in your best interest to settle the disagreement quickly. The longer it takes, the more expensive it will be both financially and emotionally.

You will be asked for money either as a loan or outright gift. It is possible you'll be asked to put up the money for someone to start a business or to help save a failing business. Generally speaking it is better to give than to loan. An unpaid loan sits between friends until it is paid. Many lottery winners regret having loaned money to friends who did not pay back the money and the friendship was damaged as a result. If you want to help someone, meet with your financial advisor to decide how much you can give away without harming your financial future. Then give with an open heart.

Funding a business or bailing out a failed enterprise can be far more involved than you imagine. If you are not experienced in business it is a good idea to pass on the opportunity.

Elation and the Spending Spree

When you win the lottery, the initial emotion you feel is usually elation, which leads to some form of celebration. You might feel all-powerful, able to use your new money to make changes for yourself, your family, and maybe the entire world. But be careful. What begins as a quiet, private celebration of good fortune often moves to the local luxury car dealership, and everyone gets a new car.

Although buying drinks or dinner for your friends and paying off your credit cards are normal initial reactions, an immediate spending spree is not a great idea. Though you may feel you deserve to splurge, you also deserve to get to enjoy the benefit of your new money for decades to come. A serious spending spree may limit your choices. *It is important to find out just how much money you have after taxes and what kind of income this after-tax amount can produce before you purchase anything.*

A large spending spree wiped out one man's entire retirement plans. He bought new houses and took all of his friends on a gambling cruise. No doubt everyone had a lot of fun. But when it was time to use the money to produce income so he could quit his job, he was out of luck. Let's look at some numbers.

If you were to win a $2 million lottery that paid out a lump sum, you would have to pay $800,000 in federal income tax and maybe another $100,000 in state income taxes. That leaves your after-tax winnings at $1.1 million. If you spent $300,000 on a house and $100,000 taking 10 friends on a cruise and gambling, you now have only $700,000 left.

If you wanted to quit your job and live off of your lottery money, you would have between $35,000 and $50,000 per year, *before taxes,* to live on. Even if your previous income was in that range, you could still be short since the new house would cost more in taxes and upkeep. Without the big spending, you would have the full $1.1 million to live on, providing you with between $55,000 and $77,000 for retirement income per year. This extra $20,000 per year in retirement income would allow you many important extras throughout your retirement years, such as more vacations and a nicer home without financial worries.

My Recommendations

Before you do anything with your new money, you should create a Bliss List (including an amount that covers the shopping you plan to do). Only after you and your advisor have done Reality Checks that take into account inflation, taxes, and any debt you have, will you know how much you really have to play with.

Do your fantasy spending on paper first, as you may find that you really don't want all of the things on the list once the exuberance wears off. Even if you have won so much money that you can buy anything and everything you ever thought you wanted, these purchases may be less important to you over time. One lottery winner, on the suggestion of his girlfriend, bought enough clothes to fill all of his closets. Several months later, his brother's financial planner stopped by to see him, and found the clothes were still in the closets with the tags still on. Eventually, he moved out of town to a place where no one knew about the lottery win. He left his notoriety—and the closets full of clothes with the tags still on—behind.

Spending Plan

Lotteries pay either a lump sum amount or equal payments over 20 or 30 years. Either way, you will have to determine how much you can spend each month by developing a cash management system based upon long-term income projections. Even if you have won tens of millions of dollars, you need to set some limits on your spending. Think about it: If you have $15 million and you spend and give away $2 million per year, you will eventually run out of money. Spending $2 million per year is not unheard of when the winner has never gotten a handle on the basics of money management.

The best approach when creating a spending plan is to set up a fixed monthly income with the help of your financial planner. That monthly income can be spent on anything you want without guilt or worry. The Bliss List and Reality Check exercises as outlined in Chapters 6 and 7 show you *how to determine* what amount you are free to spend each month without worrying about jeopardizing your future security. A true spending plan accounts for future income needs, as well as emergency or unexpected large expenses. You need to feel secure that your income will keep pace with inflation and that you have set aside some money to handle any large expense that comes up.

Replacement Plan

If your lottery payments are going to end in 20 or 30 years, you need to have a plan to replace the income. Not having a plan is a classic mistake that usually ends with the winner running out of money long before the end of the road. The strategy is to set aside enough money from each payment to fund your replacement plan. How much you need to set aside depends on how much other money and retirement income you will have. If the lottery is your only income, then you must put roughly half the annual after-tax amount into the replacement plan from the very first year. If you won the lottery a few years ago, then you need to set aside more than half to make up for the years that were missed. The roughly half estimate comes from the following assumptions:

A $10 million win would pay you $500,000 per year for 20 years. After taxes, you would have $300,000 per year. If you invested $150,000 (one-half of your lottery income) every year for 20 years and averaged 12% on your investments, you would have $12 million.

If you took an investment income based upon 6% a year you would have $720,000 per year, which replaces your lottery money and adjusts for an assumed inflation rate of 2%. If the rate of return and inflation are higher or lower, your results will be different. For this reason, it is important to check on the progress of your replacement plan each year.

Watch Out for Debt

In the beginning, it may be hard to believe that you could ever have money problems again, but it is possible—and probable—if you don't get your spending and replacement plans laid out right from the start.

When a lottery winning is received in annual payments over 20 or 30 years, it is common to get into debt as a result of a spending spree that gets out of hand and is done on credit. This becomes likely because your guaranteed lottery income qualifies you to borrow high amounts of money.

If you get into the frenzy of limitless spending, particularly buying a new home (or homes) and furnishings, you may exceed your lottery income for the first year. Rather than waiting for the next check to come, you might put the purchases on credit. When the second check comes, part of it is already needed to pay off last year's debt. If the same overspending occurs each year and more debt is added, it won't be long before you need to be bailed out.

Getting bailed out is not easy once the debt is excessive. The funds available to pay off the debt have a limit and come in once a year. The responsible way to deal with the debt is to cut back your living expenses and perhaps go back to work until the debts are cleared up. However, for most people who have developed lavish lifestyles, this is not an easy thing to do.

The Lottery Buyout

If the lottery money is your only resource and your income potential if you go back to work is low compared with the amount of debt you have incurred, then you become a candidate for a lottery buyout. There are several companies that buy your rights to the annual lottery income in exchange for a one-time lump sum of money. The catch is that the amount of the lump sum is substantially discounted.

If you have chosen to receive your payout as a series of payments, you may be offered a lump sum buyout. Until recently, many lotteries only offered the series of payments, but now that most offer a choice of a lump sum or the payment, the lump sum payment is the strong favorite. According to the Lottery Commission of the State of Florida, when they first started to offer the lump sum option, 55 out of the next 66 winners chose the lump sum. Even when the lump sum is deeply discounted, it seems to be human nature to want to be paid now, rather than later.

Winners receiving payments cannot go back to the state or Powerball and change their minds about how they receive their money, but they can sell their payments to a third party in exchange for a single lump sum. Selling your future payments may or may not be a good idea. The lottery buyout company will offer you a discount amount that is typically based upon the current interest rates.

Ryan and Molly had 15 more annual payments of $118,000 for a total of $1,770,000. The lottery buyout company offered them $1,040,000 (after tax they would have about $624,000). If they were able to invest the full amount for 15 years and they averaged a 10% return they would have $2,606,000. But if they needed to live on this money, as well as let it grow, they would find it challenging to outperform the guaranteed payments. If they dropped their income to $60,000 a year and managed a 12% annual return their money would last another 25 years—ten years longer than the lottery payments.

If you are considering a buyout offer, make sure you are willing to take the risk of the uncertainty of the investments you would be using. Some of the buyout companies are very aggressive, so don't let yourself be pressured; this is an irreversible decision. You may also encounter brokers who will assure you they can get the kind of returns you will need to make the buyout worthwhile. If the numbers work while assuming average rates of return, then it might be worth your consideration. If above-average returns are required, then spend some time thinking about the risk you are about to take.

The Carpenters won the $10 million lottery, which paid $500,000 each year for 20 years after taxes. They had already collected three years of lottery income and had 17 more payments to go. So they had a guarantee of $8.5 million, paid out over 17 years.

Any time you exchange an annuity payout over many years for a one-time lump sum, the amount of the lump sum will be less than the total of the annual income stream. The question is: How much less, and what will you do with the money that will make it worth taking such a steep discount?

Lottery buyout companies will let you sell specific years of income. So if the Carpenters needed $980,000 to pay off their debts, they could sell the next five years of income for $1.7 million, or years 13 through 20 for the same amount. The reason it would take seven years in the second example is that the buyout company has to wait longer to get paid back. Therefore, the $980,000 they need will cost $3.5 million, rather than $2.5 million of lottery payments. It is a time-value-of-money issue: The longer the company has to wait for their money to be paid back, the greater the return they will require on their money.

In the Carpenters case, it makes more sense for them to sell the next five years, because they are ready to do the necessary cutbacks and both return to work for 10 more years. They had hired a financial planner to work out a plan to help them establish long-term financial security. They realized that while they had really messed up, they still had a shot at being well-off as a result of their winning. This was the game plan:

■ Cut back on spending and go back to work for 10 years.

■ Use the bailout money to pay off all their debts.

■ Put 100% into a long-term investment plan when lottery payments resumed (in five years).

- Retire in 10 years.

- Save two-thirds of the remaining seven lottery payments, and live on the remaining one-third.

- Use the money in the long-term investment account to replace the lottery income they had been spending once the payments stop.

The planner projected that the Carpenters would not be able to replace the entire annual lottery amount, because they had not saved any of the lottery money for the first eight years. Even though they began saving 100% for five years and 66% for seven years, losing the growth on the money for those first eight years cut into their potential to fully replace the lottery income.

Note: Where most people go wrong with a lottery buyout is that they do not work out a recovery plan as the Carpenters did. Lottery buyout companies see the same people coming back for additional bailout money over and over until there are no more payments to sell. The next step is personal bankruptcy.

Taxes

Contrary to what you might have heard, *there is no way to avoid paying tax on lottery money.* Even if you give it all away to charity, you will still owe some taxes. When you give money to a qualified charity, you get a *deduction,* but it is *not* worth the full amount of the gift. So before you gift it away, make sure you will have enough to pay the remaining tax.

Federal Income Tax

The real story is that when you receive your money, 20% will be withheld for federal income taxes. You might owe additional taxes and you should meet with a specialist to find out how much more you owe, if anything. Your accountant can arrange quarterly tax payments, and tell you how much you owe each year (the amount can fluctuate).

If you receive your money in annual payments, you need to set the money aside for the necessary quarterly payments. Setting it aside means putting it into a money market account or other very conservative, interest-paying investment. The monthly interest on a large amount of money will add up. If you were to pay the tax before it was due just to get it taken care of, you would lose the interest it could have been earning for you.

State Income Tax

A popular strategy among high-income and high-net-worth individuals is to move to states that don't have state income tax. If you *win* the lottery while living in a state that has high state income tax and *then move* to a state with no income tax, you will have to *properly establish your residency in the new state.* This can become a rather technical matter and should be done with legal advice. After all, your old home state will not be happy about losing the tax on your winnings and may try to prove that you don't really live in the new state. Your old home state will do everything in its power to prove that you should pay taxes to *it*, rather than to your new home state. Establishing residency, or domicile, is different in each state, so do your research.

Note: You cannot establish residency in the new state quickly enough to avoid state taxes on your *initial* payment or on a lump sum payment.

Other Considerations—Estate Planning

If you pass away before you have collected all of your lottery payments, your heirs will continue to receive the payments. Since the money is being paid over several years and the estate taxes are due within nine months of your death, your heirs might have a problem paying the tax. Why? Because the IRS will put present value on the future lottery income and want to tax that amount right away. Therefore, it is necessary to meet with an estate planning attorney and to create a plan to deal with all the various possibilities.

Your new net worth may be high enough that your estate would be subject to estate taxes. Estate taxes are higher than income taxes and in many cases they are easily reduced or eliminated. There is a good chance you have never done any estate planning, most Americans do not even have a will. The arrival of your lottery win has created an even greater need to meet with an estate planning attorney to explore what you can do to minimize the amount of tax your heirs will have to pay before they receive your assets.

Conclusion

Winning a lottery gives your life a new range of possibilities and can be a blessing or a curse. Where your winnings take you depends on how you deal with your new money emotionally and financially. And the direction you're headed in is decided long before you arrive there.

For many people whose experiences were not positive, much of the damage occurred at the beginning of the Sudden Money Process and had its roots in nonfinancial matters. Many simply did not know how to handle the attention and emotions involved, and they were not prepared to make the decisions and set the boundaries that were necessary. You have the benefit of knowing what to expect and how to handle it. It's up to you to make your lottery win something that changed your life for the better.

Athletes and Entertainers

I f you are an athlete or an entertainer who has suddenly been catapulted into a new dimension of fame and wealth, and if it seems
that you have entered a world where all of your dreams can come
true—congratulations! As you may know, only a tiny fraction of
athletes make it to the pros, and an even smaller number make
enough money by the time they retire so that they never have to
work again. Likewise, only a small number of performers become
wealthy practicing their craft.

Like other Sudden Money recipients, you too need to acclimate
yourself to your new circumstances. After all, you are susceptible to
the same dangers as others who get windfalls. For instance, your
Chute of Emotions may be particularly difficult if it consists mostly
of very positive feelings such as elation. Elation is dangerous
because it is often accompanied by very expensive purchases.

This is why your Decision Free Zone (DFZ) is particularly important. If you take the time to process how you feel about your newfound money and, perhaps, your newfound notoriety, you will be
less likely to fall into the traps that have led many before you to
financial ruin.

The Good News

The good news is that if you have made it in your chosen field, you are among a minuscule minority. If you have talent—and sometimes even if you don't—and there is demand for someone like you, your entire life can change overnight.

- Orlando ("El Duque") Hernandez was making about $8 per month as a rehabilitation therapist until he left his native Cuba to play baseball in the United States. In 1998, at 28 years old, he signed a $6.6 million, four-year contract with the New York Yankees.

- Glenn Robinson, the top draft choice of the NBA in 1994, signed a 10-year contract with the Milwaukee Bucks for $68 million. And that was before he ever played a professional game or even graduated from college (he left Purdue after his junior year).

The Bad News—Career Lifespan

The bad news is that it could all end tomorrow. If you are an athlete, you could injure yourself and your career could be over. If you are an entertainer, particularly one without a good contract, public opinion could end your career in an instant, regardless of your talent or abilities.

According to one prominent agent, roughly half of major league ballplayers with salaries of $500,000 or more in the 1980s had little or none of their baseball earnings left four years after they retired.

The Financial Reality

The average salary of players in the National Hockey League is about $1 million (not including income from endorsements and investments), *and the average playing career is 5.5 years.* One million dollars for each of 5.5 years equals $5.5 million gross. Subtract agents' fees and taxes, and you're under $2 million. So let's say you are 32 years old and you have just retired from the NHL. You do not have any endorsement contracts, but you do have a couple of injuries that prevent you from playing on a professional level. You haven't been to college or had any other education outside of hockey, so your biggest earning days *could* be over. You are going to be around for many more decades, and you have $2 million to take you through them.

No matter what amount of money your contract or bonus is for, that is not the amount you will have to save, spend, or invest as you like. For most people in show business and for most highly paid athletes, the fees of agents, business managers, attorneys and CPAs can be 25% of the gross. Then, there's the 40% that will go to the IRS. *That leaves your net amount at 35% of the original amount.*

The Decision Free Zone

The moment word gets out that you have "made it," several new phenomena are likely to occur.

Invitations to Participate in the "Deals of the Century"

Watch out for the "can't lose" business proposition from your brother or your best friend that entails an investment of your cash. Along those lines is investment advice from your sister, unless she is a Certified Financial Planner who is experienced with clients similar to you. Bad investment advice is a veritable epidemic, and the more money you have, and the more visibility you have, the more you will become a target. Include in this category any lender who offers you an enormous loan because you are a good risk given your status. *Don't act on any investments during at least the first six months after you have received your first check.*

Being Treated Like You've Laid a Golden Egg

Unfortunately, in some families, when one member "makes it," a sense of entitlement is spontaneously generated among the other members. Some people might honestly believe that blood relation gives them the right to claim some of your money. Long-lost relatives might suddenly reappear, and those from whom you have been estranged might instantly come to their senses once they have heard of your success.

If your mailbox is flooded with requests for help and if your phone is ringing off the hook, I have two suggestions. The first is to get yourself a new, unpublished phone number and give it out on a need-to-know basis. Second, *do not give anyone any money.* Tell everyone the same thing (the truth), which is that you are not going to make any decisions about your money until your financial advisor tells you exactly how much you have and how long it will last under various scenarios. Furthermore, you need at least a couple of months to let it all sink in, and you don't want to make any decisions that are not essential.

How to Handle Legitimate Requests
for Help or Payback

Legitimate requests for help or payback should be handled the same way. In some families, all of the members have been making sacrifices, for years, for the benefit of the person who is perceived to have the talent. In such families, parents and siblings often willingly give up their own dreams in order to further the career of the artist, performer, or athlete. If this is your situation, unless there is a dire need for an amount of money that is well within your means, hold off until your advisor gives you the okay.

It's worth saying that I do not think a brand new luxury automobile goes under the category "dire need." It is perfectly legitimate to have some feelings of guilt if your entire family has put you and your dream before themselves. But before you allow that guilt to manifest as expensive gifts that drain you financially, speak with your financial advisor about each gift you would like to give.

The One Thing Everyone Should Do—Immediately

I urge every person in this category to find a financial planner *immediately.* Most of the costly mistakes of Sudden Money recipients in this category could have been avoided if the recipient had taken the time to find a trustworthy financial planner *before* making any spending or investment decisions.

There are full-service sports agencies that take care of all of the needs of athletes, from negotiating contracts to estate planning. In addition, there are individual planners who specialize in athletes and entertainers and who are sensitive to your needs and know what you are going through. There are also financial planners who do not specialize in people in this category who are just as competent. Once again, you need to do your own research and to find someone with whom you can comfortably communicate about your aspirations, your needs, and your anxieties.

Two other professionals that I recommend are an accountant and a therapist or some kind of support group to help you deal with the emotions accompanying your success. Fortunately, some colleges offer counseling programs for athletes to help them cope with the pressure of their move into the limelight. I have developed a Sudden Money Camp that devotes an entire day to your emotions, and it is led by a psychologist who specializes in this area, for those of you who want a thorough orientation to your new circumstances.

I suggest you find a good accountant if your planner does not consider her- or himself an expert in tax law. Why? For some athletes and entertainers, incorporating is a good idea, while for others it is not. And for some, expenses that people who are in the public eye incur can be deducted, such as those related to the maintenance of their appearance (e.g., personal trainers, spa treatments, cosmetic surgery). Many entertainers assume that all expenses they incur, including meals, wardrobe, and entertainment (under the guise of "research") can be deducted. This is not always the case, and tax laws change frequently, so your unique situation needs to be carefully examined by an expert.

Education—The First Line of Defense

Educating yourself about your money and the factors that affect it (i.e., taxes and agency fees) will go a long way toward helping you understand and feel comfortable with your new lifestyle. Many of the mistakes of Sudden Money recipients in this category occur because the recipients have been spending all of their time and energy training or working at odd jobs until their "big break." Career athletes and entertainers often do not have the same level of financial literacy as people who took more conventional career and education paths. For this reason, most windfall recipients of this sort need to educate themselves about the basics of personal finance as well as how their industry works (e.g., who the players are, what they do, how much of a "cut" they usually get).

In addition, this type of Sudden Money often comes in many forms other than upfront cash. Your assets may be in the form of royalties, residuals, copyrights, or several other kinds of profit participation and ownership possibilities. You should know what your gross is (was); what your net is; who gets what percentage of your money and why (including the IRS); and what, if any, guarantees you have of future income. Your DFZ should be used to help you get up to speed on the details of your income: where it comes from, what form it is in, who gets what percentage of it, and why.

Furthermore, do not sign anything that you have not thoroughly read and understood. You have the right to have every detail explained to you as many times as it takes until you understand what you are getting yourself into.

Pretend That What You Have Now Is All You'll Ever Have

Considering the possibility that it can all end tomorrow, act as if the only money you will ever have is the money you have now. If you have $4 million more than you had before you, for instance, released a hit record, assume that by this time next year no one will know your name.

The reason I recommend you do this is that if you live as if you will have an endless income, you will be in debt before you know it. After all, that $4 million is not even $2 million after taxes and fees. And $2 million can easily be spent on a house, which then has to be maintained, furnished, decorated, and taxes have to be paid. Where will *that* money come from?

Don't say, "From my next job." Entertainers and athletes have notoriously unpredictable and volatile earnings. Neither necessarily progresses from low pay to high pay to exorbitant pay in steady increments of dollars or time. Both may have long periods—sometimes years—when they have no income at all from their craft. Do not plan, save, or spend, based on anticipated future income, because there is no guarantee that you will get it. At this point, theoretically, you are just like some people who have just taken a lump sum payout—this money could be the first and last large sum you will ever see. You need to take very good care of your new money so it lasts as long as possible.

The Function of Your Money: Capital to Secure Your Future

The new money you have should not be treated as spending money. More than most individuals, you need to think about your retirement years because your high earnings might not last long and they might even come to an abrupt end without warning.

The strategies for retirement planning for Sudden Money recipients in this category include forming a corporate entity (called a loan-out corporation) through which you can adopt corporate qualified retirement plans and even profit sharing. Entertainers who belong to guilds can then have two qualified retirement plans. Check with your planner or accountant about whether this strategy is for you.

In addition to any pension plan that you contribute to, if you have a predictably short career span, you should be saving a minimum of 30% of income after all fees and taxes have been paid. Take moderate risk with the 30% (e.g., invest it in bonds and conservative stocks) so it has potential to grow, yet it will still be there when you need it. The pension money is for when you are over 60, and this money is for the event that your career ends before you are sixty.

Do Not Give Anyone the Power to Sign Your Checks

When you are suddenly catapulted into wealth and stardom, you may find yourself needing a team of people to handle the various aspects of your personal and business needs. The first step in losing control over your finances is giving one or more of those people the power to take money out of any of your accounts.

The Chute of Emotions

Because you are so good at what you do, your fans, your friends, and even *you*, might have difficulty understanding the emotional challenges success can create.

Numbness

Individuals who are taken by surprise by their success often report feeling numb, as if they are in a state of shock. They don't know what to expect financially, emotionally, or socially. They know that their life has changed, but it hasn't "hit" them yet.

The reactions to numbness range from a complete lack of interest in financial matters to huge shopping sprees with no regard for budget. Regardless of where you fit on the spectrum, you should immediately find a financial advisor and a therapist to help you with your financial and emotional transition and to keep you from making serious financial mistakes.

Unworthiness/Guilt

If your success was a complete surprise to you either because of your age, experience, or talent relative to others, you might feel unworthy and guilty about it and the amount of money it has brought you. Feelings of unworthiness and guilt often manifest themselves in extravagant spending and gifting, with the unconscious intention of ridding oneself of the money. Working with a therapist and a financial planner, from the beginning, will help to prevent you from self-destructive spending.

Take as much time as you need in your DFZ, without purchasing anything or giving any money away. Once you feel comfortable with your success and your finances, you can branch out into the world of large purchases, investments, and charitable giving.

Enthusiasm

Most people who practice something every day for years and who strive to be the best, approach other aspects of their lives with similar intensity. Two areas that they are frequently overenthusiastic about are partying and spending.

THERE'S CELEBRATING . . . AND THEN THERE'S PARTYING Celebrating your new success by throwing yourself a party and inviting some friends and family is probably not harmful when it is done in a modest way and in proportion to your finances. Flying your entire party first-class to Fiji for a week could be detrimental, depending on how much money you have and what your financial situation was before you "made it." I recommend that before you celebrate, you ask your financial planner to give you an allowance for your party, so you are certain that you are not endangering your financial future.

For some people, celebrating includes the use and abuse of alcohol and drugs, and often some gambling—and some of those people do not need a reason to celebrate. Unfortunately, this is an area in which athletes and other celebrities tend to have problems.

The personal, emotional, and social implications of addictive behavior are beyond my expertise and the scope of this book, so I will address only the financial implications here. Needless to say, if you had an addiction before you received your windfall, it has a good chance of getting worse with the arrival of your new money because you will have more to spend on it.

SPENDING As the tabloids will tell you, people in this category are notorious for going on spending sprees as soon as they get a check.

They buy themselves a car, then one for their spouse, one for their mother, and one for their favorite cousin. Then they move to jewelry, including watches. And maybe just one house. If you are asking yourself, What's wrong with that if you have a $10 million contract? then you should go back to the beginning of this chapter.

It's not really $10 million. Remember, most people have no idea how much of their money will go to taxes, agency fees, and attorneys fees. They have no idea how much money they really have, and they spend based on the gross amount they are publicized to have gotten. And they don't think about ancillary costs for the things they have purchased (e.g., maintenance of a large piece of property, insurance on three sports cars when the person is a 20-year-old single with a couple of speeding tickets).

In other words, don't spend any of your money until you have the okay from the person who knows the most about your situation and your money—your financial planner. Don't give your brother money for that restaurant he has been wanting to open, and don't give your parents a first-class ticket around the world until you know you can.

This is one of the few times when excitement can be detrimental. Many athletes and entertainers spend their entire lives waiting—dreaming—about the moment when all of their years of sacrifice would pay off. Others are caught completely by surprise because they had never dared to dream of being discovered and had spent relatively little time thinking about what would happen. In both cases, the recipient is overwhelmed and ecstatic, and that often translates into *impulsive* acts of all kinds, particularly with money.

Individuals who grew up with economic hardship are especially in danger of blowing their money fairly quickly. If your only car is a beat-up Corolla that you've had for a decade and you are suddenly able to purchase a couple of Ferraris, you might just do that—because you can.

DOWNTIME CAN BE JUST AS DANGEROUS The spending patterns of athletes and entertainers are usually a function of their schedules. During basketball season, for instance, an athlete is likely to spend most of his time training, playing, and traveling. Likewise, an actor on your favorite sitcom spends 10 to 12 hours per day taping the season's episodes, and doesn't get much time to do anything else. Therefore, most of the spending of these people occurs in their off-season and when they are between projects. And when you have a couple of months off, you can do significant financial damage.

Working Minors

To protect minors who work in radio, motion pictures, and television from parental misuse of their earnings, California and other states mandate that 25% of the net income of the minor be invested "very conservatively." However, if you are the parent or custodian of a minor, a very conservative investment strategy might not be in their best interest. And considering the percentages that will go to agents, managers, attorneys, and income taxes (yes, you must pay income tax), that 25% might be all you should put into guaranteed investments. If the other 75% is invested in stocks, the minor's earnings will have a better chance of providing long-term financial security than if it were put into guaranteed investments. Therefore, I recommend putting another 50% in growth investments.

On the upside, "making it" as a minor, or as a young adult, is definitely an infrequent occurrence, and there is plenty of time to find an alternative career if things don't progress further. A possible downside is that many young people use this time to develop some bad spending habits that will be difficult to sustain financially and even more difficult to break. And because of their age, they have a very long time before they reach retirement age. Therefore, *it is vital that minors invest whatever money they can wisely, aggressively, and for the long term.*

Cash Flow Planning

Cash flow planning is a tricky area for people whose schedules are unpredictable. One problem is that you may not be certain about how long you will have between projects. Another problem is that you could get injured and be out for a season or two or become ill and miss a performance or two (which may or may not affect your situation, depending on your contract). Then there's the possibility that the income from your future projects will not be as high as it has been if, for example, the box office hasn't been kind to you or if the critics panned you.

I recommend that you ask your financial planner to suggest a low monthly allowance for a six-month period, don't overspend, and keep track of where your money is going. At the end of that period, you should have a better idea of where you are going financially *for a time period that has similar characteristics* (i.e., you are working full-time, part-time, or you are between projects or in an off-season). You may have to discuss altering the amount, but at least you will know how much you *really need* without spending lavishly.

Because you have chunks of time that look significantly different, I suggest that you do this exercise at least twice: once while you are working, and once while you are between jobs. This way you'll get an idea of how much your spending pattern differs depending on how much you are working.

Next, *as an exercise,* ask your planner to calculate how long your money will last if you raise the allowance amount. Remember that the funds to raise your allowance have to come from somewhere—your savings and investments. In other words, the more you take now, the less you'll have for later. This exercise will help you see how spending just a little more now—or investing a little more now—can significantly impact your retirement money and your retirement plans.

Insurance Considerations

Your success has arrived with a responsibility to review and upgrade your insurance coverage. When you buy insurance, you make a purchase you hope you'll never need. What you are buying is piece of mind.

Life Insurance

You need to cover the risk that you won't be around for people who depend on your income. Just because you have a large income doesn't mean that if you are not here, the people who depend on you will be okay. You don't necessarily need to insure for the value of contracts, but you do need to ensure that those who depend on you won't have their financial lives turned inside out.

Disability Income Insurance

Most disability income insurance policies will insure up to two-thirds of your income. As your income increases, review your need to increase your coverage. The best policies (with the best coverage) might be with companies that specialize in insuring the income of athletes and entertainers.

Liability Insurance

Unfortunately, famous people are targets for all kinds of spurious legal claims. A by-product of this phenomenon is that individuals with high visibility encounter higher premium costs. But the extra cost is worth it if you end up in court.

The two areas of coverage you should look into are personal coverage and business coverage.

- *Personal* coverage can be purchased in the form of an *umbrella policy* (above your homeowner's) or an *excess-liability policy*. What it does is protect you when someone has been injured in your home, on your property, or in some other way by you. Be sure to read what is included and excluded very carefully. You may have to purchase yet more insurance for the included items, such as claims of personal injury that are intangible (e.g., libel, slander, or mental anguish).

- *Business* coverage can come in the form of business umbrella or excess-liability policies of the individual, or it can sometimes be included in the liability policy of the employer. If, for instance, you work in the film industry, you might be able to be a *named insured* in the liability policy of the production company or studio. (Named insured are entitled to full benefits, and *additional insureds* only benefit when their actions are in the scope of their employment. Be sure to have this distinction made clear to you when you are negotiating contracts.)

Property Insurance

As your income skyrockets, your ability to purchase expensive furniture, antiques, jewelry, and art increases. If you are going to spend the money to buy these things, spend the additional money to insure them.

PERSONAL Many athletes and entertainers are known for their lavish lifestyles. There are several television shows and magazines that are devoted entirely to showcasing and examining the way these particular individuals spend their money. Because most property insurance policies have a cap of one-half the value of the dwelling, it is important that you carefully authenticate and appraise your possessions to determine if you need to increase your coverage.

And when it comes to your home, make sure that any special needs are attended to if you live in a location that is prone to floods, earthquakes, or brush fires. While this extra coverage may seem expensive, particularly considering that it has restrictions and deductibles, if you ever need it, you'll be glad you bought it.

BUSINESS This probably pertains more to entertainers, as they often own the equipment they travel with. If you are in a band with expensive instruments and a huge, computer-run sound system, you'll need coverage for it and anything else that could affect your ability to perform.

Workers' Compensation Insurance

Be sure to examine the coverage you have through your employer (and if you have formed a corporation, be sure to get thorough coverage for yourself). Make sure you are covered no matter what country or state you are in, particularly if traveling or touring are at all involved in your career. Basic policies usually do not include occurrences outside of North America, and you will have to purchase foreign or worldwide workers' compensation if you travel overseas frequently.

Estate Planning

Entertainers and athletes who have reached celebrity status and do a lot of endorsement work (I'll call them all entertainers) have some unique assets that may present problems at the time of transfer. They have copyrights, royalties, residuals, and what is known as profit participation, which is a contractual right to a percentage of future profits.

In addition, because these people (except for creative artists such as painters) are not ordinarily known for the tangible items they produce, when they do produce something, it becomes more valuable. Upon their death, its value increases more. For example, if Michael Jordan were to take up sculpting, his sculpture would be worth more than mine, regardless of how talented he is deemed to be with his clay. In 100 years, his clay sculpture would probably be worth several times more than the present, hypothetical amount.

Your estate may be made up of several illiquid but taxable assets, such as royalties and memorabilia. Without knowing it, you may put your family in a terrible cash flow position while they settle your estate. Estate taxes go up to 55%, and they must be paid within nine months of death. Your liquid investment may be wiped out to pay taxes, leaving only your home and other difficult-to-sell assets. The life you now enjoy may not be sustainable your loved ones if you don't do serious estate planning with your team of advisors.

Charitable Giving

Many athletes and entertainers feel a desire to give back, particularly to the communities they came from. This is especially true for people whose socioeconomic status changed drastically as a result of their success. From Magic Johnson, Sammy Sosa, and other NBA stars, to Jimmy Smits, MC Hammer, and other entertainers, charity begins at home and quickly returns there.

As I have said elsewhere, anyone contributing to charitable causes is responsible for finding out just how much of their donation is tax-deductible. This tells you how much money is really going to the cause you are supporting. If you go to a fund-raising dinner and pay $500 for your ticket, the full amount is probably not tax-deductible, because the cost of your meal and the event site (unless it was donated) has to come from somewhere. It wouldn't be unusual for $200 of your $500 to go to expenses, thereby making your actual donation $300.

If this is not okay with you, then you should find a different way to demonstrate your support. For instance, you can forego the dinner and send a straight donation, volunteer your time at the event, or donate your possessions (the value of which may have increased as a result of your success). In other words, where there is a philanthropic desire, there is a way to realize it.

If you have vague philanthropic inclinations, then there are two things you need to do. First, you need to decide what exactly it is that you feel passionate about. Second, you need to research thoroughly the different ways you can support your cause, including their tax implications.

Chapter 14, "Giving and Sharing," explained how to go about creating a meaningful philanthropy plan. I suggest a collaborative effort with your financial advisor when you start out, in which you provide the passion and the ideas, and your advisor tells you how to realize them.

Conclusion

Though your fame may come and go, your fortune does not have to. Since it is difficult to measure your future income and the value of your endorsements, seize the opportunity you have today. Be conservative with spending and commitments until you have a solid base. As you have more time in the limelight and earn more, you can afford to stretch out and live a little higher and then a little higher. Again, the heights to which you eventually escalate won't make you dizzy if you have built a strong foundation. Wouldn't it be great to know that no matter what happens, you and your family will have financial security? That is your possibility, and you can make it a reality.

Retirement Benefits Package

The receipt of a retirement benefits package is the most common form of Sudden Money. It represents the time and effort that you put into your career and it is not an unexpected event. However, the receipt of your retirement benefits may trigger many emotions and challenges similar to those of the other Sudden Money events.

Your retirement package requires you to make management decisions that may be both unfamiliar and life-altering. You have new opportunities, responsibilities, and challenges, and they are not without stress. In addition, just as with the other Sudden Money events, the amount you are about to receive may be the single largest amount you have ever had available to you. And it may be the only time in your life when a Sudden Money event happens. The choices you make will have far-reaching consequences, and you need to understand your options thoroughly before you make any decisions.

This chapter will explain the various types of retirement plans and their parts in order to help you make the most appropriate decisions for your lifestyle, your goals, and your risk tolerance.

Chute of Emotions

Whether you have permanently retired or you have been downsized, your day-to-day existence has been dramatically altered, particularly if you are retiring. There was a consistency and a predictability to your life that you might suddenly be thinking about *because of its absence.* Much of the emotional component of this type of event is a result of the change in your daily routine, and much of it is really depression manifesting in different forms. I recommend psychotherapy to everyone who experiences such a radical change in lifestyle, as its effects are broader than you might think.

Following are some of the basic emotions that you are likely to feel and some of the other issues that arise for retirees. Remember that while you are in your Decision Free Zone (DFZ), you should take as much time as you need to acclimate to your new circumstances, and you shouldn't make any decisions that are not essential.

The Fear of Losing Money

While you are employed, there is some predictability of income. Naturally, the primary fear of retired people is running out of money and having to go back to work or having to rely on friends, family, or charity. But that fear is easily combated by doing your best to minimize the likelihood that it will occur.

For example, if you fear losing money through investing, stick with investments you understand and that meet your objectives. Keep track of your investment progress rather than blindly assuming everything is okay. Meet with your advisor regularly (once a quarter or twice a year), and take time to review your investment account statements each time they arrive in the mail.

Perhaps a more obvious way to make sure that you will hold on to your money is to not spend it. You should develop a spending plan right from the start, and keep track of your expenses using a system like Quicken. If you have skipped over it, Chapter 3 has a cash management plan designed to keep you from spending principal without realizing it.

When doing any kind of planning, remember to assume increases in taxes and inflation for your long-term income projections (see Chapter 7, "The Reality Check"). Try to structure your spending plan to meet these higher conservative assumptions. This may mean spending less money than you would if you thought everything was going to stay the same.

Finally, unexpected medical expenses can be dealt with by buying an excellent health insurance policy. When you are eligible for medicare, buy a medicare supplement policy. If you are worried about catastrophic illness, consider buying a catastrophic policy or getting a rider added to your existing policy. Keep some money in a liquid guaranteed investment such as a CD, U.S. Treasury bill, or money market account for additional help in covering emergency medical expenses.

There will always be unknowns, but if you have worked out all the possible scenarios, you know that you will have a way of dealing with them if your level of income drops dramatically. No one likes surprise expenses, so take some time during Phase One to use your imagination to anticipate future problems. Taking the surprise out of the surprise is half the battle.

Loss of Identity

Retirement can be very stressful socially because when you stop going to work each day, you lose the daily, predictable contact you had with a group of people, whether you liked or disliked them. In addition, when you lose the job title that defined you for many years, you might initially feel lost. You might feel as if you don't know who you are anymore, and you might not know how to present yourself to others.

In order to alleviate this feeling, I suggest that you look to your community or to a nonprofit organization you believe in. You don't have to seek a position you will be paid for, but something that gives you a sense of purpose and satisfaction. My only caveat is to decide, before you go out looking, how much time you are willing to give. Most nonprofits and community organizations are understaffed and will gobble up your time if you allow them to. If you have—and stick to—a predetermined schedule, you won't feel as though you are being taken advantage of.

A CEO of a large international corporation retired to Cape Cod. He had the management skills to run the homeowners' association and even the entire town. However, rather than taking a position with a lot of responsibility, he has found satisfaction volunteering for a local social service organization. He drives homebound citizens to their doctor appointments and delivers meals to them several times a week. He likes to see for himself that he is making a difference in the lives of the people in his community. He reports that his hands-on experience is more rewarding than many of the committee decisions he made as a CEO. In addition, his volunteer work allows him to meet other retirees in the area and the flexibility to travel with his wife.

Your Spouse's Reaction

Your spouse may have a difficult time understanding your need to reestablish your identity. I recommend discussing your feelings and intentions and perhaps consider working together on one or two projects. If a joint project does not work, at least reach an agreement on how much time you will spend on any new commitments.

In addition to giving you a sense of identity, your career probably gave you some autonomy as well. "Married for better or worse but not for lunch" is an old saying that rings true in many retirees' households. Neither you nor your spouse may be prepared to spend all day, every day, together. Problems that were acceptable before retirement because you were so busy, distracted, and/or fulfilled with your career, may suddenly seem insurmountable. Many couples have experienced this and have successfully dealt with it. If you are unable to conquer it by yourselves, try enlisting the help of a therapist. It's always easier to have an experienced, objective third party guide you through difficult times.

Sadness and Depression

Sadness is a common result of not working and consequently becoming isolated, and so is depression. It may take some time and effort to decide what you want to do with your time now that it is not scheduled for you each day. It is a good idea to pursue an interest or to become involved in a community volunteer program or enroll in courses to learn about something that interests you. Elder hostels are great ways to learn while traveling and meeting new people. Most colleges have programs for nonmatriculated students, and the courses are usually low cost and interesting. Use your time constructively, but have fun doing it.

Stan retired and lived alone, and he felt lonely. He didn't have a lot of money, but he figured he was better off than the people at the homeless shelter. Each day he went to the shelter to have lunch and just talk to the guys who frequented it. He befriended many and often stayed around for the afternoon to help out. Without saying a word to anyone, Stan changed the beneficiary of his life insurance policy to be the shelter. When he died, the money from the policy was gratefully received and used to make badly needed improvements that made the shelter more comfortable and uplifting for its residents.

Overwhelmed

When you leave a company, with benefits, you have many financial decisions to make and they can seem overwhelming. You will need to decide how to receive money from pension plans; you will need to find out about the tax consequences of your decisions; and then you will need to make spending and investing decisions. But you do not have to do anything alone. Your company benefits department can help you understand what your options are for receiving your money, and your financial advisor can help you determine which choices are best for you and your unique situation. If you have a therapist, that person can help you through the emotional transition from your corporate career. Some companies have support groups and free counseling for new retirees. So what may seem like too much for one person to handle is actually more doable once you realize that you have help.

Insecurity/Intimidation

You may feel ill equipped to make the kinds of decisions that will be required of you. To be successful in your job, you probably had to be completely focused on it, and you may not have had too many long-term financial decisions to make. Taxes were regularly withheld from your paycheck, and your investing may have been limited to your 401(k) plan and saving money to pay for your children's college tuition. Suddenly, you need to make decisions that have lifelong consequences. You are not alone if you feel paralyzed and intimidated. When you are able to work through some of that insecurity, you might find it empowering to think about creating your own financial security.

A Note on Substance Abuse

Research shows that it is not uncommon for retirees and those who are in between jobs to become dependent upon alcohol or drugs. Because you are not expected to show up somewhere each day, you may become isolated. Therefore, if you have a substance abuse problem, it will be difficult for others to detect it and to help you. There are special programs for retirees and for downsized employees that offer counseling and help with substance abuse, but you have to make that first step.

Know Your Benefits

You and your advisor might want to make a six-column chart of each of your retirement benefits.

Column 1. The name of the benefit (e.g., profit sharing plan)

Column 2. The estimated value

Column 3. The action that needs to be taken as to how to take the distribution

Column 4. The important dates (e.g., expiration dates), estimations of how long it takes to transfer the money, and cutoff dates for paperwork to be received

Column 5. The contact person (usually in the human resources or employee benefits department) and their phone number

Column 6. Taxes (and keep track of how much additional income you expect this year)

It is not uncommon for the numerous deadlines and cumbersome paperwork to result in enough confusion to cause you to overlook some important opportunities and requirements. There are several strict rules to be followed if you want to maximize your benefits, and some of the rules are easy to miss even if you are organized.

If you have worked for many companies over the years, or if the company you worked for has had several owners, do a careful search for possible forgotten benefits. You may have left some money in company plans, or you may be entitled to age-sensitive benefits you were not eligible for when you left the company.

Key Advice: Think Long Term

A common mantra is that retirement money is long-term money, meaning you should plan to keep ahead of inflation and taxes, usually by investing for growth. The general advice is to invest this money for your future retirement, which is usually presumed to be a long way off. For you, however, it is not a long way off. You have, or are about to have, access to the money that will help support you throughout your retirement.

It does not matter if you are changing jobs or if you are ready to retire completely, your retirement benefits still need to be treated as long-term money. A typical mistake in retirement planning is not planning for a sufficient period of time. Because life expectancies are increasing, it is conceivable that you will spend more time retired than you did working.

Not Retiring Yet?

If you are changing jobs somewhere in the middle of your career, it may be tempting to cash in your retirement benefits in exchange for a boat or a home improvement project, or to pay off credit card debt or numerous other seemingly pressing current expenses. However, falling into this kind of spending trap robs you of some of your future financial security. Let me help you make those words come to life. Undoubtedly, you have heard them before, but if you are considering spending your retirement money now, the words did not sink in.

Melanie's husband Mort changed jobs and received his $85,000 401(k) money as a direct payment. He had intended to spend some and roll the balance into an IRA within 60 days from the time he got the check. Mort and Melanie were in their mid-30s, and this was their first opportunity of having a lump sum of money.

They wanted a new kitchen and they wanted to pay off their credit cards so they would have plenty of credit available for their upcoming three-week trip to Europe and Africa. After setting aside $23,000 for their dream kitchen and $17,000 to pay off the credit cards, they planned to roll $45,000 into the IRA. They reasoned that at their age they had plenty of time to save for retirement. The $45,000 would grow impressively in the 30 years before they retired. (At an average growth of 10% per year for 30 years, it would grow to $785,000).

If they had done a Reality Check before they put their plan into action, they would have discovered the following: Twenty percent would be $17,000 withheld for taxes, so only $68,000 would actually be received. When the $40,000 was set aside for the kitchen and credit cards, that would leave $28,000 to roll over. Their full income tax and 10% early withdrawal penalty will be calculated on $57,000 ($85,000 − $28,000 = $57,000). The total income tax and penalty is $22,800. They have already paid $17,000 due to the 20% withholding. When April 15th comes along, they will owe an additional $5,800.

The long-term impact of spending immediately versus letting the full $85,000 stay invested is as follows.

If they retired in 30 years and their IRA rollover money averaged a 10% return per year, the full rollover ($85,000) would produce three times more retirement income than the $28,000 partial rollover. The full rollover account would have grown to $1.48 million and could produce $88,000 in annual income. The partial rollover would have grown to only $488,000 and could produce $29,000 per year.

If they survived for 25 years after retiring, they would have an additional $1.5 million from the full rollover. It can also be projected that they would have $1 million more to pass to their heirs with the full rollover.

My advice is to get your financial security covered as soon as possible. Even if you have many more years of retirement saving time, the money you have today will have more time to work for you than money saved in the future. Time is a huge asset: $85,000 invested for 20 years at an average annual rate of 10% grows to $570,000, versus $1,480,000 if you had just 10 more years of growth. Investing it for the long term today may bring you the freedom to make choices such as early retirement. It may give you more protection if life deals you an unexpected blow, such as a disability, the death of a spouse, or a major change in your industry resulting in periods of unemployment. New kitchens and vacations should be paid for with nonretirement money.

If you are changing jobs, read the section on how to roll over 401(k) plans and other retirement benefits. Run your numbers and plans through the Reality Check before you take any money out. Don't forget to account for the 10% penalty, along with the income tax on any money that you don't roll over. The amount taken along with your regular income for that year could put you into the highest tax bracket (39.6%), and when you add the 10% penalty and the cost of not rolling the money over, you lose almost 50%.

If you truly need some of the money, for a life-threatening disease perhaps, then transfer the full amount directly to an IRA rollover first. Keep the money in a money market account within the IRA rollover. Take money out as you need it, leaving the balance tax-deferred as long as possible. Take distributions only as needed (not all at once up front), possibly allowing you to spread the tax consequence over two years. Don't forget to set money aside for the taxes, thereby avoiding nasty surprises when it is time to pay your taxes.

Long term should also be the theme *if you are retiring for good*, as you will not be getting any more paychecks. Years ago, the advice was to get more conservative when you retire. This would translate into buying guaranteed bonds and living off of the interest. If your retirement package is truly vast compared with your income needs, you may be able to follow this tradition. However, the tradition was strong and appropriate when the average numbers of years spent in retirement were lower. Because we are living longer, we need to plan for income to last on an inflation-adjusted basis until our mid-90s. *Don't groan and say you will never make it that long, or that you don't want to live that long. The point is that you don't know what the future is, so be prepared to be financially self-supporting, even if you don't live that long.*

Reality Checks

Before you commit to an investment plan with your retirement money, go through the Reality Check using the assumption that you will live longer than you expect. Use conservative assumptions for inflation, taxes, and investment returns. Run one set of numbers assuming investing 100% in bonds, one assuming 100% in stocks, and then one with various combinations of stocks and bonds. You will figure out what rate of return you need to average on your retirement portfolio and what combination has the highest probability of providing the returns you need.

Insurance

Your Sudden Money retirement planning should include a review of your insurance needs. The review should cover health, life, disability, and long-term care insurance. If you had relied on employer-provided benefits, you may have the opportunity to take them with you for a limited period of time. *Health insurance* is portable, and under the COBRA rules you have the right to continue this insurance at your own expense for 18 months. This will give you time to find alternative coverage or perhaps reach the age qualifying you for medicare insurance. Include the cost of health insurance in your annual budget. Even if you qualify for medicare, you will still want a medicare supplement policy. If your retirement package includes lifetime health insurance, this benefit is taxable annually.

Traditionally, *life insurance* is used to replace the income of a wage earner. Therefore, if you are no longer going to be a wage earner, you have no need for life insurance, right? Not necessarily. You might need life insurance if you have a substantially younger spouse and enough retirement assets to cover your expected life span only. If your net worth is high enough to be subject to estate taxes (which begin at 37% and go up to 55%), you might need life insurance to provide cash to pay estate taxes. The younger you are when you apply, the lower the cost will be. If you will need permanent life insurance and you are healthy and can afford it, don't delay. You never know when you may no longer be insurable.

Disability income insurance is no longer needed if you are going to fully retire. If you are changing jobs and you had this coverage with your last employer, make certain your new employer will provide this benefit. It is a good idea to have a privately owned policy to be sure you will have uninterrupted coverage during your career years.

The need for *long-term care insurance* depends upon your ability to self-insure, meaning, to pay for at-home or nursing home care yourself. When you do your Reality Check, add an assumption that either you or your spouse will need long-term care. Use the current cost for your area and account for inflation, and if you can afford to handle the hypothetical expense, don't buy the coverage. If it would be a burden to pay for one of you to have five years of care (the average stay in a nursing home is three years, so assuming five years is a more conservative assumption), then shop around for a policy while you are insurable and younger.

However, buying this kind of policy in your 50s may be too early, as most people don't need the coverage until they are in their 80s. That's a long time to be paying premiums. Unless you have health considerations or a family history that would dictate buying earlier, it is good to buy while you are in your 60s.

To Move, or Not to Move . . .

Remember, while you are in your DFZ, you should not make big decisions such as selling your home and moving to another area. Instead, visit the new area; rent an apartment; go shopping; go out to dinner; join the clubs, churches, or synagogues you would belong to if you lived there; check out property taxes and homeowners' association fees; and don't forget to pay attention to the general attitude of the people. It is important that you feel at home in the new area. Before you retired, you may not have lived in an area where homeowners' associations were common, and the kind of rules they impose may take getting use to.

Income Tax Planning

Your income tax position will most likely be altered due to your retirement package, even if you are continuing with your career. It is likely that you will be better off deferring taxes by transferring qualifying accounts into an IRA rollover, leaving them with your old employer, or transferring them to the new employer.

If you take a distribution directly, you will owe income tax plus a possible 10% early withdrawal tax. The combination of federal and state income tax and a possible 10% penalty can mean a cost of over 55%, which is certainly high enough to be avoided whenever possible.

However, some benefits cannot be transferred or rolled over. The following will be subject to current income tax, usually in the year you separate from the company.

- Stock options frequently must be exercised within 90 days after you leave the company or they will lapse. Nonqualified stock options (NQSOs) are taxable when they are exercised. The difference between the exercise price and the stock price when exercised is subject to both income and FICA tax.

- Any payments representing unused vacation or sick leave will be subject to income and FICA tax.

- Nonqualified deferred compensation accounts cannot be transferred into an IRA rollover account. The full amount is subject to income tax the year it is received.

- Company stock owned inside profit sharing plans, 401(k) plans, stock bonus plans, and employee stock ownership plans (ESOP) have a special tax advantage if the rules are followed. If the shares are distributed to you (usually to a brokerage account in your name), they are considered net unrealized appreciation (NUA) assets. You will owe income tax on the cost basis of the stock (the price when it was acquired). If the stock price has appreciated significantly, this may be a great bargain. (For instance, if the stock cost $10 a share and it now sells for $100 a share, it is a deal to only owe capital gains tax on $10 a share.) When you eventually sell the stock, you will owe capital gains tax on the appreciated amount. Using the previous example, you would owe capital gains on $90 if you sold the stock. But you do not have to sell the stock—you may keep it in a brokerage account and hold it as long as you like. NUA treatment is only available for company stock distributed to you. The advantage is lost if the shares are rolled over to an IRA.

MEET WITH YOUR ACCOUNTANT Meet with your accountant to get an estimate of the tax you will owe and to discuss making quarterly tax payments. If you are permanently retiring, you need to set up ongoing quarterly tax payments. For the first year of retirement, you will most likely be in a different tax position than in later years. The quarterly withholding amount should be reviewed annually, as it could change each year.

Estate Planning

While you are in the process of dealing with retirement income decisions, you are also involved with estate planning. Retirement benefits have built-in complexities when it comes to estate planning. Whether you are going into full retirement or you are just changing jobs, the elections you make regarding each of your retirement benefits will have an impact on how and to whom these assets transfer.

Qualified retirement plans are great lifetime assets, as they were created to provide for retirement income. However, they are not great estate assets. The rules governing how qualified plans transfer after you are gone are complex and unfamiliar, even to most financial advisors. When you are involved in the financial planning surrounding your retirement benefits, don't overlook the estate planning implications of the decisions and elections that you are about to make.

- You are making estate planning decisions when you list the beneficiaries for each of your retirement plans, including IRA rollovers.

- You will have to elect how to calculate your required minimum distribution (RMD) from your IRA if you are age 70½. This is an irreversible estate planning decision.

- You will have to consider decisions that have estate tax implication and that are also irreversible if you have a company pension plan offering you a choice of a lump sum option or life income options.

■ You would be wise to know your overall estate planning position so you can make the most suitable choices before you make decisions on life insurance policies that you have available to you.

As you address each benefit, in addition to considering the current income tax and potential income, find out about the estate planning implications of the choices you have available. In many cases you will have to weigh the lifetime advantages against the estate advantages and make a choice.

Keep All the Paperwork

Keep all of the relevant paperwork on your IRA rollover. The penalties for not meeting the 60-day rollover requirement or for adding more money to the IRA rollover accounts are steep. When you receive one lump sum payment, you should have a statement of what it is composed of. It is possible that you will receive several statements and several checks, so keep them all, even if you think they may be duplications.

Also, keep copies of the checks, and keep the envelopes they arrived in. For extra protection, I suggest that you give your financial advisor a copy of all statements. If you need proof years down the road, perhaps after you have moved several times, your advisor's records may be more complete than yours and easier to find. Advisors can move and change careers too, so consider their records a backup to yours.

Liza took an early retirement package from her long-time employer and she rolled her lump sum into an IRA rollover account. She and her husband decided to go into the real estate development business, and they planned on using her money in 20 years when they really retired. As luck would have it, 10 years later the area where they were developing property was hit by a major natural disaster. Many of the people in their community were suddenly in financial difficulty, and personal bankruptcy started to be commonplace. So were lawsuits.

One of their previous buyers decided to take advantage of the difficulties and began suing many people for almost any reason. When Liza and her husband were named in one of his lawsuits, their lawyer advised them that the money in her IRA rollover was protected from claims of this potential creditor if it had been legitimate qualified retirement money and had met all of the rollover requirements. It had always been their largest asset, and now it was the only remaining asset left after the storms and floods.

The first thing their lawyer did was to make sure that the IRA rollover was done correctly. The paperwork kept by their financial advisor clearly showed the dates and the amounts. If they could not have proved this, the potential creditor would have had something to fight for. Because proof was produced at the deposition, he dropped the suit and went after bigger fish. Liza and her husband were able to rebuild their lives without having to take time and money to fight a frivolous lawsuit.

Replacing Your Paycheck

Your retirement income may come from several sources; company pension, social security, withdrawals from an IRA rollover, and personal investment accounts are the most common. There are two essential questions to answer: How much money can you spend each year without going broke, and where will that money come from?

- The answer to the first question comes from doing the Reality Check exercise. After you run various scenarios, you will know approximately how much you can spend each year. I say approximately because unless you are receiving a fixed company pension and social security without any other source of income, your income will vary each year. The Reality Check will give you a good guideline of how much you can spend; yet, each year you will need to review your overall income position making adjustments as needed and desired.

- Once you have done the theoretical exercise of the Reality Check, then comes the very practical question, Where does your money actually come from, and how do you get it? My advice is to set up a system that sends a predictable monthly income to your operating checking account. (Review the cash management system in Chapter 3.) This amount should cover your monthly expenses.

- Consolidate accounts as much as possible. It won't be practical or allowable to combine all your accounts; IRA accounts and personal accounts will always be separate, but you can keep them all with the same advisor. Many brokerage firms and independent advisors can produce a consolidated statement showing all of your various accounts on one statement. This will help you keep track, meet required minimum distributions, and manage your cash flow more efficiently. It is a good idea to take income from taxable accounts first, allowing tax-deferred accounts to grow for future use.

- Identify one or two accounts that will produce your monthly income to cover your fixed expenses. Your advisor's firm should have the ability to collect all of the interest, dividends, and systematic withdrawals distributed by your various investments into an interest-paying money market account. At the end of the month, one check should be sent or transferred to your operating account.

- Identify specific investments or savings to be tapped for large annual expenses like property taxes and insurance premiums. Also know which investments or accounts you will use for the fun stuff, such as vacations, gifts, and splurges.

Jeff and Amy have projected that they will need $180,000 in after-tax income now that they are retired. Their fixed expenses, including mortgages, homeowners' association fees, utilities, food, and entertainment, run $10,000 a month. They have $9,500 in property taxes and $10,000 in insurance premiums as annual large expenses. In addition, they are generous with their children and have an adventurous appetite for travel.

The $10,000 a month comes from the investment account created when they transferred the company stock in his stock bonus plan and 401(k) to an account set up by their advisor. They sold 75% of the stock to diversify and kept 25%. This account is invested in bonds and stocks. The income comes from the interest from the bonds and the systematic monthly liquidation of shares of their stock mutual funds. On the last day of the month, $10,000 is transferred directly to their operating checking account.

Their combined social security is $22,000 a year. They save their check each month and use this money to pay the annual property taxes and insurance premiums.

The fun money comes from their personal investment account. Each year, they take 5% of this account for travel and gifts. The actual amount varies each year, depending upon how their investments fared.

Once they reach age 70½, they will make withdrawals from the IRA rollover. If the extra income is not needed to offset inflation at that time, they will start giving money to their children.

You will have a greater sense of control and security once you understand where your income will come from and how to access extra money when you need it.

The Retirement Package

Retirement packages are all different; they have different components, timetables, and requirements. You will need to understand what your benefits are and how to access them and determine which are the best choices for your personal needs.

Most benefits will be guaranteed, but some will not. Some will disappear if you fail to meet specified time requirements. For instance, if you pass the deadline for exercising your stock options, you may lose the options. If you leave money in a non-qualified deferred compensation plan, you could lose all the money if the company goes out of business. It is your responsibility to know your package, the timetables, the choices, and the tax consequences.

Jennifer's husband died suddenly at age 58. She was devastated and grieving; for months she put off anything that had to do with sorting out her new financial position. Eventually, she sold her house and moved to another state where she had relatives.

When she met with a financial planner whom her aunt had recommended, she found that one of her husband's retirement benefits worth $50,000 had to have been applied for within six months of his death. The financial planners petitioned the employer, and the response was that a committee would have to meet and vote on whether the circumstances warranted an exception to their rules. Several months later, the committee voted to pay Jennifer the $50,000. The vote was not unanimous, and no interest was credited for the many months during which the money was held up.

The point of planning is to coordinate all the benefits to support what you need now and in the future. Before they can all be used together as a whole, each benefit should be understood on its own.

How to make the best use of your retirement benefits is a big and cumbersome topic. You will not have all of the possible variations listed and explained in this chapter, so turn to the sections that do apply to you and skip the rest. The following elements of the package are covered in the balance of this chapter:

- Unused vacation pay and sick pay
- Qualified retirement plans
- 401(k) and savings plan money
- SEP-IRA
- Profit sharing
- Company pension benefits
- Nonqualified plans
- Deferred compensation plans
- Company stock options

Vacation Pay and Sick Leave Pay

Vacation pay and sick leave pay come directly to you, usually as separate checks, and are subject to income taxes. It is up to you to find out if taxes were withheld. If your company did not withhold taxes, you must set the tax money aside. Check with your accountant to determine if you should be making quarterly tax payments the year you receive your severance benefits.

When you meet with your financial advisor, discuss how to best use the after-tax money you are receiving. How you spend or invest this money will depend upon your current and anticipated cash flow. If you find you will have plenty of income and all your bases are covered, spend it and have a great time. If you have any doubts about your cash needs, avoid the temptation of thinking of your lump sum as splurge money earned by not being sick and not taking all of your vacation time.

If you do need cash to cover potential shortfalls or emergencies, this is the money you should use first. You have already paid taxes on this money, unlike the money that is still in tax-deferred retirement accounts, such as IRA rollovers. It is better to let the retirement account money grow tax deferred and to use money outside these accounts that has been set aside for unexpected needs.

Qualified Retirement Plans

There are basically two kinds of qualified retirement plans: *defined benefit plans* and *defined contribution plans*. Your company pension plan is a defined benefit plan governed by a government agency, the Pension Benefit Guaranty Corporation (PBGC). The funding for these plans comes from employer contributions, not from employees. The IRS gives the employer a tax deduction for the money contributed each year and sets rules for how much needs to be in the plan in order to meet future obligations.

Your defined benefit plan benefits are guaranteed by the employer. When you qualify for benefits, you will be offered either a one-time lump sum or guaranteed monthly income. If you choose to take the lump sum, you become responsible for how to invest, when to take income, and when to pay taxes. Choosing the guaranteed monthly payments means that you are relying on the company to make the promised payments. The PBGC guarantees you only a small monthly income if the company is unable to meet their pension obligations.

Your 401(k), profit sharing, ESOP, and SEP-IRA are all defined contribution plans. Defined contribution plans are funded by a combination of employer and employee contributions. When you either retire or leave the company, you become responsible for this money. You will have three choices: (1) leave the money with the old employer if it is allowed; (2) transfer the money to an IRA rollover account to avoid paying income taxes immediately; or (3) receive the money directly and pay taxes and possible penalties.

DEFINED BENEFIT PLAN DECISIONS Your defined benefit plan document will describe the exact options you have for taking your benefits. When you become eligible to take your benefits, you will probably have a choice between the lump sum option or life income option. Which one may be right for you is a personal matter. Review the following pros and cons to help make a decision.

The *advantages* of taking the lump sum are as follows:

- If you choose the lump sum option, you maintain control, deciding where to invest, how much income to take, and when to pay the taxes.

- If you don't need the income when you first get the money, you can let it grow tax deferred until you do need it. This gives you the chance to increase the current amount and to increase your future income as well.

- If you take the lump sum, you have the possibility of still having money in your rollover account to be passed on to your loved ones. The life income option doesn't leave money behind for your children or other heirs.

- If you take the lump sum, one of the most important advantages is that you will have the chance to keep your income adjusted for inflation. The life income options are not usually adjusted for inflation; therefore, it is as if the income is shrinking over the years.

- If you need access to a large sum of money because of illness or a problem within your family, you would have it if you take the lump sum. Once you make the life income choice, you give up the rights to your money in exchange for the monthly income.

- If you someday change your mind and feel a fixed monthly income is what you want, you can always purchase your own life income annuity from an insurance company. Depending upon interest rates and whether the IRA rollover account has grown or shrunk, you may have a higher or lower monthly payment than your company is now offering. This can be an important option for a financially inexperienced surviving spouse to have available.

The *disadvantages* of taking a lump sum are as follows:

- If you have serious debt problems, the annuity is a better way to go. It will be tempting to use your lump sum money to pay off your debts. If you have not recovered from your overspending habit, you are likely to recreate the problem by piling up new debt and not having any additional "bailout" money to rescue you. In this case, it is better to structure a monthly payment using your pension income and to keep your living expenses low to accommodate the debt reduction plan. Because of taxes and penalties, it may take $1.30 to $1.50 to pay off $1 of debt.

- If you have a gambling problem or a history of being a lousy and/or speculative investor, the annuity is a better bet. If you lose all you have at the track, at least you still have an income check coming in each month.

- If you have a low stress threshold or a history of mental illness, it may be better to keep things simple and just get a predictable and guaranteed monthly income. Managing a lump sum payment for growth and inflation-adjusted income will be stressful at times, particularly when the stock market has dropped. To be successful as an investor, it is important to be committed to your investment strategy in good times and bad. If you don't have the inner strength to withstand the tough times, don't take the lump sum.

GET PROFESSIONAL ADVICE The decision you make is irreversible and may have lifelong influences, so get professional help. Even if you are good with numbers, it is still best to do this strategic planning with an experienced financial advisor. There is no changing your mind once you have made the election. Before you decide, work through the possible scenarios within the Reality Check exercise. As I have recommended previously, make conservative, realistic assumptions.

Remember that the success of taking the lump sum depends upon your investment success. If you take the lump sum to attempt to receive higher income than the life income options and to keep that income increasing with inflation, you will need stocks or stock mutual funds in your lump-sum portfolio. You might need to have 50% or more in these growth investments; this means you will have ups and down in your portfolio. Become familiar with investment cycles and make sure your expectations are realistic.

How to Receive Money from the Company Pension Plan

Your company pension plan benefit may be your largest single retirement asset. You are likely to have to choose from the following ways to receive this money.

LUMP SUM If you choose the lump sum option, you must inform the benefits department of how you want the money paid to you. The two general choices are to take the money directly, which will cause you to owe income taxes on the full amount, or to have the money transferred to an IRA rollover account and continue to defer taxes.

If you choose the IRA rollover route, the check should be made out to the company that will act as your IRA custodian. *The check should not be made out to you.* If it is made out to you, 20% will be withheld for taxes. This sets up a difficult sequence of requirements to get the withheld money back, and frequently it is never recouped, even though your intention was to put all of the money into the IRA account. The problem can be avoided by having the check made out to the receiving custodian. Let me fully explain the dilemma.

When you take the rollover route, you actually receive a check made out to you, and you have 60 days to put this money into a new IRA rollover account. When an employer withholds 20%, a problem is created. The problem is you have to put 100% of the money into the IRA rollover account and you only have 80% of it. If the 20% balance is not made up, you will owe taxes. Depending upon your age, you might also owe an early withdrawal penalty.

Let's assume that you roll over a lump sum of $200,000 and that 20% ($40,000) is withheld, so the check you actually receive is for $160,000. But you have to put the entire $200,000 into the IRA rollover, or you will owe taxes and maybe penalties on $40,000. You will also lose the future tax protection on that $40,000 afforded you now by the qualified plan.

If you can't come up with the $40,000 from savings or other investments, you will owe taxes and a possible penalty for a combined cost of as high as 50% on the $40,000. If you can deposit the $40,000 and avoid paying taxes and penalties, you can apply for a refund when you file your taxes. The refund will be for less than $40,000.

This is an easy problem to avoid. Just be sure to pay close attention to the paperwork and deadlines when you retire or separate from an employer. If the check does arrive in your name, instead of cashing it, return it and request a new check properly made out to the new custodian. Make sure the replacement check arrives in a timely manner to avoid missing the 60-day rollover requirement.

The transfer should not take more than two to three weeks. Once the money has arrived in the IRA account, IRA rules apply. You will be required to make withdrawals once you reach age 70½, and you will be penalized if you take money out before age 59½. With the money in the account, you can now invest it to meet the goals and income requirements set out in your financial plan.

LIFE INCOME OPTIONS If you choose to take one of the income options, you have the security of knowing the payments are guaranteed. Your employer will give an insurance company enough money to guarantee your income. Your checks will usually come from the insurance company, not your ex-employer. If the employer goes out of business, your money is still guaranteed by the insurance company.

When you are considering the life income option, you will have to examine your specific alternatives. Each company's plan may be different. The general choices are:

- Life only
- Life with 10-year certain
- 50% joint and survivor
- 100% joint and survivor

Life only. This option pays the highest monthly amount because payments continue for your lifetime only. When you are gone, so are the payments. Even if you die soon after you retire, your spouse and your heirs won't receive anything. This option makes sense if you are single, if your spouse has his or her own pension benefits that are adequate to meet his or her needs, or if you have planned to take this option ahead of time and purchased life insurance to replace the lost pension income.

Life with 10-year certain. This is the second highest monthly amount. It pays lifetime income but guarantees at least 10 years of payments. If you should die two years after you retire, your spouse would receive eight years of payments and then the payments would stop. This option works well if you are in good health and if you have enough money invested to replace your pension should you die before your spouse, or if you have a sufficient amount of life insurance.

50% joint and survivor. The amount you will receive will be less than the life option will pay. With this option, your surviving spouse receives 50% of what you had been receiving before you died. Since the combined life span of two people is longer than one life, the company assumes it will be paying for a longer period of time, so the payments while you are alive will be lower than the single life options. Before you select this option, make sure your spouse can either live on the lower amount or has a way to make up for the decrease in income. If you have a life insurance policy on your life with your spouse as beneficiary, or if you have money set aside to make up for this future drop in income, this option may be a good choice.

100% joint and survivor.   The amount paid with this option is the least because your surviving spouse continues to receive the same monthly pension after your death. This spreads the monthly pension payments over two lifetimes; there is no reduction in the benefit if you die first. This option is probably the safest choice if you do not have much money invested or saved.

GET ADVICE Once you have made your decision, you cannot change your mind. This is one of those times when you will absolutely need professional advice. Even if you are good with numbers, you still need to do some strategic planning. The answers are not always obvious, and the decision you make needs to be based on realistic assumptions. In the vast majority of cases, taking the lump sum is the most advantageous choice.

If you choose to take one of the life income options, you have the security of knowing the payments are guaranteed. Your employer may make the payments out of the money they have set aside each year to meet their pension obligations. If the company is small, they will probably turn the money over to an insurance company, buying an annuity to cover your payments.

Defined Contribution Decisions

As you either retire or move on to another job, you will be required to make decisions regarding your 401(k), SEP-IRA, ESOP, and profit sharing assets. You must take responsibility for your money inside these qualified plans; the decisions are yours, not the company's. You have three basic choices:

1. Take the money and pay taxes.

2. Transfer the money to an IRA rollover and defer taxes.

3. Leave the money in your old employer's plan if allowed.

If you take the money directly, you will owe income tax on the entire amount and possibly an early withdrawal penalty of 10%. It does not make sense to pay taxes if you can avoid it. The longer your money grows tax deferred, the better off you are. Keep this money tax protected even if you intend to start drawing income from it or if you think you will need it as a lump sum at some point in the near future. It should cost very little if anything to transfer the money. Try to draw income and handle expenses from your taxable accounts before tapping into your tax-deferred account.

The total tax cost to access this money may be up to 55%. The full amount is considered taxable income the year you receive it, and the withdrawal plus your earned income may temporarily put you in the highest tax bracket, 39.6%. You may also owe state income taxes, averaging 5%, and if you are under 59½, tack on a 10% penalty. Instead of the $110,000 balance you think you have in your 401(k), you may end up with only $49,500.

Most advisors will recommend that you go with the IRA rollover because you will have the widest range of investment choices and distribution flexibility. If you prefer the convenience of leaving the money with your old employer:

- Make sure you have excellent investment choices.

- Get a written copy of the plan document detailing how to make investment changes or how to begin to take income.

- Get a written copy of the annual cost.

- Find out how long you may leave the money there.

There are times when you should not use an IRA rollover, including the following:

- If you are at least 55 years old, but not yet 59½, you can access your 401(k) money without owing the early withdrawal penalty if it is kept in the company plan. Once you roll the money over to an IRA, this advantage disappears.

- If the amount is small and you are temporarily in a low-tax bracket, it may be the cheapest time to take the money out.

- If you have company stock that is held in your 401(k), ESOP, or profit sharing plans, don't roll it over. Take a single distribution of all of the shares of the company stock, and roll the remaining plan assets into the IRA rollover. Company stock held in these accounts will qualify for unrealized capital gains treatment, which is usually substantially lower than your ordinary income tax rate. To qualify, the shares must all be withdrawn as a one-time lump sum. If you take more than one withdrawal, you lose the qualification. The share may be transferred to a brokerage account and held for as long as you want. If this stock represents a large percentage of your assets, work out a plan to sell and diversify.

ROTH IRA Created in 1997, the Roth IRA offers an interesting tax twist: Qualifying withdrawals from Roth IRAs are tax free. To qualify for tax-free withdrawals, the money must have been in the plan for five years and you must be age 59½. Though the income is federally tax free, your state may tax Roth withdrawals as income.

Since this is a new retirement option, you won't have much money accumulated in a Roth IRA unless you converted money from a regular IRA account to a Roth. The cost of the conversion is the income tax you would owe on the converted amount of the regular IRA. The benefit is that the money in the Roth continues to grow tax deferred and eventually comes out tax free.

Now that you are making retirement benefit decisions, you might consider converting a company plan into a Roth IRA. You can do this by first transferring the money to an IRA rollover and then converting. You can't go from the company plan directly to the Roth. Whether this is a good idea depends upon:

- If you will be able to pay the taxes from other sources (i.e., not from the rollover/conversion money)

- If you will be able to let the Roth money grow without taking income for a sufficient time (you need time to make up for the cost of paying the taxes)

In addition to the income tax advantage of a Roth, you will not have to start taking required minimum distributions at age 70½. This may allow you to accumulate money for your heirs or for income much later down the retirement road.

To be eligible for a Roth conversion, you must have less than $100,000 income, whether you are single or married. The amount of the conversion is not included in the qualifying $100,000. You may convert a portion of the IRA account; you don't have to convert 100%.

REQUIRED MINIMUM DISTRIBUTIONS OVER AGE 70½ The government offers the tax-deferred incentive to encourage you to save for retirement. Once you are of retirement age, it is expected that you will be withdrawing money and paying taxes on those withdrawals. To ensure that this happens, there is an RMD beginning April 1 of the year after you turn 70½.

The penalty for not making an RMD is steep—50% of the required amount not taken. So, if you are required to withdraw

$10,000 and you don't do it, the penalty is $5,000, *plus* you would still owe regular income taxes on the $10,000. And if you take only a portion of what is required, you will owe the 50% penalty on the amount left in. If you are required to take $10,000 and you take only $7,000, you would owe the penalty on $3,000.

There are several ways to calculate the RMD. Not only are there income and taxes to think about, but there are also estate planning implications. This is another one of those irreversible decisions, so take your time and do your planning well in advance of the cut-off date.

Your lifetime objective in this planning exercise is to come up with the lowest possible required distribution. You can always take more money out each year than is required. But you don't want to be forced to take out more than necessary in an attempt to keep your income tax bill as low as possible. However, by taking the lowest possible RMD, you may create undesirable estate consequences.

Your estate objective will be to allow your heirs, a spouse, or a nonspouse the option of extending the tax deferral for as long as possible. The choices you make focus on how you will calculate your life expectancy, whom you choose as your beneficiary, and whether you include your beneficiary in the life expectancy calculations. The RMD is based upon the amount in retirement savings accounts and your life expectancy. Naturally, the IRS would like you to have withdrawn all the money and paid all taxes before you die. Your objective may be to leave some money in these tax-deferred accounts for as long as possible.

You can choose either the fixed method of calculation, or the recalculation method. With the fixed method, your RMDs are higher and you run out of money faster, but your heirs have more choices once you are gone. With the recalculation method, the required withdrawals are lower, and you might stretch the time period out until you are over 100 years old.

Deferred Compensation Plans

If you have a deferred compensation plan, your employer has put money aside for you that you have yet to pay taxes on. These plans can vary quite a bit, even within a company. It is not uncommon to have more than one deferred compensation plan because companies may have offered different plans to different levels of management. As you moved up the ladder, you may have been given a better version with the move. No matter how many plans you have, the money you take out of them is always taxable at your ordinary income tax rate.

Variations may be found in how much time you have to take the money out. Some plans have a mandatory policy for taking the money, all in one lump sum, or spread out over a set number of years. Other plans allow you to determine your withdrawal schedule.

Until you take the money out, your employer technically owns your deferred compensation money. If the employer goes bankrupt, your money may be lost for good. Therefore, you don't want to leave the money in the plan for years and years, even if you are allowed to.

Unless you have a plan that was designed specifically for you and that allows for a wide range of investment opportunities, the plan will probably be invested in guaranteed investments. Some compensation plans are not even funded; all you have is the company's word that they will pay at a specified date.

Your best bet is to develop a withdrawal plan that complements your other taxable income. The plan should include how the taxes will be paid and how you will use the after-tax money. This money may be used for living expenses, allowing qualified plan money in an IRA rollover to grow tax deferred until the deferred compensation money runs out. Another option is to add the after-tax money to your long-term investment portfolio.

Stock Options

A stock option is a right granted by your employer to buy the company stock at a predetermined price called the *exercise price* or the *strike price.* You would exercise an option when the price of the stock exceeds the strike price. The value of the option is the difference between the strike price and the current value of the stock. It logically follows, then, that a stock option has no value until the fair market value of the stock exceeds the strike price. For example, if you have the option to buy the stock at the exercise price of $15 per share, and the fair market value of the stock is now $25 per share, you would have a profit of $10.

There are two basic kinds of stock option:

1. Incentive stock options (ISOs)

2. Nonqualifying stock options (NQSOs)

If the ISOs meet certain holding requirements, they are not taxed when you exercise, but they may be subject to alternative minimum tax. If you hold the optioned stock for two years from the grant date and one year from the exercise date, you will be taxed at the favorable long-term capital gains rate.

Nonqualifying stock options are taxable when they are exercised. The difference between the exercise price and the price of the stock when exercised is taxable at ordinary income tax rates, plus FICA. The NQSOs do not qualify for capital gains tax and do not have the same holding period requirements. How and when you exercise your stock options depends upon your evaluation of the stock's future prospects and your need for the money. The tax advantages are important but should not be the driving consideration.

Options will have expiration dates or lapse dates. Typically, options have to be exercised within 90 days after you leave the company. However, in many situations, extensions are granted. If you have the ability to delay exercising and you believe the stock price will increase at least at the same rate as an alternative investment, it is better to delay exercising. If you need to turn the options into income-producing investments, you won't have the luxury of waiting until expiration.

When you do your planning, take into consideration the cost to exercise, taxes, transaction costs, and the cash to pay for the optioned stock. Then account for the capital gains tax. If you are going to delay exercising and you want to use a projected value for your overall planning, run scenarios with a range of stock prices to get an idea of your possibilities. See Chapter 16 for more on stock options.

HOW TO EXERCISE ISOS To exercise your options, you need to have a way to pay for the cost of the stock at the exercise price. If you have a strike price of $10 and 1,000 options, you need $10,000 to settle the trade. The simplest way to pay for the transaction is to come up with the cash. However, if you do not have the cash or if you do not want to use it, then consider one of the following possibilities:

- *Option exercise loan.* Sometimes it is necessary to borrow money in order to exercise your options. Typically, the loan comes from your company's stock option loan program or a bank. Brokerage firms are not allowed to make margin loans until the option is exercised. You can use the company's plan to exercise and then use a margin loan from the brokerage firm to pay off the company's loan. You may need to hold on to the stock for a year to qualify for capital gains treatment, so calculate the cost of the margin loan into your planning. If you do not want to have a margin loan, you can sell enough shares to pay off the loan and keep the balance of the shares for at least 12 months.

■ *Stock-for-stock exchanges.*   Rather than paying cash for the exercise transaction, you can exchange shares of the company stock that you already own. There will be no income tax on the transaction; however, the difference between the cost and the fair market value is a preference item for alternative minimum tax purposes. Again, you must hold the remaining shares for 12 months to get the capital gains treatment.

HOW TO EXERCISE NQSOS The NQSOs typically expire 90 days after you leave the company, although your options agreement may allow an extension of up to five years. The cost to exercise and the taxes due as a result will erode what you might have considered to be the value of your options. Before you make plans to use this money, find out what the net value will be. Run the numbers assuming different prices for the stock so you get an idea of how price fluctuations will affect your value.

Managing your stock options can be confusing. It is a good idea to list each block of options by the date they were granted. You may be dealing with several different exercise prices and expiration dates. Read Chapter 16, "Stock Options," for planning points on managing stock options.

If it seems that you have a lot of work to do when you retire—you're right—you do. But it will decrease with time. You will not need to be as intensely focused once you have made your core decisions and implemented your retirement investment plan. There should be plenty of time to enjoy yourself and your new freedom. Meet with your advisor team quarterly or semiannually, read your monthly statements, make sure your cash flow system works, and fine-tune as you go along.

Net Income Worksheet
Annual

GROSS INCOME

Salary and earned income _____

Child support and alimony _____

Pension and social security _____

Rental income _____

Dividends _____

Interest _____

Capital gains _____

EXPENSES

Mortgage payment/rent _____

Homeowner's Association _____

Vacation home mortgage _____

Auto loan(s) _____

Auto maintenance and gas _____

Personal loans/
    charge accts _____

Credit cards _____

Child support and alimony _____

Other _____

TAXES

Federal income taxes _____

State and intangible taxes _____

Local and property taxes _____

INSURANCE

Life insurance _____

Health insurance _____

Disability income
    insurance _____

Auto insurance _____

Homeowner's insurance _____

Other _____

VACATION AND TRAVEL

Air travel _____

Hotel _____

Other _____

SAVINGS AND INVESTMENTS

Monthly investing _____

Retirement savings _____

Other _____

PHILANTHROPY

Religious   _____

Charitable   _____

HOUSEHOLD EXPENSES

Personal

Clothing   _____

Doctor and dentist   _____

Prescription drugs   _____

Professional fees   _____

Education expenses   _____

Day care/elder care   _____

Personal care   _____

Electricity, gas, fuel   _____

Telephone   _____

Water   _____

Garbage/pest control   _____

Home maintenance   _____

Pool maintenance   _____

Security system   _____

Home furnishings   _____

Veterinarian and pet care   _____

Fun

Club dues   _____

Entertainment   _____

Children

Tuition   _____

Lessons   _____

Allowances   _____

Gifts

Total Annual Income   _____

Total Annual Expenses   _____

Annual Net Income   _____

Universal Dos and Don'ts

As you now know, Sudden Money comes in many forms and sizes and has many origins. In addition, each individual situation is composed of its own unique set of circumstances, personalities, and feelings. Despite all of that variety, however, there are still many commonalities in the experiences of the recipients. I compiled this list of dos and don'ts after analyzing those commonalities and separating the ones that contributed to the financial success of the recipients from the ones that contributed to their financial downfall. If these universal truths are accepted and my guidelines are followed, you will be less likely to experience many of the problems that typically plague windfall recipients.

A note before we begin: At first, some of the points on the list may seem obvious. But don't just brush them off. It is possible that you are experiencing the rush and the excitement of your new money and that you are not really thinking things through as you would in other situations. Many people whose money materialized as a result of a loss may still be in too much pain to see clearly, and these points won't have much meaning at the beginning. Therefore, I suggest that you go through this list several times over a period of weeks, or even months, until you are certain that all points are covered appropriately. This list is particularly helpful as you go through your Phase One work; use it to gauge how you are doing and to keep you going in the right direction.

Universal Dos

Do take the time to settle into your new circumstances. Your new financial position creates new possibilities and new responsibilities. Some people find this overwhelming and/or confusing. You must allow time for the flood of confusion to dissipate; only then can you attain the clarity necessary to begin making plans and decisions.

This is the time to establish a Decision Free Zone (DFZ), wherein only essential decisions are made. This time should be used to learn about your new circumstances while postponing all investment, gifting, and spending decisions. The amount of time that you will need is up to you; it is okay to take months— or even a year—before you feel prepared to make these kinds of decisions.

Do find a financial advisor to work with. Accompanying your sudden, large amount of money is often a flash flood of advice. It is normal for most of your friends and family to have an opinion about what you should do with your money. The advice will be plentiful and you won't even have to ask for it. However, the best and only advice you should take in the beginning is to find a good financial advisor. But you will hear much more than this.

Remember that others might have their own agenda for your Sudden Money. They might use all kinds of emotional pressure to convert you to their way of thinking. The most common tactic is to make you feel guilty or obligated. Keep in mind at all times that *it is your money.* You are the one who will pay the taxes on it and support yourself with it, and only you will have to live with the consequences of your financial decisions. Therefore, when the pressure gets to you, always defer to your financial advisor. Ask for a written evaluation of what you are being asked to consider, and tell whomever has given you advice or asked you for something that you cannot do anything until you have consulted with your advisor. There isn't anything that can't wait until after you have sought expert advice.

Whether your Sudden Money is tens of thousands of dollars or tens of millions of dollars, it should be used to create your highest good. You cannot begin to do that, however, until you take care of some crucial financial details. An advisor can help you determine which bills to pay off, what amount of income your new money can safely support, what your tolerance for risk is, which investments are appropriate for you, and how to minimize your tax burden.

Even if you are an experienced investor, maybe even a Certified Financial Planner, you still need an advisor to help you through the maze of decisions that Sudden Money creates. The advisor you are looking for should have experience working with others in your position, good professional credentials, and integrity. Equally important is that your ideal advisor should be someone you can communicate with and ask questions of without hesitation.

Do know your range of possibilities. If you are not experienced in dealing with the kind of money you now have, you have a limited frame of reference when it comes to the possibilities that exist for you. Even high earners have difficulty dealing with a large lump sum of money; often, they are unsure of what the boundaries of the money are.

People tend to feel one of two extremes: (1) that they can do anything and everything they want, or (2) that they will never have enough. The result of both extremes is that they don't spend or enjoy. Before inventing a new lifestyle that is fit for the likes of Robin Leach, have your advisor show you your new range of choices. You might be able to do anything you want, but you probably cannot do *everything* you want.

Do know which decisions are irreversible before you make them. The last thing you want to do is make a decision that you cannot reverse— at least not until you have all the facts. It is likely that you will face one of these decisions at the start, when you have to commit to how you want to receive your money. Getting the dry facts may be easy; either you'll receive a one-time lump sum payment or a stream of much smaller payments over a period of time. Knowing which is best for you is not always easy. This is one of the times you absolutely need a good advisor or team of advisors.

Irreversible decisions can also come up with investments. A standard question to ask when making an investment decision is the following: If I don't like this investment for any reason, how do I get my money back? Most investments are easily sold, but some may tie your money up for a long time and obligate you to make future payments.

Giving money away to another person or to a charity is irreversible, as is putting money into an irrevocable trust (hence the name). I suggest you postpone all irreversible decisions *that are not entirely necessary* until you have your financial plan completed and you are sure you know what you want to do with your money.

Do set short- and long-term goals. Use your money with intention; it is a tool that you can use to fulfill your goals, to support your lifestyle, to help others, and to create a secure future. Take time to do the goal-setting exercise, and spend extra time creating your Bliss List. When you know what you want to manifest in your life and you know when you want the manifestation to occur, you can then use your money appropriately.

Do diversify your portfolio. Putting all of your money, or even a large percentage of it, in any one investment, is called gambling, not investing. There is no one perfect, all-weather investment. Every investment has its pluses and minuses; the goal is to select investments that have different degrees and different kinds of risk. When one is not doing well, others may be having a good year. A well-diversified portfolio will not be risk free, but if it is designed properly, it should have stability and inflation protection. On the other hand, a poorly diversified portfolio will be subject to either volatility accompanied by a high probability of loss, or erosion due to inflation.

Do keep a vigilant eye on your tax situation. It is a fact of life in America that when you earn money, you pay taxes. This includes money from the lottery, pension money, some insurance settlement money, and alimony. Of course, it also includes the money that you earn on your investments.

Therefore, when you are calculating the returns that your investments have produced, you need to make the taxes that you will owe part of the calculation. The tax consequences of some investments can make an otherwise reasonable return become disappointing. Your objective is to use your new wealth to create long-term financial security; to do this, your investments must at least keep pace with inflation. Unfortunately, taxes on interest, dividends, and capital gains make this goal more challenging. Eliminating, delaying, deferring, or otherwise minimizing taxes should be part of your investment strategy. Your objective is to find investments that pay you the highest return after taxes are paid. Here are some tax strategies that will help you to control when and how much tax you will owe on your investment portfolio.

- *Eliminate taxes.* One way to eliminate tax is to buy tax-free municipal bonds. These are bonds issued by state or local governments and agencies. The federal government gives these bonds tax-free status to help state and local governments build roads, schools, and make other necessary improvements. They pay lower interest than corporate or U.S. government bonds because the interest is tax-free.

- *Defer taxes.* In some cases, such as with individual stocks and real estate, deferring taxes is relatively easy. Though you will have to pay tax on the *income* these investments produce as you go along, you won't have to pay the tax on the *profits* until you actually sell them. Long-term capital gains taxes are due when you sell investments you have held for at least one year. For some investors, the maximum 28% long-term capital gains rate is lower than their ordinary income tax rate.

  Other investments, such as some mutual funds, do not allow for the deferring of taxes. Mutual funds that invest in stocks must distribute 99% of the long-term capital gains earned throughout the year by December 31. This means their investors pay taxes on these gains even if they still own the fund.

  When buying mutual funds outside of a tax-protected retirement account or a variable annuity, it is a good idea to look at their capital gains record. This can be obtained from the fund or from the Morningstar report on the fund, and it will give you an idea of what to expect each year. Funds that have a high turnover rate (i.e., do a lot of buying and selling) will have more tax consequences than funds with a low turnover rate. Some funds achieve their success by actively buying and selling each year, whereas others purposely keep this activity low to manage the tax bite. Neither way is superior. In the end, it is the net after-tax return with which you should be concerned. Knowing what tax consequences to expect will help you and your accountant plan accordingly.

  The most common way to defer taxes on investments is to own the investments within a qualified retirement account. The word *qualified* means that the money that is put into the account qualifies for a federal income tax deduction. It also means that the investments within the account are not taxed until you withdraw the money at a later date.

You can contribute money to qualified retirement accounts only if you have earned income. If your Sudden Money has allowed you to stop working, you can no longer add money to this kind of retirement plan. It will be important to allow money already in IRA, 401(k), or other retirement plans to remain tax-protected for as long as possible.

Although it is important to consider the tax consequence of an investment, taxes should not be the most important consideration. Many investors who are overly concerned with taxes make some fundamental mistakes as a result. For instance, the strategy of buying only municipal bonds and paying no taxes at all is okay if you have other earned income that keeps you in a high tax bracket. However, if you are retired and investment income is all you have, you are better off buying some taxable bonds and creating a 15% or 29% tax bracket. This way, you will have a higher after-tax income, even after paying the tax on the few taxable bonds.

Universal Don'ts

Don't give up access to your money. This is the number one area of trouble for Sudden Money recipients. No matter how much you don't want to manage your own money, never give up your right to control it. In the beginning stages, the money management process may seem overwhelming or simply unappealing. It is not only okay to hire a professional to help you, but I strongly recommend that you do so. Hiring financial planners, CPAs, and lawyers does not mean you have given up control; you always have the right to fire the person or firm you have hired. Furthermore, it is rare for any of these professionals to require their clients to sign long-term contracts. If a service contract is signed, it is normal to allow the dissatisfied party to cancel with written notice.

Don't loan money to friends or relatives. There will be times when you want to help someone you care about. You know the old saying: Neither a lender nor a borrower be. Well, it applies doubly to people close to you. Everyone has their own "stuff" about money and in nonmarital relationships it is usually best to keep money separate. When your friends and relatives know you have lots of money, they may feel entitled to a portion of it and ask you for a loan that they wouldn't have dreamed about asking you for prior to your windfall.

A good way to handle this is to tell them the truth—that you have no idea where you stand with your new finances and new taxes until you have worked through the numbers with your advisor. Later on, you can tell them that it just is not possible. If you feel an overwhelming desire to share your new money, work with your advisor to determine an amount you can safely *give away*. Then, make it understood that you are giving the most you can and that you expect nothing back. In this way, you have set a safe, realistic limit, and the relationship will not be jeopardized if the money is not repaid.

Giving is far more satisfying than lending, especially when it is part of your financial plan and you know you can afford to do it. Many of my Sudden Money clients receive great pleasure from giving money away, so I build this into their cash flow planning every year.

Don't quit your job until you know that you can afford not to work. Until you have determined what level of income your new money will support for life, don't dive into early retirement. Receiving $1 million or $2 million may support you if you are 65 years old, but not if you are in your 40s. Even a large amount of money can get eaten up by inflation over long periods of time.

Before you retire, buy a new home, and start living the good life, make sure your new lifestyle is sustainable. Work with your advisor to determine the longevity of your money under various income scenarios. If you find that you don't have enough to support the kind of income you would like, either adjust your income goal or invest the money for future growth and put retirement off for a few more years. Whether the money is enough to allow you to retire today or at some point in the future, it is more than you had before; if you handle it correctly, your retirement will be more abundant and more secure than it was before your windfall.

Don't take too much—or too little—investment risk. Risk is personal, and how much risk you can and should take depends upon your overall financial picture and risk tolerance. As defined in Chapter 8, your risk tolerance is determined by evaluating the following:

- *Your investment time frame.* For example, money needed within a couple of years for school tuition should be invested for safety, not for growth. The longer you can leave the money alone to grow, the more risk you can take.
- *Your objective.* Will you need income from the investments, or will you be able to let them grow for future use? An investment objective is what you want the money to do (i.e., pay you income, grow, or both).
- *Your tolerance for market fluctuations.* Can you still sleep at night when the stocks in your portfolio are going down? If you can, your investments could include more stocks than not.

Too much risk means investing outside of your risk tolerance or your comfort zone. What is too risky for one investor may not be for another. Similarly, taking too little risk and ignoring the impact that inflation can have on your money is another way to jeopardize your lifestyle and your financial security.

Not taking enough risk implies that you don't have a plan to deal with inflation. Not planning for inflation means that you are at risk of running out of money, or at least that you have to continually redefine (i.e., decrease) your lifestyle once you retire and inflation catches up with you. This risk is referred to as *purchasing power risk,* and the way to deflect it is to add (more) stocks to your portfolio, because stocks have historically outperformed inflation and bonds.

Don't try to time the market. One of the most powerful ways to make money is to put time on your side. A popular saying among financial planners is: "Investment success is achieved with time, not timing." Over the years, it has been proved that timing the stock market has been difficult, if not impossible. Many money managers have made names for themselves by calling a steep market drop and getting their investors out before it took place.

Although it feels better to be out of the market as it is crashing, the real talent is to know when to reenter the market before it starts to go back up. Trying to determine the stock market's highs and lows has preoccupied many otherwise intelligent persons for decades. So far, no one person or mutual fund has an impressive record. What does make an impression is the result of lost opportunities that you would have suffered by missing just a handful of the best trading days while waiting to time your reentry.

Don't invest in illiquid investments. Most investments are easily sold if you are not satisfied with them or if you need your money for something else. However, some investments, such as limited partnerships, are designed to be illiquid. Although not all partnerships are bad investments, this is not the time to be making investments you cannot get out of. Real estate is another example of an illiquid investment. You have no way of knowing if there will be a willing buyer who agrees to the price you have set at the precise moment you want to sell.

Most stocks, bonds, and mutual funds can be liquidated the same day that you give the instruction to sell. The money should be in your brokerage account within a day or two. If you are dealing directly with a mutual fund company, it may take a week or so to get your money.

While you are getting comfortable with your new money, stick to the basic investments that can be bought and sold as you wish. Those same basics have worked for both the wealthy and the monthly savers for generations. Illiquid investments add an element of risk that you don't need to deal with.

Don't sink your new wealth into a new business. New businesses are the ultimate illiquid investments. They have a very high failure rate, and they usually require more money than anticipated, and more and harder work than anticipated. In addition, they take more time to pay off than the investors and owners ever thought possible.

People go into new businesses with a range of hopes and dreams, many of which are unrealistic. For a combination of reasons, elite athletes and entertainers frequently invest in restaurants, and for a combination of reasons they frequently fail. The money lost in such business ventures is rarely recovered.

Remember that the stock market has a history of dropping 20% in a severe correction, and then recovering and going higher than it was before the drop. Money lost in the stock market has a far better chance of being recovered than money lost in a new business. *Again, stick to the basic investments that have less risk and good return potential.*

Just because you have come into a large sum of money does not mean you are ready to invest in more speculative ventures than you invested in prior to your Sudden Money. Ordinarily, you would not be asked to put money up for "big deals" if you were perceived to be an average investor saving money for retirement. However, when the word gets out that you now have new wealth, it is possible that you will be invited to join "the big boys" in venture capital deals. Due to the amount of money you now have (or that all of these people think you have), others may assume that you can afford the added risk of these deals.

Venture capital deals involve funding a new business that has perceived potential, but lots of ground to cover before it becomes profitable. What's worse is that investors are often called upon to contribute more money, and if they cannot or do not, their ownership percentage may be decreased. You don't have to look very far to hear stories about investors adding more and more money to a deal just to protect their initial investment. The phrase *throwing good money after bad money* frequently applies. Venture capital deals can be very profitable, but the risk you take to get to the profit is probably far greater than you should take.

INDEX

THE SUDDEN MONEY™ CENTER

The Sudden Money Center is dedicated to education, training, and on-going research regarding the Sudden Money phenomenon.

We would love to hear from you; please contact us at the address below with your Sudden Maney story.

Also contact us if you would like more information on:

- Sudden Money Camps, multi-day workshops designed to help families and individuals become oriented and comfortable with their Sudden Money
- Our latest research, articles, audiotapes, and support materials
- Training programs for financial advisors
- Corporate programs designed to help prepare for company related Sudden Money
- Sudden Money financial advisors

The Sudden Money Center
141 Green Point Circle
Palm Beach Gardens, Florida 33418
888-838-9446
www.suddenmoney.net

ABOUT THE AUTHORS

Susan Bradley has been a Certified Financial Planner for nearly 20 years. She is the founder of The Sudden Money Center, a research and education company in West Palm Beach, Florida. She speaks, gives seminars and multi-day workshops, and trains financial advisors in the Sudden Money Process. She designs Sudden Money programs for families, financial service companies, law firms, and corporations.

Mary Martin, Ph.D. is a writer living in Palm Beach, Florida. She received her doctorate in Applied Linguistics from New York University and has been writing and developing curriculum for over a decade.